ISTANBUL

At Your Fingertips

*A complete book
to discover
Istanbul.
A cultural and
practical guide
with maps to
make life easy
for visitors.*

GÜLSEREN RAMAZANOĞLU

This guide has been prepared especially for the use of the guests staying at the Istanbul and Parksa Hiltons.

The aim is to answer practical questions and supply a bit of information on the historical and the cultural aspects of Istanbul. The map of Turkey will remind the readers of the fact that there is much more than Istanbul to discover.

As the guide will be published annually, corrections will be made and the material updated. Therefore, your comments and suggestions are welcome. In view of the latest economical difficulties some shops or restaurants may be closed after publication of this guide and some establishements might stop accepting the credit cards. Telephone numbers without area codes belong to the European side. When calling from the Asian side make sure you dial first the area code 0212.

Publisher's other titles:
Turkish Cookery
Turkish Cooking
Turkish Embroidery

First published in May1994
by DAMKO A.Ş.
Edited by Gülseren Ramazanoğlu
Chief Contributor: Anna G. Edmonds
Other contributors:Berter Üner, Gülseren Ramazanoğlu,
Lorraine Hanson, Susan Ritter, Verda Sorgun
Electronic typesetting: Ekin Sökmen
Cover: Aydın Erkmen (Artist's impression of Istanbul)
Maps: Dr. T. Levent Erel
Old Istanbul Plan: Selim Ramazanoğlu
Map illustrations: Kemal Molu
Legends: Levent Curabeyoğlu,Tuncer Özer
Printed by Kaya Basım, Istanbul, Turkey
Copyright Gülseren Ramazanoğlu 1994
All rights reserved in all countries
Publisher's address: Ebe Kızı Sokak 16, Sosko İş
Merkezi A Blok 56, Osmanbey, Istanbul, Turkey
Tel. (0212) 247 4527 - 230 4372 Fax. (0212) 248 9195

ISBN 975-7489-11-5
Printed in Turkey
1994 Edition   **Printed on recycled paper**

LEGENDS

Baths (Turkish)

Bridges

Cafes

Castles

Churches

Columns

Drinks, Bars

Exceptional views

Markets, Shopping

Mosques

Museums

Recipes, Restaurants
Turkish Cuisine

Recommended in its category

Schools, libraries, booksellers

Synagogues

Transportation

Contents

Intriguing, golden, magnificent — İstanbul has for centuries been characterized in superlatives. A sprawling, crowded, badly-polluted megalopolis today, the city still commands an incomparable geographic position across two continents, and a magic that captures and holds the imagination of those who visit it.

Geography. Greater Istanbul includes the old walled city (sometimes called ("Stamboul"), the "new" city of Galata and Beyoğlu (both these old and new regions are in Europe), the Asian cities of Kadiköy and Üsküdar, the villages that reach north on either side of the Bosphorus, and the new suburbs now stretching out in a rough semicircle from the Seraglio Point. The area is 253 km^2.

Like Rome, the old walled city sits on seven hills. The First Hill includes the Topkapı Palace, the Blue Mosque, St. Sophia, and the Hippodrome. The Second Hill centers around the Mosque of Nuruosmaniye, the Covered Market, and the Burnt Column (Çemberlitaş). The Mosque of Süleyman the Magnificent sits on the crest of the Third Hill, while the Mosque of Fatih Sultan Mehmet is on the Fourth, and that of Selim II is on the Fifth. The top of the Sixth Hill is at the Mosque of Mihrimah and the Edirne Gate in the land walls. The Seventh of the hills, characterized by the Byzantines as "dry," slopes from Millet Caddesi to the Sea of Marmara. The whole area makes a triangular peninsula about 6 1/2 km wide on the western side and 7 km long.

The walls of the city from the Sea of Marmara to the Golden Horn were built early in the fifth century by Theodosius II as a protection against Atilla the Hun. Wars, earthquakes, and city planners have each exacted their toll on them more than once. The sea walls were started before these land walls; bits and pieces of them around the Seraglio Point date from the time of Constantine. They sustained their greatest damage in the winter of 763 when huge icebergs crashed against them bringing down a large section. A chain from the end of the sea walls across the Golden Horn to Galata acted as part of the defense on the third side of the triangle. It was the Golden Horn walls that the Fourth Crusaders scaled in 1204.

Of the regions that lie immediately beyond the land walls, Eyüp is the holiest place of pilgrimage in Europe for Moslems. Located at the western end of the Golden Horn, it is sacred because Eyüp Sultan, the companion and standard bearer of the Prophet Mohammed, is buried here, and there is a mosque dedicated to him. Many people have chosen the cemetery near his mosque for the place of their burial.

The southern edge of the "new" European city is on the Golden Horn in Karaköy (Galata). Once a community of Genoese merchants that owned the land between the places of the present quay, the Galata Tower and the Atatürk Bridge, with increasing rapidity in this century the city has expanded through Beyoğlu (Pera),Taksim, Nişantaşı, Mecidiyeköy, and on beyond the Levents up to Maslak and Emirgân hills.

Across from the Seraglio Point are the regions in Asia of

Kadıköy, Haydarpaşa, and Üsküdar. All of the imperial mosques in Asia are worth a visit, as is also the room in the Selimiye Barracks that has been set aside for a museum to Florence Nightingale. From the crest of the Çamlıca hill on a clear day there is a panoramic view of the Princes' Islands, the Seraglio Point, and the Bosphorus north to the hills above Beykoz.

Each of the many bays on both sides of the Bosphorus is known by the name of its village that formerly was accessible only from the water. Some of them were fishing villages; some were summer residences. Ferries zigzagged from Eminönü to Üsküdar to Beşiktaş to Çengelköy to Bebek and farther up. Today two great suspension bridges carry the stream of traffic between Europe and Asia.

The Bosphorus is the strait between the Black Sea and the Sea of Marmara. About 30 km long from north to south and between one and five km across, it divides Europe from Asia here. The average surface current flowing from the Black Sea is about one meter per second. The channel is deeper at the entrance to the Black Sea than at the Sea of Marmara.

An archipelago known as the Princes' Islands (they used to belong to the Byzantine royal family) lies about 15 km southeast of Istanbul in the Sea of Marmara. Four large and five smaller islands are mainly summer residences.

Climate. Istanbul's climate is generally mild. The temperatures range from around 38^0 C on a hot summer day to -5^0 C during a blustery winter storm. Occasionally there may be hotter or colder spells. Several winds influence the climate. It's claimed that the north wind (*poyraz*) and the southwest wind (*lodos*) identify the seasons more than the months of the year. Spring is a pretty time with many flowering trees and vines in bloom. The weather is usually good from May into November. February can be dreary with gray skies and sometimes heavy snowfalls.

History. For the first thousand years of the history of the peninsula, from the time of the legendary Byzas (667 BC) until the fourth century AD, Byzantium did not attract much attention. Darius took it for the Persians (512-479 BC), and Philip of Macedon tried but didn't get it (340 BC). (His son Alexander didn't bother.) Then the Romans captured it in 196 AD, but gave slight value to what they owned until Constantine decided to make it his new capital (330).

In strengthening his empire, Constantine added the power of the Christian church to his geographic and political power. This combination of church and state, centered in Constantinople, occurred at the time that Rome was declining under the attacks of the barbarians.

For several centuries after Constantine, his city flourished due to the guidance of strong emperors and churchmen.

To give two examples, in the fourth century the bishops (among them Basil of Caesarea and Gregory of Nazianzus) led the Church to define its faith and its role in government. Two hundred years later in the sixth century Justinian (527-565) put the laws of the state in clear and usable order; he added to the geographical extent of the empire, and gave the city a majesty in its major buildings. All of the later history of the Eastern Roman Empire was built on these foundations.

By the end of the twelfth century, however, the rulers and the people of Constantinople had lost their earlier vigor and were vulnerable to attack. The strength that had been apparent in the fourth century Church decisions had given way to rivalry, misunderstanding, and schism. Thus when a Fourth Crusade went awry it was Western Christians who pillaged and razed the treasures of Eastern Christian Constantinople (1204). Mehmet the Conqueror (1451-1481) understood well both the military and the psychological victory he won with his capture of Constantinople. He also was conscious of the importance and vitality of the past when he converted St. Sophia to a mosque. But he was much more than a military strategist; he was a statesman. Through the *millet* system he legalized the position of the minority religious groups, giving them authority in such areas as worship, education, and charity, but reserving criminal justice for the Moslem courts. In this he reflected the Moslem tolerance for the "peoples of the book." The comprehensive system of education which he devised for the Palace School was probably influenced somewhat by Byzantine culture. Again a combination of religion (Islam) and politics produced a viable government. The Ottoman Empire reached its climax in two hundred years at the time of Süleyman the Magnificent (1520-1566), and maintained sufficient stability to continue for almost six hundred years.

With the pressures of the twentieth century (exploding population, communications, international politics and economics), a new Turkish Republic (1923) took the place of the Ottoman Empire. Istanbul marked time briefly when Ankara took over as the capital. Today the excitement of Istanbul is not only in the many layers of its history but also in its present residents, the individuals, the great variety of their backgrounds (cultural, economic, educational), and the opportunities each creates to produce a richness of ideas and activities.

Personalities. A few individuals stand out for the major contributions they have made to the life and art of the city. In historical order they are these:

Constantine the Great (288-337). Constantine was the first Christian Roman emperor; his support of the Church determined the future of Christianity.

Having made Constantinople his capital in 330, he then embellished it with columns and statues, churches and a palace, fountains and squares, and enough art (much of which he removed from Rome) to make his entire city a museum.

Justinian (463-565). When Justinian became emperor Theodora was crowned with him. Justinian was the emperor of the Eastern Roman Empire during its most brilliant period. In spite of the Nika riots which were sparked by his harsh fiscal policy and in which 30,000 people were massacred, he is known not only for the majestic Church of St. Sophia, but also for the laws which he codified.

Theodora (c.500-548). Theodora was Justinian's wife; she exercised considerable influence in governing the empire. The inspiration of her courage and firmness during the Nika riots saved Justinian's throne.

Henricus Dandalo. A not-too-noble age is marked in a name inscribed in the balcony of St. Sophia. Henricus Dandalo was the Doge of Venice who led the Latins' Fourth Crusade against Constantinople in 1203-1204. When the city was captured and ransacked, the Crusaders broke, burned, melted down, or carted off to Europe almost everything of value. Dandalo ruled part of Constantinople, including St. Sophia, until his death the next year at the age of 91.

Theodore Metochites. Sixty years after the Byzantines regained Constantinople, a top man in government dedicated his money to beautify a small church on the outskirts of the city. The mosaics and frescoes which he instructed be put on the walls of St. Savior in Chora (Kariye Camii) rank among the world's masterpieces.

Mehmet the Conqueror (1432-1481). He was bold, stubborn, courageous, a poet and a diplomat, a general and a linguist (he spoke Turkish, Greek, Slavic and Arabic). He had a love of learning. He founded the great Palace School which educated the military and government leaders of the empire for almost 400 years. He also organized the education of the women of his harem.

The Ottomans considered that his conquest of Constantinople signalled their government's change from a minor principality to a world-class empire. Mehmet moved his capital from Edirne to the city that gradually came to be called Istanbul. He repopulated it with merchants and craftsmen from among all the ethnic groups of his realm. He built roads and public buildings. He founded several mosque complexes and built both a residential palace and a governmental palace, now called Topkapı.

Süleyman the Magnificent (1494-1566). He is known first as the lawgiver. Abroad the splendor of his reign continues to distinguish him as "the magnificent". From the wealth that Süleyman acquired in his military victories, he embellished the city with a number of public buildings, notably his mosque and its dependencies.

Roxelana (?1504-1558). Known in Turkish as Hürrem Sultan, Roxelana was Süleyman's wife and the mother of Sultan Selim II. Her contributions to Istanbul were mostly through her power over her husband, but her mosque (the first built by Sinan in Istanbul) should be mentioned.

Many of the women of the palace — mothers and daughters of the sultans — contributed one or more public buildings to the city: Esmahan Sultan, daughter of Selim II, built the Mosque of Sokollu Mehmet Paşa in Kadırga. (Its architect was Sinan.) Safiye Sultan, the mother of Mehmet III, began the

building of Yeni Cami in 1597; Türkhan Sultan, mother of
Mehmet IV completed it in 1663. A large mosque complex in
Eyüp with its school, still-functioning soup kitchen, and foun-
tain, was built in 1794 by Mihrişah Sultan, mother of Selim III.
The mosque of Pertevniyal Sultan, mother of Abdülaziz, was
built in 1871 in Aksaray.

Sinan (1489-1588). Conscripted into the janissary corps at an
early age, Sinan rose to become the Chief Court Architect.
During the fifty years that he held the position he built over
450 bridges and fountains, schools and hospitals, soup
kitchens, hans, and mosques. Of the latter, his masterpieces are
the Mosque of Süleyman in Istanbul and the Mosque of Selim
II in Edirne.

Florence Nightengale. As a young girl, she had defied her
family and the contemporary prejudices to study nursing.
Appalled by the conditions of the hundreds of sick and
wounded soldiers in the Crimean War, she offered her services
to the British Secretary of War. From 1854 to 1856 she was in
the Selimiye barracks in Haydarpaşa. Nightengale's small
room in the north tower of the barracks is maintained by the
Turkish army as a museum dedicated to her.

Pierre Loti. Many of the romantic, oriental images of the 19th
century were captured by the French writer, Pierre Loti. Some
of his writing he did at a table in the outdoor coffeehouse
above the Eyüp cemetery. The coffeehouse in his name is still
there.

Halide Edip Adıvar. She was a novelist of the first half of the
20th century. Like Loti, her plots were romantic, she portrayed
the struggles for independence of which she had been a part.

Mustafa Kemal Atatürk (1881-1938). No listing of the people
whose visions have colored Istanbul is complete without tribute to the Republic's first president Atatürk. He never settled in
Istanbul, although he died in the Dolmabahçe Palace. Among
his homes were one in Şişli (now a museum), and a room at the
Pera Palace Hotel (also a museum). For Atatürk, Istanbul represented the corruption and inactivity of the defunct Ottoman
Empire. With his wish to start a redefined, vigorous country,
he moved the capital to Ankara in 1923.

Atatürk united a defeated, divided country and transformed it
in 1923 into the democratic Republic of Turkey. His reforms
include secularization, education, language and alphabet
reform, women's suffrage, and Western legal codes. His
watchwords were, "Peace at home; peace abroad." He turned
the country around from being the "Sick Man of Europe" and
started it on its course to become the pivotal force it is today in
Middle Eastern affairs. He was outstanding in many areas: he
was a general, a politician and an orator. Every year on the
anniversary of his death at five minutes after nine on
November 10 traffic stops, sirens ring while the country
remembers this president and his legacy.

Çelik Gülersoy (b. 1930). Stimulated by Çelik Gülersoy's
vision and enthusiasm, the Touring and Automobile Association of Turkey, of which he is the General Director, has

restored a number of historic buildings and parks in Istanbul.
A prolific writer, he set up an Istanbul Library based on his
personal collection on Soğuk Çeşme Sokağı where the
Ayasofya Pansiyonları (also restored by the Touring and
Automobile Association of Turkey) are located.

The excitement of the city endures in the visions of its people.

Language, Vocabulary

Turkish is written with a phonetic, modified Latin alphabet.
Each letter represents only one sound. The vowel sounds are
these:

a	as the "a"	in	father
e	as the "e"	in	set
i	as the "i"	in	with
ı	as the "ee"	in	beet
o	as the "o"	in	oh
ö	as the "ur"	in	urge
u	as the "ue"	in	blue
ü	as the "ew"	in	few

A few consonants are markedly different from English:

c	as the "j"	in	just
ç	as the "ch"	in	church
g	as the "g"	in	gate
ğ	no sound; it lengthens the vowel it follows		
j	as the "s"	in	measure
ş	as the "sh"	in	shall

Meanings of Turkish words are modified by adding suffixes.
You will notice these frequently:

-*lar*, -*ler* plural form: *kitap* (book), *kitaplar* (books)

-*i*, -*ı*, -*in*, -*si* possessive: *cami* (mosque), *Bayezit Camii* (Mosque
of Bayezit)

-*dan*, -*den*   from   *Ankara'dan* (from Ankara)

-*a*, -*e*, -*ya*, -*ye*   to   *müzeye* (to the museum)

You will smooth your visit if you can use a few common
Turkish phrases. (Note that all letters are pronounced in
Turkish words, and that the syllables are without accent.)

Civilities

Thank you	*Mersi,* or *Teşekkür ederim.*
Hello	*Merhaba,* or *Alo*
How are you?	*Nasılsınız?*
Thank you. I am well.	*Teşekkür ederim. İyiyim.*
	(the answer to "How are you?")
Good morning.	*Günaydın.*
Good evening.	*İyi akşamlar.*
Good night.	*İyi geceler.*
Welcome.	*Hoş geldiniz.* (said to the guest)
We're glad to be here.	*Hoş bulduk.* (answered by the guest)
Good-by.	*Güle güle.* (said by the host)
Good-by.	*Allaha ısmarladık.* (said by the guest)
I'm sorry.	*Pardon, affedersiniz.*
Please excuse my fault.	*Affedersiniz.*
I hope your work is easy.	*Kolay gelsin.*

I hope you recover quickly.	*Geçmiş olsun.*
Bon appetit.	*Afiyet olsun.*
This is good.	*Bu iyidir.*
This is very beautiful.	*Bu çok güzel.*
God bless you.	*Çok yaşa.*
What is the time?	*Saat kaç?*
Can you help me?	*Bana yardım edebilirmisiniz?*

Titles

Mr. *Bay* before the man's name: *Bay Süleyman Demirel.*
Bey after the man's given name: *Süleyman Bey.*
Miss, Mrs. *Bayan* before the woman's name: *Bayan Tansu Çiller*. *Hanım* after the woman's given name: *Tansu Hanım.*
Sultan for the ruler, before his name: *Sultan Mehmet;* for the queen, after the name: *Hürrem Sultan.*
Pasha after the man's name: *Rüstem Paşa.*

Addresses

apartment	*apartıman*	
avenue	*cadde*	as in *İstiklâl Caddesi*
boulevard	*bulvar*	*Atatürk Bulvarı*
floor	*kat*	
office	*daire*	
road	*yol*	*Divan Yolu*
square	*meydan*	*At Meydanı*
street	*sokak*	*Soğukçeşme Sokağı*

Buildings

Bosphorus summer home	*yalı*
bridge	*köprü*
caravansary or inn	*han*
church	*kilise*
covered bath	*hamam*
department store	*büyük mağaza, galeri*
dervish convent	*tekke*
fruit and vegetable store	*manav*
grocery store	*bakkal*
hospital	*hastane*
kiosk, pavilion	*köşk*
market	*çarşı*
mausoleum	*türbe*
mosque	*cami*
mosque fountain	*şadırvan*
mosque school	*medrese*
mosque soup kitchen	*imaret*
movie theater	*sinema*
museum	*müze*
night club	*gece kulübü*
palace	*saray*
school	*okul*
store	*dükkan*
synagogue	*sinagog*
theater	*tiyatro*

Do's and Don'ts

Courtesy and a smile make as good mileage abroad as they do at home. When visiting a mosque, you will be expected to be dressed modestly and to take your shoes off before entering. Women may be asked to wear a scarf on their heads. Don't sit on the floor.

Offer to take off your shoes when you enter someone's home. They may have slippers at the door which you can wear inside. When you are visiting a home, take a small present (flowers, candy) to your host and hostess.

Observe the formalities of greeting each person in a room individually, and of saying good-by again to each one individually. In general, social situations are more formal in Turkey than in the US. You will notice this first perhaps in the formal phrases repeated over and over in these situations.

Be extra careful in traffic. Don't expect all the traffic rules to be observed by the other person. Walk defensively, and drive defensively. Seat belts are required for people in the front seat of a car.

Protect your valuables, but expect that most people are honest. The taxi drivers will give correct change, as will clerks at a store. But watch the gas station attendants.

Build into your time schedule the probability that you will have several long periods of waiting: waiting in traffic, waiting for an appointment, waiting to change money, or just plain rushing somewhere in order to wait.

Mosques and Islam

Most Turks are orthodox Moslems; their religion is Islam. Their prophet is Mohammed; the book that God (Allah) revealed to him is the Koran.

Mosques are the public buildings for Moslem worship; they are usually open to everyone. However, if you are not participating in the Moslem service, it is courteous to wait until people have finished praying before you enter. For this reason, mornings are the best times for non-Moslems to visit a mosque because there are no organized prayers between sunrise and noon. The Friday noon prayer is the one most attended.

A mosque is always oriented so that the worshippers face Mecca. If the building has been converted from a church the prayer niche (*mihrap*) will probably be set at an angle so that people may arrange themselves correctly.

The Islamic calendar is lunar; it is divided into twelve months of 29 or 30 days. It gains about 10 days a year in relation to the Western calendar, moving around it about once every 33 years. Turkey uses the Western calendar and observes Sunday as the day of rest. The Islamic calendar is noted during the month of fasting (*Ramazan*), Religious Holdiday (*Şeker Bayramı*) and the Festival of Sacrifice (*Kurban Bayramı*).

Islam is a religion, a social organization, and a political force. Islamic law (*sheriat*), like the Koran, was divinely revealed. It includes public and private, national and international law, and also details of ritual and ethical conduct. To it are added the traditions (*hadith*) of what Mohammed is believed to have said or done that are not included in the Koran.

Suggested Itineraries

One-Day Tours
If you have but **one day** in which to glimpse Istanbul:
MORNING: **Topkapı Sarayı** and **the harem** (Get to the palace when it opens and see the harem first because waiting to get in it may take most of your time.) **St. Sophia** (Don't skip the gallery — open 9:30-11:00 am, 1:00-4:00 pm — with the view of the nave and the remarkable mosaics.)
AFTERNOON: **Blue Mosque, Hippodrome, Kariye Müzesi**.

Two-Day Tours
If you have **two days**, see the places listed in the first day, and then add these to those sites:
MORNING: **Archaeological, Museum, Museum of the Ancient Orient, Çinili Köşk** (Tiled Kiosk)(These three are grouped together.)**Yerebatan Sarayı** (Basilica Cistern) **Ibrahim Paşa Museum.**
AFTERNOON: **Covered Market.**

Five-Day Tours
If you have **five days**, add these places in your desired order to those listed above. But note that the Archaeological, St. Sophia, and Ibrahim Paşa Museums are closed on Mondays, and Topkapı Sarayı and Kariye Müzesi are closed on Tuesdays.
THIRD DAY:**Mosque of Süleyman the Magnificent, Spice Market, Mosaic Museum, Golden Horn** (walls, Greek Orthodox Patriarchate, Bulgarian Church), **Galata** (Arap Camii, Rüstem Paşa Han, Yeraltı Cami.)
FOURTH DAY: **Palace of Dolmabahçe, Bosphorus cruise, Rumeli Hisar, Palace of Beylerbeyi, Çamlıca.**
FIFTH DAY: **Mosque of Eyüp, Teahouse of Pierre Loti, Kariye Müzesi** (a second time perhaps) **Tekfur Sarayı, Yedikule, St. John of Studion, Kumkapı** (for lunch)**Küçük Ayasofya, Mosque of Sokollu Mehmet Paşa.** In moving around the city, either during your one-day visit or your longer time, you should notice these places which you may pass by, or which you can see from afar:
IN THE OLD CITY: city walls, Golden Horn, Eminönü, bridges across the Golden Horn and the Bosphorus,Valens aqueduct, Mosque of Şehzade, Istanbul Belediye building, Istanbul University, Mosque of Bayezit, Çemberlitaş, St. Irene, IN BEYOĞLU, Taksim Atatürk Cultural Center, Beşiktaş and statue of Barbarossa, Galata Tower,Tophane (cannon foundry) Pera Palas Hotel, Istiklâl Caddesi. IN ASIA: Sea of Marmara, Princes' Islands, Kadıköy, Haydarpaşa, Selimiye barracks, Karacaahmet cemetery, Üsküdar, Leander's Tower, Çamlıca, Beylerbeyi Palace and mosque, Küçüksu Palace, Anadolu Hisar.

H I L T O N

T U R K E Y

"Take me to the Hilton."

THE HILTON · THE HOTEL

Buses

An inexpensive method of transportation, buses are frequently overcrowded. You can get buses on Cumhuriyet Caddesi going from the Hilton to Taksim, Şişli, or beyond. Outside rush hours you'll get a seat more easily.

Purchase tickets at kiosks by the bus stops before you board. Or you may find enterprising people along the line selling tickets with a little profit for themselves added on. You can buy tickets in any quantity.

Destinations are marked on the front and the side of each bus. Drop the ticket in the box when you enter, and push the exit button just before the stop where you plan to get off. There are no transfer tickets.

Double-decker buses

The most comfortable means of public transportation. No standing passengers are allowed. The fare is double the normal bus rates. The upper deck provides better view of the sites. Buses #200 and #201 operate every half hour between Taksim and Bostancı, buses #211 and #212 between Taksim and Kadıköy and bus #71T between Taksim and Ataköy. As one can always come back to the starting point, one can explore Istanbul on one's own. A third line operates between Sultanahmet and Bebek following the coastal road. It is worth a ride for the lovely view of the Bosphorus.

Minibuses

Cheaper than the buses, the minibuses mostly operate on longer distances. Unless you are adventuresome, they are not recommended because both the seats and the speed of the driving are uncomfortable.

Dolmuşes

Necessity is the mother of invention! When public transportation first was not sufficient and taxis were expensive, the shared taxi (*dolmuş*) system sprang up. Dolmuşes operate on certain routes; they have fixed fares. The best way to use a dolmuş is to go to the terminal for a particular route and queue up. For instance, if you want to go to the Ataköy Galleria for shopping, you can take an Ataköy dolmuş from Taksim. From two dolmuş terminals you can go to the Asiatic side, one in Taksim next to the Atatürk Cultural Center Car Park, and the other in Şişli on the street opposite the mosque. Just for the sake of the experience you should try one long-distance dolmuş ride. You might make friends and have a jolly chat. If you are lucky your carriage might be a 1940 Chevy.

Taxis

Yellow taxis (*taksi*) are in abundance on the streets of Istanbul. The cars have meters adjusted to day-time and night-time rates. Tipping is not customary. Most of the drivers do not know the city as well as they should. They like to play loud Turkish music and to smoke. Yet when asked to do otherwise, they will turn the radio off and extinguish their cigarettes.

Underground

The Tünel, the world's second oldest and the shortest underground railway, built in 1877, operates between Beyoğlu and Karaköy. From Taksim you can ride the old-fashioned streetcar to the end of İstiklâl Caddesi where you will find the top end of the Tünel. From the bottom end you can walk to the Kadıköy ferries or across the Galata Bridge to the Spice Bazaar.

Ferry boats

The ferries are the most pleasant public transportation. Their routes include Sirkeci-Üsküdar, Üsküdar-Beşiktaş, Sirkeci-Kadıköy, Beşiktaş-Kadıköy, Sirkeci-the Islands, Bostancı-the Islands and Yalova, up and down the Golden Horn, and up and down the Bosphorus. For tourists there are special cruises every day from the Eminönü quay (#3 landing) at 10:35 am to Anadolu Kavağı, a fishing village at the north end of the Bosphorus on the Asian side. There people can have lunch ashore before returning on the same boat. The recommended menu is fried mussels, fried fish, and salad. For more information call   522 0045.

İstanbul Deniz Otobüsleri (water buses)

The high-speed and most comfortable air-conditioned catamaran water buses operate to and from all major ferry landing spots except the ones on the Bosphorus.
European Side. From Kabataş, Bakırköy, Yenikapı to Bostancı, Kadıköy and Yalova.
Asian Side. From Bostancı, Kadıköy, Kartal to Kabataş, Karaköy, Yalova, Yenikapı, Bakırköy. And between Kartal and Yalova. In summer months the water buses operate from Kabataş, Bostancı and Bakırköy to Büyükada (the largest of the Princes' Islands). The water buses are very frequent. For more information and exact schedule call (0216) 362 0444. From the Kabataş landing there are free shuttle bus services to Taksim.

Banliyö Treni (Local Trains)

On the European Side. Between Sirekci and Halkalı.
On the Asian Side. Between Haydarpaşa and Gebze.
Very crowded during rush hours. Mediocre standard.

Hızlı Tramvay (Metro Trolley)

They work between Sirkeci and Topkapı. It may be an experience to get on it from Sultan Ahmet, after finishing sightseeing, to go to Sirkeci to take a boat to Beşiktaş (to avoid hectic traffic) where one can take a taxi to go to the Istanbul or Parksa Hilton.

Istanbul Metro

Under construction and is expected to be finished next year. It will operate between Taksim and Levent.

Bazaars (Markets)

In Ottoman times there were three main kinds of markets: the *bedesten*, the *çarşı*, and the *pazar*. The bedesten and the çarşı were both under a roof; the income from each went to the pious foundation (*vakıf*) they supported. The pazar was an outdoor market, usually without any permanent structure, of a more informal nature. These names still persist, but the distinctions between them have become blurred.

Originally the bedesten was the place to buy *bez*, that is, valuable cloth such as silk. Because its doors were locked at night it also became both the market for gold and jewels, and the safety deposit for such.

The çarşı was built around the bedesten. It housed the shops of manufactured goods: shoes, hats, towels, copperware, saddles, for instance. Both the bedesten and the çarşı were constructed of heavy stone or brick walls; their roofs were pierced with skylights which provided the only light. No open flames were permitted because of a well-founded fear of fire.

Each street in the çarşı was devoted to the products of a particular guild. The shops were controlled by the relevant guild. Names of some of the old crafts still linger in the streets of the Covered Bazaar in Istanbul: Tuğcular Sokak (Street of the Makers of Horsetail Pennants), Kalpakçılar Caddesi (Avenue of the Makers of Fur Caps).

The large markets were almost towns in themselves. They had their own mosque, their own water supply, their own firemen, their own government. They opened early; usually they closed at the time of afternoon prayers since the interior would be too dark for business after prayers. The merchants sat on raised platforms; they kept their merchandise in cupboards, and their display areas were often not much larger than the reach of their arms.

Although the pazars were active every day, some of them had special days when their goods were more varied or more abundant than others. Those markets have left their names in areas of the city: Salıpazarı (the Tuesday Market), for instance, is near the Kılıç Ali Paşa mosque. Like the bedesten and the çarşı, they were patrolled by government inspectors who checked the accuracy of the weights and measures, and the fairness of the prices. Punishment for infraction was a bastinado — a severe beating on the soles of the dishonest merchant.

Among the permanent specialized pazars were the flea markets (*bit pazarı*) in several locations, the book market (*sahaflar*) just outside the Covered Market in Bayezit, and the slave market near Çemberlitaş. The slave market no longer exists; the locations and the merchandise of the flea markets have changed over the years. The book market continues as an excellent place to hunt for unexpected treasures.

Two covered markets in Istanbul are famous. **The Covered Market** or **the Grand Bazaar (Kapalı Çarşı)** between the Nuruosmaniye and Bayezit mosques is thought to date from the time of Mehmet the Conqueror. The bedesten inside may be considerably older than the rest of the building. The streets of the market form a rough grid with some streets on the edges angling off or ending in one of the many adjacent caravansaries.

While for foreigners the Covered Market is almost a museum, for local residents it is a working market where they shop for bargains in foam rubber, quilts, furniture, carpets, and gold. Some shops are known for their ceramic ware, some for their leather coats, and others for their brass and copper. Shopping is unhurried; both merchants and buyers linger over a cup of coffee or hot apple juice as they discuss politics, world news, mutual acquaintances, and, salted among the topics, the price of the article in question. Never mind that you don't speak Turkish. Either the shopkeeper or his assistant will be fluent in whatever language you prefer.

Inside the Covered Market there are two bedestens. The **Sandal Bedesten** near the Nuruosmaniye entrance is one of the more recent additions to the market, having been built in the 16th century. For years it was the location of a bi-weekly auction when eager buyers perched on wooden tiers of seats while the sellers spread out their stacks of rugs and carpets. It has lost its old Istanbul character in the many tourist items sold there now.

The Inner Bedesten (İç Bedesten) maintains an aura of fabled riches. The elaborate calligraphy that you may be shown may have been done by one of the sultan's official scribes. Perhaps the brass bell that was too expensive really was from one of the Ottoman navy's ships that survived the Battle of Lepanto. You know that antiques may not be sold or exported, but are you sure that the small gold coin in your hand is not an authentic louis d'or? Or could the diamond brooch have once been worn by a 19th century Russian princess? Or can you make up your own tale?

The second covered market, the **Spice Bazaar (Mısır Çarşısı)** is located just north of Yeni Cami in Eminönü. An ell-shaped building much smaller than the Covered Market, it houses about 100 stores inside while another 50 line its outside walls. Large containers of henna (a greenish powder) at the entrance or dry linden blossoms identify the shops selling spices and herbs. Next to them may be shops with equally large furry skins that hold *tulum peyniri* (a kind of cheese aged in a bag of goat skin). A little further on you will find bags of pistachios and roasted chick peas in one shop while across the street may be a shop selling Turkish Delight and *helva*.

Outside is an open nursery offering vegetable plantings, fruit trees, house plants and, here and there, pet stores of fish and parakeets. Many local people shop here for their gardens.

Hisars, Kules (Castles) 🏰

The castles of Istanbul were built primarily as strongholds, not as residences for the emperors or sultans. Thus, in contrast to some European castles, they appear inelegant and stripped of their equipment. Although not in the center of the city, three of the castles are fairly easy to visit: Yedi Kule, Rumeli Hisar, and Anadolu Hisar. A fourth, Anadolu Kavağı, has recently been opened to foreigners.

All have towers joined by curtain walls. Soldiers running along the upper patrol paths of those walls were protected by crenellations. Engravings of them show the towers and turrets capped with conical lead roofs into the 19th century. None suffered major damage in any war; the cracks you see are the results of the passage of time and of natural disasters. Two were political prisons into the early 19th century; now they are used as museums.

Anadolu Hisar, the first Ottoman holding on the Bosphorus, was built between 1390 and 1395 by Sultan Bayezit I. It overlooks the Göksu (one of the Sweet Waters of Asia); in history it was called Güzelcehisar — the Pretty Fortress. Lew Wallace, the author of Ben Hur and one-time United States Ambassador to the Sublime Porte, wrote "The Prince of India," a romantic tale which he located in this fortress.

Anadolu Kavağı (near the north end of the Bosphorus) holds memories of Jason, King Prusias I (for whom Bursa is named) and all of the Byzantine emperors. During the 14th century it was a Genoese castle, and several times during the Ottoman Empire it was taken by Russian forces.

The fortress of **Rumeli Hisar** was built between March and August of 1452 by Sultan Mehmet II. It was the Ottomans' first post on the European side of the Bosphorus. By then the Byzantine emperor was so weak that Mehmet took the land with little more than armed protest from the local residents. Its Turkish name, Boğazkesen, is a play on words: cut-throat or strait-cutter. The words describe the control of the Bosphorus that it, combined with Anadolu Hisar opposite, exercised.

Mehmet's three generals built the towers: Grand Vizier Çandarlı Halil Paşa the east tower near the water, Saruca Paşa the north, or black, tower (Kara Kule), and Zağanos Paşa the south, or rose, tower (Gül Kulesi). Mehmet himself was responsible for the turrets and the curtain walls.

In honor of the 500th anniversary of Mehmet's conquest, Rumeli Hisar was repaired in 1953. The patrol walk is open to visitors; the Halil Paşa tower is occasionally, but the other two towers are not. On good summer nights the sloping enclosure is used as a theater, often with a historical drama being the evening's entertainment.

Yedi Kule (the Seven Towers) originally was only the Golden Gate over the Via Egnatia, through which triumphant emperors returned to their capital. On the gate was inscribed in Greek the words, "Long live the Emperor! God has brought you back." When the land walls were stretched west by Theodosian in the 4th century the gate was included in them, and then four towers were added. Mehmet the Conqueror built three more towers in 1458, enclosing a hexagonal area.

During Ottoman times it was a state prison and a storehouse for palace valuables. In keeping with the custom of the time, foreign diplomats of those countries with which the Empire was at war were imprisoned for the duration of the hostilities. Besides French, Russian and Venetian gentlemen, there were also prisoners from Germany and Hungary. One ambassador was held because his country owed money; another escaped; and more than a few died.

In 1622 Sultan Osman II (Genç Osman) ran afoul of his janisaries when he plotted a reform of the army. They captured him in the palace, hauled him to Yedi Kule, and here in the south pylon tortured and killed him.

Like Rumeli Hisar, Yedi Kule has been used more recently as an open-air summer theater.

Bridges

At present there are three bridges across the Golden Horn and two across the Bosphorus.

In the sixth century Justinian built an arched stone bridge across the Golden Horn beginning at Blachernae; it was destroyed in 1204. Until the next one was built between Eminönü and Galata in 1835, people crossed by row boat. That small boat traffic continues parallel with the new bridge. The **Atatürk Bridge** between Unkapanı and Azap Kapı was built in 1935; both it and the **Galata Bridge** have leaves that open to permit large ships access to the shipyards of the Horn. During the political disturbances of the 1970s those leaves were opened on occasion to prevent surging mobs from crossing easily. At that time the only passage was north of Eyüp across the Alibeyköy stream (one of the Sweet Waters of Europe). The third bridge, the **Haliç Köprüsü** is near the place of Justinian's; it carries the traffic of the E-5 highway.

The first bridge across the Bosphorus was a pontoon bridge of boats built by Darius the Great in about 512 BC for his army. It probably crossed between Anadoluhisar and Rumelihisar, the narrowest point. Having served its purpose it was dismantled at once.

The first permanent bridge, the **Bosphorus Bridge**, between Ortaköy and Beylerbeyi was opened on October 29, 1973 to celebrate the 50th anniversary of the Republic. The **Fatih Sultan Mehmet Bridge**, opened on July 3, 1988, was built because of the success of the first and because the amount of traffic was too great to be handled by only one. Both of these are suspension bridges.

One other large bridge in the city is more commonly thought of in another context. The Valens Aqueduct is a typical double Roman bridge, originally about 1,000 meters long and twenty meters at its greatest height.

Caravansaries

In Istanbul caravansaries or *hans* were hotels, warehouses, and offices for the out-of-town merchants. The rooms were arranged around a central open courtyard.

The larger ones such as the Büyük Valide Han were two or three story buildings. The entrance gate was both high to allow the camels and their loads easy access and strong to protect their goods.

Stables, storerooms for fodder, baggage rooms and a blacksmith were on the ground floor while the sleeping quarters and toilets were upstairs. In some the baggage rooms served as offices for the merchants. Other rooms became workshops to complete the manufacture of the raw materials. The large caravansaries now are almost entirely given over to manufacturing.

Many of the caravansaries were built to bring income for a mosque. That of the Büyük Valide Han went to Yeni Cami. The second largest han in the city is the Yeni Han across the street from it; the oldest may be the Vezir Han near the Mosque of Nuruosmaniye.

In the cities the caravansaries were located in the market area: a number of them open off the streets of the Covered Market. On the main roads outside the cities they were spaced about a day's journey from each other.

Cemeteries, Mausoleums

The largest cemetery in Istanbul is the Moslem one of Karacaahmet. From a distance it is marked by the forest of dark cypress trees on the hill between Üsküdar and Kadıköy. The name commemorates a folk hero reputed to be buried here, Swarthy Ahmet, who rode through Anatolia healing the mentally sick. The popularity of this place is because it is on the same continent as the holy cities of Mecca and Medina.

Another favorite burial spot is the area around the Mosque of Eyüp. A newer cemetery is that at Zincirlikuyu. Most of the mosques have cemeteries in their precincts.

The engraving on the stones in Moslem cemeteries, particularly the older ones, is often a work of art. Until about 1830 the men's stones were decorated with turbans that identified their profession and rank. The women's tombstones had designs of flowers, fruit, or jewelry. The inscription told something about the character of the person. Those on the women's gave their father's name, but not their husband's.

Between 1830 and 1926 the men's stones were capped with a *fez*. Today both the men's and the women's are without decoration except for the name, the dates, and a request that those who read them recite the Fatiha (the first *sura* of the Koran) in memory of the dead.

The dead are buried in wooden caskets or wrapped in shrouds. Moslems are placed on their backs with their heads turned to Mecca. There is no cremation in Turkey.

A mausoleum (*türbe*) in a Moslem cemetery is a small domed building containing the tombs of important people. Usually more than one person is buried in the mausoleum. The buildings are oriented towards Mecca with the *mihrap* directly opposite the door. The bodies are buried in the ground; above them are the cenotaphs. The head of a man's cenotaph was indicated previously by a turban or a fez: those of the sultans carried their owner's turbans. A woman's cenotaph was covered only with a cloth.

The most recent mausoleum/memorial, above Adnan Menderes Caddesi, is the burial place of Prime Minister Menderes and of President Turgut Özal.

Among the Christian cemeteries, there are the Greek Orthodox and Armenian Orthodox in Şişli. The cemetery at Balıklı Kilisesi for several hundred years has been the burial place of a number of Greek Orthodox patriarchs. Earlier patriarchs were buried on Heybeliada.

At one time the oldest Armenian church was that of Surp Kirkor Lusarovitch (St Gregory the Illuminator) in Karaköy where some of their patriarchs were buried. (The present 20th century building is like the patriarchal church of Echmiadzin.) Roman Catholics and Protestants have shared adjacent grounds in Feriköy since the mid-19th century.

There is also an Anglican cemetery in Haydarpaşa established for the burial of those who died in the Crimean War.

Jewish cemeteries are located in Arnavutköy, Bağlarbaşı, Kadıköy, Ortaköy, Şişli and Nisbetiye.

Christian Communities, Churches ☖

The Christian communities in Turkey were recognized historically by their *millet* (nationality according to religious creed). The millet system was devised by the Turkish sultans as a means of ruling their minority peoples. Many of the distinctions between these communities are related to the decisions of seven major ecumenical councils that met between 325 and 787 and that intended to determined belief, practice, and relative political standing.

In outline, the main church bodies which have members resident in Istanbul are these: The Eastern Orthodox (Greek Orthodox) Churches recognize the authority of the decisions taken in the Seven Ecumenical Councils. The Oriental Orthodox (Armenian and Syrian) Churches separated from Eastern Orthodoxy after the Third Council which took place in Ephesus in 431.

The Eastern Rite Catholic Churches include groups that united with Rome in the last 400 years (the Armenian Catholic and the Greek Catholic, for instance), and one group (Maronite) which considers that it never broke its communion with Rome. Some of the members of the Latin (Roman) Catholic Church in Istanbul are foreigners more or less permanently resident there; some few have distant family ties to the 12th century crusaders.

The Protestant community is largely the result of European and American missionary activity. The European began with the Huguenot presence in the early 17th century that was protected by the Dutch embassy. The American influence dates from 1820.

In 1054 the Eastern Orthodox and Latin Catholic Churches pronounced mutual anathemas against each other. The most dramatic moment of this action took place when Bishop Humbert placed a papal Bull of Excommunication against Bishop Cerularius on the altar of Saint Sophia on July 16. These anathemas were finally annulled in 1965. Since then Pope Paul VI visited Istanbul in 1967 and Pope John Paul II in 1979.

Relations among all the Christian communities have become increasingly cordial in the last thirty years.

Columns, Monuments

The oldest column in Istanbul is the monolithic obelisk in the Hippodrome that originally was erected by Ptolemy III in Karnak in 1471 BC.

Both Constantine and Julian the Apostate ordered the governor of Egypt to send them an obelisk, but it wasn't until 390 that this one was erected here by Theodosius I. That feat is shown in high reliefs on its base.

Next to it, the small bronze Serpentine Column is also an import: it came from the Temple to Apollo in Delphi where it symbolized the Greek struggle for freedom against the Persians in the Battle of Platea in 497 BC.

The Goths' Column in Gülhane Park is thought to have been put up either during the time of Septimius Severus or of Constantine. It is supposed to commemorate a victory by the Romans over the Goths at Nish in 259 AD. Çemberlitaş or the Column of Constantine, was erected during the reign of Constantine and was topped by a statue of him crowned with a sun symbol of seven rays. It has suffered in storms and earthquakes, and the drums have had to be reinforced several times. It was only one of many columns that supported statues of Byzantine emperors.

A monument visible from the E-5 highway close to the Çağlıyan exit is the Abide-i Hürriyet (Column of Liberty), a memorial to the soldiers who died fighting to overthrow Sultan Abdül Hamit in 1909.

In the Taksim square is the memorial arch honoring the founding of the Republic. On the east face is Mustafa Kemal Atatürk flanked by İsmet İnönü on his right and General Fevzi Çakmak on his left. Behind him are the civilians and the army.

Two admirals are remembered with modern statues: the 16th century Admiral Barbaros Hayrettin Paşa's statue is in the park in Beşiktaş, while 19th century Cezayirli Gazi Hasan Paşa and his pet lion are at the ferry landing of Kasımpaşa.

Mosques

The mosque (*cami* in Turkish) is the Muslim building for communal worship. The domes and the minarets of the largest ones are important elements of Istanbul's distinctive skyline. Wherever they are in the world, mosques are situated so that when worshippers face the front wall (*kıble*) they are oriented to Mecca. (In Istanbul this is southeast.) Formerly only those mosques founded by sultans had more than one minaret. All minarets have at least one balcony from which the *müezzin* used to give the call to prayer (*ezan*); now the call is more often broadcast electronically.

In addition to an outside fountain and/or a series of spigots where men perform their ritual ablutions before entering the mosque, there is a courtyard which helps distance the religious role of the mosque from the secular character of the city. (Women wash themselves at home if they are attending the mosque.)

The inside of a mosque is a large sanctuary. There are no seats: they would be in the road of worshippers performing their prayers (*namaz*). The floor is covered with rugs or matting.

In the middle of the front wall is the prayer niche (*mihrab*); to the right of it is the stepped pulpit (*minber*) from which the preacher (*imam*) gives the Friday noon sermon. In front of it is a free-standing raised platform (*müezzin mahfili*) used by chanters in some services. On the east wall is a raised chair for the *imam* during other services. (Although the imam is present at each service, he is not an intercessor; each Muslim addresses God directly.)

The sides and the back of the sanctuary may be screened off for use by women or for classes given by the imam. Everyone entering a mosque must be dressed modestly and must remove his or her shoes.

Above the mihrab are plaques with the names of Allah and Muhammed. Similar plaques around the room have the names of the first four caliphs, Ebu Bakir, Ömer, Osman, and Ali, and Ali's two martyred sons Hasan and Hüseyin.

Islam does not permit pictures of people, but mosques may be brilliantly decorated with geometric and floral designs in marble, tile, and wood. Usually there are also stylized calligraphic quotations from the Koran in medallions and along the string-course.

Devout Muslims pray five times a day: at sunrise, at noon, in the afternoon, at sunset, and at night. The exact hours change according to the season. (Note also that the Muslim calendar is lunar and therefore moves about ten days every year. Thus while one year the month of fasting — Ramazan — may fall in the spring, ten years later it will come in winter.) Performance of prayer follows a pattern of standing, kneeling, and bowing to the ground.

Before starting, the worshipper states his belief in God and in Muhammed as God's prophet. During the prayer he recites one or more of the *suras* of the Koran. Although it is thought to be more valuable to pray as a community, individuals may pray any place as long as they and their prayer space are clean. To protect themselves from being interrupted during their prayers they may stand so that a wall blocks their view; if they are distracted they must start at the beginning. Because of this it is considerate of visitors not to walk in front of worshippers.

The majority of Muslims in Turkey are Sunnis (orthodox). The Shi'ites (followers of Ali) are the majority group in Iran, but in Turkey they are a minority. Popular Islam found expression through the leadership and devotion of a number of mystics whose way of life became centered in the dervish orders. This movement is known as Sufism; members of one of these orders are the Whirling Dervishes (Mevlevi Dervişleri).

Surrounding the larger mosques are several dependencies which once would have been schools, a caravansary, a hospital, a soup kitchen, an insane asylum, a market, and a time keeper's quarters. Collectively these are called a complex (*külliye*). Income from them helped support the mosque. Only a few of these buildings are still used for the purpose for which they were built: the caravansary of Atik Valide Camii has become a prison, and the school of İskele Camii is a clinic; however the Spice Market of Yeni Cami continues as it was, and the soup kitchen of the Mihrişah Complex in Eyüp still serves about 500 people daily.

Walls

The walls of Constantinople make a triangle of the Golden Horn, the Sea of Marmara, and the land walls. Their circumference is about 20 km. At first the walls protected only the summit of the First Hill. Septimius Severus's walls in 196 AD enclosed a larger area from present-day Eminönü up the hill to the Hippodrome and then down to the sea near the Saray Point. Constantine moved them west of the present Atatürk Bridge, from where they went over the hill and back down to the sea at Samatya. Little if any of these land walls still exists.

The Golden Horn side of the city was protected not only by the walls but also by a heavy chain that reached from near Eminönü to Karaköy. Part of the chain is in the Naval Museum of Sultans' Kayıks in Beşiktaş. The walls are most visible in the area of Balat. There you can find a plaque in memory of Mehmet the Conqueror whose fleet almost miraculously appeared in the Horn on the morning of April 6, 1453, having been skidded up over the Galata hill from the Bosphorus. Before that event the walls had been breached by the Latins in 1204 when they ran their ships up and fastened boarding bridges against them.

Like the Golden Horn walls, the sea walls were a single line that was extended each time the city was expanded. Near the Point the walls carry an inscription in Greek which identifies the Emperor Theophilos (829-842) as one of the builders.

Both the Byzantines and the Ottomans had small palaces on the water where they could enjoy the summer breezes. The Palace of the Boukoleon, which Justinian is said to have built for Theodora, still has a number of its marble window frames. Marble lions in the Archaeological Museum were once part of its façade.

A near-by pretty Pearl Kiosk was a 16th and 17th century sultan's recreation pavilion. At the west end of the Sea Walls is the Marble Tower, possibly also an imperial palace. It's a stone's throw from the Golden Gate and the Seven Towers (Yedi Kule) at the southern end of the Land Walls.

The fifth century Theodosius II was the main builder of the land walls. They stretch 6 1/2 km from the Sea of Marmara to the Golden Horn. The walls had a moat 20 meters wide, an outer wall 8 1/2 meters high, a terrace, and an inner wall that was between 18 and 20 meters high. The two walls were studded at alternating intervals with 96 defense towers each. A few of the gates such as the Edirnekapı and the Fifth Military Gate retain their original character. In recent years a part near the Belgrat Kapısı has been elaborately restored. Close to the Horn is the Palace of Blachernae, the residence of the last Byzantine rulers.

All of the walls have suffered from military attacks, from earthquakes, from weather, and from city modernizations such as railroads and broad avenues.

Water Supplies

Water for Istanbul has always been one of its sources of both strength and of difficulties. Almost surrounded by salt water, the Sea of Marmara and the Golden Horn were the natural moat for its citizens. Those bodies plus the Bosphorus and the Black Sea favored them with commercial highways that needed little outlay for upkeep until the latter part of the present century.

However, drinking water has been more problematical. Throughout its history there have been frequent accounts of water shortages in the city caused by military sieges, by breaks in the pipes, and by a population too great for the existing system. Each age has added to the complexity of the supply.

The first sources of fresh running water were a number of streams and springs. The Sweet Waters of Europe that empty into the Golden Horn were once a part of the main supply and were piped into a cistern in the center of the old city. (The story of the water supplies for the Asian side parallels that of the European.) There were — and still are — also a number of springs throughout the city. From their earliest days the residents considered a spring holy; the water was both refreshing and purifying. Known as a holy well or "*ayazma*," the spring was a goal for pilgrims who hoped for cures from its supernatural power. Even yet, a formal thanks to the one who has given you a drink is "*Su gibi aziz olasın*" — "May you be as blessed as water."

Hadrian is thought to have been the first ruler to channel the water from outside the city walls; by the time of Constantine some of it was being brought from Saray about 150 km to the west. The source of more was the forested hills north of the city where it was collected in dams and then directed over a number of aqueducts. The **Great Dam** (Büyük Bend or Belgrat Bendi) in the Belgrade Forest dates from Byzantine times; other dams include the **Valide Bendi** and the **Mahmut Bendi**. The water of **Lake Terkoz** (a.k.a. Durusu) was added to the Istanbul reservoir system towards the end of the 19th century. In the last twenty years the **Alibeyköy Reservoir** has been built to meet the demands of the rapidly growing population.

Among the aqueducts in the Belgrade Forest are the **Mahmut I Aqueduct** which you drive under as you approach from Büyükdere, the **Long Aqueduct** (Uzunkemer) and the **Bent Aqueduct** (Eğrikemer) near the village of Kemerburgaz , and the **Pretty Aqueduct** (Güzelcekemer) and the Justinian's Aqueduct or **Maglova Kemer** near the Alibeyköy Reservoir. The most frequently seen aqueduct is that built by the Emperor Valens in 378 which crosses Atatürk Boulevard near the Istanbul Municipal Buildings. Chief among the Ottoman builders, Süleyman and Sinan repaired and restored many of the city's dams and aqueducts.

For most of the distance from the lakes and dams the water is channeled through pipes underground. Twice those channels are reputed to have figured in Byzantine history: the Emperors Justinian II in 705 and Michael Paleologus in 1261 stole through them unseen into the city, each to regain his throne.

Every household once collected rain water in barrels or cisterns. A number of those private cisterns are still functioning. The large public cisterns have been the central distribution reservoirs (*taksim*) around the city. The one near the Atatürk Cultural Center in Beyoğlu gives its name to that region. Three very large cisterns were turned to other uses as far back as Byzantine times: Aspar, Aetios and Mocius. A 10th century cistern near St. Sophia is currently a restaurant (**Sarnıç Taverna**). The Basilica Cistern (**Yerebatan Sarayı**) has become a museum noted for its many columns, two of which, it was discovered when the water was drained out, were supported by handsome marble Medusa heads.

In several places around the city (for example between St. Sophia and the Basilica Cistern and by the parking lot of the Divan Hotel) you will see a tall dressed stone tower similar to an obelisk, called "*su terazisi*" in Turkish. The towers are part of the mechanics of the water system. They both allow water to flow from one point to another without having to travel downhill all the way (like a siphon), and they regulate the pressure in the pipes. The water comes into the tower from a source slightly higher than its height; it is pushed to the top where there is a small collecting pool; from there it runs down again through one or more distribution pipes. Not only the problems of insuring themselves with a sufficient supply of good water but also of maintaining its cleanliness continue to beset Istanbul residents.

By the 1980s pollution around Istanbul had become a noxious offense. As part of the solution Mayor Bedrettin Dalan began a general project of sewage collection and treatment plants for the entire metropolitan area in cooperation with the Istanbul Water and Sewage Administration.

Baths

The Roman institution of the public baths is preserved in Istanbul (and throughout the country) in the *hamams*. Among the larger and better-known ones are those of Mahmutpaşa, Çemberlitaş, Cağaloğlu, Ortaköy, and Galatasaray. They are usually domed buildings with either separate sections for men and separate ones for women or separate times for each sex. The buildings are without windows, but the domes are pierced with many glazed holes which admit the daylight. They are heated often by a system of ducts under the floors and up the walls which conducts the hot air of the furnace. Water is heated also by that furnace.

Bathers enter a hall where they pay for their bath and where they find a stall where they may undress. Towels, soap, and wooden clogs may be furnished by the establishment. Depending on the facilities, the bathers may then go either

through a second room (*soğukluk* in Turkish) or directly into
the steaming hot room (*hararet*).

Often the floors and walls of these rooms are covered with
marble. There may be several recessed compartments where
people can bathe privately. Both in them and in the large open
room water flows into marble basins arranged against the
walls. Small wooden stools for people to sit on are in front of
the basins.

Etiquette prescribes that the water in the basins (which have
no drains) is used only for rinsing. Each bather is furnished
with a metal bowl (*hamam tası*) to scoop up the water from the
basin and pour it over himself. The rinse water runs out
through drains in the floor.

After the first washing a bather may enjoy a massage and
scrubbing by a masseur (or masseuse) on the central flat stone
(*göbek taşı*) before a final wash and rinse.

Many people also enjoy resting with a cup of Turkish coffee or
nibbling some fruit following the bath. Historically the
hamams were important social institutions where people met
their friends for a leisurely visit. Even today some of the
hamams are more than just places to take a bath.

The **Termal** is a spa outside of Yalova which has a variety of
facilities including hotels, a movie theater, a greenhouse, picnic
areas, and mountain walks. It also has a very old indoor pool
and a large outdoor one where bathers can swim. The water
here comes from a hot mineral spring that has been popular
since at least the third century BC. Constantine and his mother
St. Helena sought healing at this spring, as did the Empress
Theodora. Behind the movie theater are a number of columns
from the Church of the Archangel built by Constantine and
restored by Justin II in the sixth century.

Modernized by Atatürk in 1928, the facilities are again being
renovated.

Map of Turkey

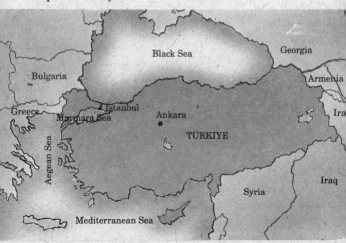

Hello! This is the Istanbul American Hospital.

The American Hospital of Istanbul is a full specialty and fully equipped general hospital. Emergency service is given 24 hours a day by a professional team of specialist physicians and nurses.

Centrally located in Nişantaşı, the American Hospital is easily accessible from many parts of the city. In case of emergencies, we have a 24-hour ambulance service. So, keep our number at hand: **(212) 231 40 50**

AMERICAN HOSPITAL

Güzelbahçe Sokak, Nişantaşı-İstanbul Fax: (212) 234 14 32

This list is to enable you to find the places under their Turkish names, given in bold face below. When they are sub-listings under another category, the notation is: **Balık Pazarı** (*see* **Çiçek Pasajı).** If the English name and the Turkish name are similar enough that both should be recognizable, only the English is given below. The Blue Mosque is listed under both its English and its Turkish names because both are the common reference; the Palace of Topkapı is likewise under both names. If only the English name is common, the Turkish name is omitted: British Crimean Cemetery. The same applies if only the Turkish name is common: **Anadolu Hisarı**, not the Anatolian Castle. A few items are listed in more than one category. For instance, the **Çiçek Pasajı** is both a MARKET and a PLACE OF ENTERTAINMENT.

AQUEDUCTS: **KEMERLER** 27
  Bentler: **Eğri Kemer** (*see* **Belgrat Ormanı)** 45
  Pretty: **Güzelce Kemer** (*see* **Belgrat Ormanı)** 45
  Justinian's: **Maglova** (*see* **Belgrat Ormanı)** 45
  Long: **Uzun Kemer** (*see* **Belgrat Ormanı)** 45
  Valens 88

BATHS: **HAMAMLAR** 28
  Baths of Roxelana: **Ayasofya Hamamı** 43
  Cağaloğlu Hamamı 50
  Çemberlitaş Hamamı 54
  Galatasaray Hamamı 61
  Mahmut Paşa Hamamı 71

BRIDGES: **KÖPRÜLER** 21
  Atatürk Köprüsü 41
  Bosphorus: **Boğaziçi Köprüsü** 48
  Fatih Sultan Mehmet II Köprüsü 59
  Galata Köprüsü 60

CARAVANSARIES: **HANLAR** 21
  Rüstem Pasha Caravansary: **Rüstem Paşa Hanı** 77
  Valide Kösem Sultan Caravansary: **Büyük Valide Han** 49

CASTLES: **HİSARLAR** 19
  Anadolu 38
  Anadolu Kavağı 38
  Genoese (*see* **Anadolu Kavağı)** 38
  Rumeli 76
  Seven Towers: **Yedi Kule** 90

CEMETERIES: **MEZARLIKLAR** 22
  Balıklı Kilise 43
  British Crimean 48
  Eyüp 58
  Feriköy 59
  Mausoleum of the Prophet Joshua: **Yuşa Nebi Türbesi** 92
  Karacaahmet 68

CHURCHES: **KILISELER** 23 ⛪
(Except for the Monastery of Constantine Lips, the Church of St. Euphemia, St. John the Baptist of Studius, and those that are now mosques or museums, the following are functioning and open for Christian worship at stated times.)

Armenian Orthodox Patriarchate: **Ermeni Patrikhanesi** 58
Balıklı (Church of Fishes) 43
Cathedral of St. Esprit 50
Church of St. Andrew in Krisei *(see* **Koca Mustafa Paşa Camii**) 69
Church of St. Antoine 51
Church of St. Euphemia *(see* **Kadıköy**) 66
Church of St. George in Fener 77
Church of St. George (Galata) 51
Church of St. Irene *(see* **Saint Irene**) 78
Church of St. Louis 51
Church of St. Mary Draperis 52
Church of St. Savior in Chora *(see* **Kariye Müzesi**) 68
Church of St. Sophia *(see* Saint Sophia) 78
Church of SS. Sergius and Bacchus *(see* **K.Ayasofya Camii**) 70
Church of St. Stephen of the Bulgars 52
Church of the Holy Apostles *(see* **Fatih Sultan Mehmet Camii**) 58
Church of the Kyriotissa *(see* **Kalenderhane Camii**) 66
Church of the Theotokos Pammakaristos *(see* **Fethiye Camii**) 59
Church of the Pantocrator *(see* **Zeyrek Camii**) 92
Crimean Memorial Church 53
Dutch Chapel 57
Greek Orthodox Patriarchate: **Rum Ortodoks Patrikhanesi** 77
Monastery of Constantine Lips 73
St. John the Baptist of Studius 78
Surp Astavdzadzin *(see* **Ermeni Patrikhanesi**) 58

CISTERNS: **SARNIÇLAR** 27
Cisterns of Aetios, Aspar, and Mocius 52
Basilica: **Yerebatan Sarayı** 91
Fildamı 59
Thousand-and-One Column Cistern:**Binbirdirek Sarnıcı** 46

COLUMNS: **SÜTUN, TAŞ** 24
Built (Column of Constantine Porphyrogenitus) *(see* **At Meydanı**) 41
Burnt (Column of Constantine): **Çemberlitaş** 54
Column of Marcian 53
Egyptian Obelisk *(see* **At Meydanı**) 41
Goths: **Got Sütunu** 62
Serpentine *(see* **At Meydanı**) 41

ENTERTAINMENT: **EĞLENCE, KÜLTÜREL ETKİNLİK**
Atatürk Cultural Center: **Atatürk Kültür Merkezi, AKM** 41
Belgrade Forest: **Belgrat Ormanı** 45
Beyaz Köşk *(see* **Emirgan**) 57
Cemal Reşit Rey Konser Salonu 51
Çadır Köşk *(see* **Yıldız Sarayı**) 91
Çırağan Palace: *(see* **Çırağan Sarayı**) 54

MUSEUMS: MÜZELER

SCHOOLS (LYCEES), UNIVERSITIES: **LİSELER,
ÜNİVERSİTELER** (General listing is under "Schools" or
"Universities")

SYNAGOGUES: **SİNAGOGLAR** 27

TOWERS: **KULELER**

WALLS: **SURLAR**

A-A-A

Açık Hava Tiyatrosu
(Open Air Theater) in Harbiye
During the summer there are a variety of theatrical and musical events staged in this theater. It is one of the venues for some performances during the International Istanbul Art Festival (June 15-July 31). It has also hosted classical ballet and folklore dancing.

Akıntı Burnu
(Cape of the Devil's Current)
The swift Bosphorus current off the point of land between Arnavutköy and Bebek has defeated more than one small boat plying upstream. On land now it is a favorite perch for amateur fishermen. In the 19th century in the ceremony of the Baptism of the Waters the Greek Orthodox patriarch would throw his cross into the water here on Epiphany (January 6); youths would then dive into the icy water to retrieve it and be rewarded with honors for the rest of the year. (That ceremony is now observed in Yeşilköy.)

Aksaray Meydanı
(Aksaray Square)
One of the largest squares in the old part of the city, Aksaray is located about where the Forum Bovis was in Constantinople. The marble Roman forum has been replaced by a concrete cloverleaf of streets and avenues.

Anadolu Hisarı
(Asian Fortress)
The small fortress on the Asian shore of the Bosphorus was built about 1390 by Sultan Bayezit I as part of the attack he planned on Constantinople. It was the first permanent structure built by the Ottomans on the Bosphorus. Defeated and captured by Tamerlane in Ankara in 1402, his plans had to wait for his great grandson Mehmet II to realize the dream. The fortress and the surrounding Asian land remained in Ottoman control although the Byzantines continued to hold all of the European side of the Bosphorus for another fifty years. Anadolu Hisarı originally consisted of a square tower, four smaller circular towers, a dungeon, an outer, and an inner curtain wall. Most of the curtain walls were destroyed to make way for the coast road early in this century. The stream next to it is the Göksu, one of the Sweet Waters of Asia, a most favorite and romantic picnic site during the Ottoman days.

Anadolu Kavağı
It is the village farthest north on the Asian shore.
Inexpensive fish restaurants here cater to people who arrive by the noon or late afternoon ferries. On the hill above the village is the "Genoese Castle." Legend says that Anadolu Kavağı was one of the places that Jason built a temple on his return from

finding the Golden Fleece. In pagan times there were twelve temples to the gods of Mt. Olympus on the hill, and also a lighthouse. The temples were richly endowed from the gifts of pilgrims. They weren't the only ones who wanted to claim it: The Bithynian King Prusias I (for whom Bursa takes its name) had a castle here in the 2nd century BC. At the end of the 8th century AD Harun al-Rashid, Caliph of Baghdad, besieged it. Several times in its history it was taken by Russian forces. A coat of arms with a flowered cross by the main gate is a reminder that it was held by the Genoese from 1350 for about 100 years.

Arap Camii

(Arab Mosque; Church of St. Paul and St. Dominic) in Karaköy The building has been attributed to an Arab general who besieged Constantinople in the 8th century. Its present outlines suggest that it was constructed as a church between 1323 and 1337 during the Latin occupation of Constantinople. In the early 16th century it was turned over to Moorish Muslims fleeing from Spain. The square tower at the southeast end of the building, now a minaret, was the bell tower.

Arasta

in Sultanahmet

A shopping street behind the Blue Mosque, the merchants in this Arasta specialize in rugs and carpets.

Arkeoloji Müzeleri

(Archaeological Museums) in Sultanahmet. Tel. (212) 520 7742; entrance fee 45,000TL (covers Çinili Köşk Museum and Museum of the Ancient Orient); Archaeological Museum open 09:30 am to 05:00 pm except Mondays. Çinili Köşk Museum open on Tuesday, Thursday and Saturday. Museum of the Ancient Orient open on Wednesday, Friday and Sunday.

Three separate museum buildings on the slope of the land between the First Court of Topkapı and Gülhane Park house a number of historically important and artistically beautiful items. The main building of the original Archaeological Museum was built by Osman Hamdi Bey, one of Turkey's foremost painters, in 1892 to house the important finds that had been collected from around the Ottoman Empire. Its first major items were the sarcophagi from Sidon, including the so-called Alexander Sarcophagus and the Mourners' Sarcophagus. A gigantic statue of Bes, the Tabnit Sarcophagus, the Ephebe of Tralles, fragments from the excavations at Magnesia-on-the-Meander, and a number of busts of Roman emperors do not begin to exhaust that list. Since 1992 a new wing has been opened for displays of "Neighboring Cultures of Anatolia" and "Anatolia and Troy Through the Ages." Among these items is some of the gold found by Heinrich Schliemann in Troy. The 14th century frescoes depicting St. Frances of Assisi, originally in the church of the Theotokas Kyriotissa (Kalenderhane Camii), are also now here. **Çinili Köşk** (Tiled Kiosk) Çinili Köşk Museum, the second building of the Archaeological

Museums, is the oldest secular Ottoman building standing in Istanbul. Built by Mehmet the Conqueror in 1472, he used it in part as a pavilion from which he watched his men playing *cirit* (a game in which men throw spears at each other as they ride past on horseback). The museum's register includes about fifteen hundred pieces of tiles and ceramics of which about five hundred are on display. The objects cover the chronological development of Turkish ceramic art. In addition to retaining much of its original architecture, some of the tile revetments have survived to our day making the building an unrivalled location as a Museum of Turkish Tiles. **Eski Şark Eserleri Müzesi** (Museum of the Ancient Orient) This is the newest building of the three. In one of its cases a fragment of baked clay inscribed in cuneiform records an acknowledgement that "from eternity the god does not permit the making of hostility" between Egypt and the land of the Hittites. The date was 1269 BC; the event was the treaty signed following the Battle of Qadesh. The museum treasures some of man's oldest and most singular finds - Mesopotamia pottery from 5,000 BC, Sumerian, Assyrian, Babylonian, Egyptian and early Anatolian statues, vases, pottery, jewelry, reliefs and writing from about 3,000 BC. And most rare are the late BC and early AD pre-Islamic statues and reliefs from southern Arabia.

Armenian Patriarchate
(see Ermeni Patrikhanesi)

Asian Fortress
(see Anadolu Hisarı)

Askeri Müze
(Military Museum) in Harbiye; next door to the Istanbul Hilton; Tel. (212) 233 2720 (5 lines); open 09:00 am to 05:00 pm except Mondays and Tuesdays; entrance fee 15,000TL.
A wide range of military items — costumes, armaments, pictures — dating throughout Ottoman history is displayed in the buildings of the Military Museum. In addition, from 3:00 pm to 4:00 pm when the museum is open, a costumed janissary band (*mehter takımı*) performs the music that sent shivers down the spines of European troops in the 16th century, and that added new themes and new instruments to the works of Haydn, Mozart, Beethoven and others.

Aşiyan Müzesi
(Home of Tevfik Fikret) Tel. (212) 263 6986; open 09:00 am to 05:00 pm except Mondays and Thursdays; no entrance fee.
Tevfik Fikret was an early 20th century poet who inspired many of his young Robert College students with republican and socialist ideals. His home (called Aşiyan) just beneath the campus of Boğaziçi University, the former Robert College continues as a trysting place for young idealists.

Atatürk Cultural Center
(see Atatürk Kültür Merkezi)

Atatürk Köprüsü
(Atatürk Bridge)
The bridge between Unkapanı and Azap Kapı was built in 1936
to ease the growing traffic across the Golden Horn over the
Galata Bridge. It replaced an iron bridge that had served for a
record 63 years.

Atatürk Kültür Merkezi
(Atatürk Cultural Center) Tel. (212) 251 5600 (6 lines).
The AKM in Taksim is the home of the Istanbul Opera and
Ballet, the Istanbul State Theater, and the Istanbul Symphony.
Privately sponsored events are held in the small hall; the foyer
often has art exhibits. The opening concert of the annual
Istanbul Festival is held here, as are also international confer-
ences and exhibitions throughout the year.

Atatürk Müzesi
(Atatürk Museum) Halâskârgazi Caddesi 250, Şişli; Tel. (212)
240 6319; open 09:30 am to 4:30 pm. Closed on Sundays and
Thursdays; no entrance fee.
The house in which Atatürk lived briefly is preserved as a
museum of pictures and documents relating to the revolution
which overthrew the sultanate and initiated the Turkish
Republic.

Atik (Eski) Valide Camii
(Queen Mother's Mosque) in Üsküdar
The largest of the mosque complexes in Üsküdar and second in
size only to that of Süleyman was founded by the mother of
Murat III, Nur Banu Sultan. The architect of the original
mosque was Sinan; it was completed in 1582 before Nur Banu
died. The walls of the relatively large *mihrab* are covered with
beautiful İznik tiles; the *minber* is carved marble. The second
plan, completed by another architect, doubled the size of the
mosque to its present outlines. Besides the mosque, the complex included several schools, a bath, a hospital, an *imaret* (an
Ottoman institution which provided food and shelter to the
needy) and a caravansary. There was some work done on it in
the 1960s, but more is needed to preserve the complex which
comprises one of Sinan's greatest architectural achievements.

At Meydanı
(Hippodrome) The grassy park beside the Blue Mosque at
Sultanahmet is the place of the Hippodrome (or race course) of
Constantinople.
It was a sports arena with high wooden bleachers around the
two long sides and the rounded end. (The supporting sub-
structure of that southwestern end is visible below from Nakil
Bent Sokak in the Akbıyık region.) Built first by Septimius
Severus in 203 and enlarged by Constantine the Great, the

Hippodrome was big — 480 meters long and 117.5 meters wide: almost five times as long as a football field in the United States. It could hold 100,000 spectators. This was the emotionally-charged sports center of the old city where the most popular entertainment was the chariot races.

Constantine raided Rome for works of art to decorate it. Among the treasures he brought are four handsome bronze horses which had first been at the entrance to a temple in Corinth. Part of the booty from the Fourth Crusade, they went to St. Marks Cathedral in Vienna, then to the Arc de Triomphe in Paris, and then, when Napoleon was defeated, back to Venice.

Other statues included a large brass eagle that clutched a snake in its talons, an angry elephant, and a Helen that was so beautiful that no one could disbelieve the reason for the Trojan War. Cedrenus, a contemporary historian, remarked disapprovingly that all Constantine needed to complete his city were the souls of the dead Romans. Through the years other statues were added until in the 12th century another historian grumbled that there were as many heroes and gods seated in the Hippodrome as there were live people. The worst uprising in Constantinople began in the Hippodrome in January 532. Rival sports groups, the Blues and the Greens, rioted over a mixture of politics, theology, and a harsh economic policy.

The Emperor Justinian failed miserably to quiet the mob who called him a donkey and told him to shut up. He was forced to run for his life back through the secret passage to his palace, from where but for his wife Theodora he would also have run away from his throne. Shamed by her, he sent his general, Belisarius, back to the Hippodrome and, with the army, he trapped, slaughtered, and buried thirty thousand rebels. Three monuments left from the Byzantine Empire stand in the Hippodrome.

The oldest is the monolithic Egyptian Obelisk rising almost 20 meters. (At one time it was a much taller stone.) It was first raised by Pharaoh Thutmose III in the 4th century BC near Thebes. The ceremony when the Emperor Theodosius I stood it up in Constantinople in 390 is depicted on the marble frieze beneath it. A second tall pillar (the Built Column or the Column of Constantine Porphyrogenitus) may date from the 4th century. It's thought that the bronze which sheathed it was removed to make weapons during the Fourth Crusade. Between the two pillars is a second piece of Constantine's booty, the Serpentine Column. It came from the Temple of Apollo at Delphi where it was a monument to freedom, having been cast from the shields of Persians slain in the Battle of Plataea in 479 BC. The column once was three twined snakes, the heads of which were gone by the beginning of the 18th century.

The column with its heads intact appears in several 16th and 17th century miniatures showing the sultan being entertained by parades and acrobats in the Hippodrome. One other interesting item in the Hippodrome is the German Fountain, gift of Kaizer Wilhelm II.

Ayasofya Hamamı
(Baths of Roxelana) in Sultanahmet Meydanı
The double baths built by Sinan have been restored recently with
marble floors and walls. While they maintain their original character with the private cubicles and an occasional brass water
spigot, the rooms currently house the rug and carpet salesrooms
of the Turkish Ministries of State and of Culture and Tourism.

Ayasofya Museum
(see Saint Sophia)

Ayasofya Pensions
(see Soğuk Çeşme Street)

Aynalı Kavak Kasrı
(Palace of the Mirrored Poplar) in Hasköy;Tel. (212) 250 4094
open 9:30 am to 4:00 pm except Mondays and Thursdays.
(Closed until June 1994 for restoration; enterance fee 30.000TL).
The museum exhibits historical objects. The Palace of Mirrors
was built in the late 18th century by Sultan Ahmet III. Its
pleasing interior details show the overlay of Ottoman design
motifs onto the European Baroque architectural style. A peace
treaty between the Ottoman Empire and Russia in which
Russia regained the Crimea was signed here in 1783 during the
reign of Abdül Hamit I.

Azap Kapı Camii
(Mosque of Sokollu Mehmet Paşa) in Azap Kapı
One of a number of buildings that Sinan built for Grand
Vizier Sokollu Mehmet Paşa, it was completed in 1577/78. It
stands raised above the ground level; originally there were
shops underneath the prayer hall whose rents contributed to
the upkeep of the mosque. The minaret is unusual in that it is
not attached to the main building but can be approached from
the porch of the mosque. Mehmet Paşa was born in Sokol in
Bosnia. As a *devşirme* (converted) conscript, he went through
the palace school for pages, becoming the Treasurer, the
Admiral, the Beylerbey (governor) of Rumelia, and finally
Grand Vizier. He married Selim II's daughter, Esmahan
Sultan. One of the other buildings he gave the money for was
the bridge at Visegrad (1577/78) that has been immortalized in
Ivo Andric's "Bridge on the Drina". Mehmet Pasha was
stabbed to death in the Divan (Council of Ministers) in 1579 by
an insane soldier.

B-B-B

Balıklı Kilisesi
(Zoodochus Pege, Church of Fishes) in Silivri Kapı
The present church building over a sacred pool is recent in
date — 1833, but the pool has been famous since Byzantine

times. Byzantine emperors and their families often spent a
week or so here around Ascension Day (40 days after Easter)
enjoying the benefits of the pool. The fish in the pool figure in
tales associated with the fall of the city. Tombstones inscribed
in Karamanlı script (Turkish words written with Greek char-
acters) and decorated with figures indicating the profession of
the persons they commemorate pave the courtyard floor. In
the church's small graveyard are buried several Greek
Orthodox patriarchs, their tombs bearing the symbols of the
cross and the Byzantine double-headed eagle.

Barbaros Hayreddin Paşa Türbesi
(Mausoleum of Barbarossa) in Beşiktaş; not open to the public
except on the Republic Day on October 29, the Maritime Day
on July 1 and the anniversary of the victory of the Sea Battle of
Preveze on September 27,1538. On those days it is open to the
public all day.
The sea battle of Preveze took place between the Ottoman
Navy under the command of Admiral Barbaros Hayreddin
Pasha and the Crusaders' Navy composed of Venetian,
Genoese, Portuguese, Maltese and Papal vessels under the
command of Genoese Admiral Andrea Doria. The crusaders'
navy was badly defeated. Barbarossa lived during the time of
Süleyman. To the Ottoman Navy he was known as Amiral
Barbaros Hayreddin Paşa; to the Western world he was the
justly-feared pirate Barbarossa. A handsome statue to him
stands in the adjacent park. When they were in port, his war
ships were tied to the quay at Beşiktaş.

Basilica Cistern
(see Yerebatan Sarayı)

Bath at Çemberlitaş
(see Çemberlitaş Hamamı)

Bath at Galatasaray
(see Galatasaray Hamamı)

Bath of Mahmutpaşa
(see Mahmutpaşa Hamamı)

Bath of Roxelana
(see Ayasofya Hamamı)

Bayezit Camii
(Mosque of Bayezit II)
Built between 1501 and 1506, this is the oldest of the great
mosques of the city. Its courtyard area and the prayer hall are
both squares of equal size; the minarets are at the extreme ends
of the side wings of the mosque. The prayer hall is unobstruct-
ed except by the massive piers supporting the dome, allowing
worshippers a free view of the *mihrap* (prayer niche) and *minber* (an elevated seat reached by a flight of steps). It is among
the earliest of the centrally planned mosques, the previous

style being often a series of smaller domes over the central area. Sultan Bayezit and one of his daughters, Selçuk Sultan, are buried in a *türbe* (small mausoleum) in the garden of the mosque. It is not open to public. Among the dependencies of the mosque was the *imaret* which has been converted into the Devlet Kütüphanesi (State Library). Another dependency, the *medrese* (school) is also a library — the Belediye Kütüphanesi (City Library). In a courtyard beside the mosque is the shaded **Sahaflar Çarşısı** (Market for Old Books). While it is not the only place to look for collectors' items, it has a special charm. A statue in the middle of the walkway is of İbrahim Müteferrika, the first person to print books in Turkish in Turkey (1732).

Bayezit Kulesi
(Bayezit Tower)
One of the prominent landmarks of the city, the marble Bayezit Fire Tower standing on the campus of Istanbul University was built by Mahmut II in 1828 replacing a wooden structure. It is now closed to the public.

Belgrat Ormanı
(Belgrade Forest)
The name of this large area seems to be derived from the village which Süleyman the Magnificent founded here for Serbian prisoners of war from Belgrade whom he brought after his capture of that city in 1521.

They were charged with maintaining the water system of the dams and streams of the forest which for centuries has been part of the Istanbul water supply. The trees of the forest are mostly deciduous —oaks, beech, and chestnuts— and it is home to an interesting variety of flowers, mushrooms, birds and other animals. The forest has been a place of refuge for people from Istanbul.

Lady Mary Wortley Montagu, wife of the British ambassador, described the idyllic life of the rich community in Belgrade Village when she was there in 1717: "The heats of Constantinople have driven me to this place which perfectly answers the description of the Elysian fields. The village is wholly inhabited by the richest amongst the Christians, who meet every night at a fountain forty paces from my house to sing and dance..."

As you approach the Belgrade Forest from the Bosphorus village of Büyükdere the first aqueduct you see was built by Sultan Mahmut I in 1732. Not too far from it is his dam, the **Mahmut Bendi**. This water is still directed into the reservoir at Taksim from which it is distributed.

The **Eğri Kemer** (Bent Aqueduct) and the **Uzun Kemer** (Long Aqueduct) near the village of Kemerburgaz were built by the architect Sinan, and he rebuilt the **Maglova Kemer** (often called Justinaian's Aqueducts) and the **Güzelce Kemer** (Pretty Aqueduct). The city's increasing need for water has caused new dams to be built in the forest. **Terkoz Gölü** (Lake Terkoz) is the largest of the lakes in the forest; it is one of Istanbul's reservoirs.

B
A
R
_
B
E
L

Beylerbeyi Camii
(Mosque of Beylerbeyi)

The present Beylerbeyi Mosque sits on the edge of the Bosphorus; an earlier mosque had been built here by Ahmet I. Although Sultan Abdülhamit who built this one in 1776 asked that it be named for his mother, Rabia Sultan, instead it has kept the name of the village. For a time the whole village was so busy and splendid a place that it was called Ferahfeza (meaning Increasing Joy).

Beylerbeyi Sarayı
(Beylerbeyi Palace) in Beylerbeyi. Tel. (216) 321 9320; open 9:30 am to 12:30 pm and 1:30 am to 4:00 pm except Mondays and Thursdays; entrance fee 50,000 TL.

Sultan Abdül Aziz built this elegant little palace between 1861 and 1865 to be a summer palace for himself and a residence for visiting royalty. The Empress Eugenie was here in 1869; her rooms duplicated her private apartment (since lost) in the Tuileries.

Marble features in abundance in the construction. Large Japanese and Sevres vases, crystal columns from Venice, and Bohemian glass chandeliers grace the grand salon, and frescoes painted by Italian artists decorate the walls of the reception rooms.

The dining-room is distinguished by the furniture which Abdül Aziz carved himself. The garden was designed by Murat IV in 1639; during Abdül Aziz's time it had a menagerie that included ostriches and Bengal tigers.

Beyoğlu

Its ancient name Pera meant " beyond" in Greek, indicating that it lay beyond the walls of the old Galata. Along its main street (the Grand rue, now İstiklâl Caddesi) were located the residences of the foreign ambassadors who headed their correspondence "from the vines of Pera."

The crossroad was at Dörtyol where the Kumbaracı and Asmalı Mescit streets met. Close by was the house of the son of the last emperor of Trabzon whom Mehmet the Conqueror had brought to Istanbul. Tradition has it that the present name is a long-forgotten reference to that ruler's (bey) son (oğlu). Later that place was the Russian embassy; now it is a quiet building.

Binbirdirek Sarnıcı
(Cistern of a Thousand and One Columns) in Cağaloğlu. Not open to the public.

One of the large, covered cisterns of the city, Binbirdirek probably dates from the time of Constantine. It is sometimes known by the name of its principal builder, the Roman senator Philoxenus. The columns bear the names of patricians who helped with its building; some of them are placed upside down, and all are recorded in Greek, not the Latin that would have been the contributors' native tongue. (One wonders if they ever saw them!)

Bit Pazarları
(Flea Markets)
A number of flea markets can be found in various quarters of
Istanbul (near Istanbul University, just east of the Üsküdar
ferry landing). While much of the stuff on sale is flea-bitten
junk, occasionally unusual items come for sale at unusual
prices. Broken bedsteads and love seats minus a leg are jum-
bled together with chiming clocks, tile stoves, escritoires and
Tiffany glass lamp shades. Depending on the day and on how
keen your eyes are, you might spot a mahogany Hepplewhite
chair that merely needs its leather seat replaced.

Blachernae
(Palace of Blachernae) in Ayvansaray
Built into the corner of the walls of the Golden Horn and the
Land Walls, the Byzantine Palace of Blachernae is represented
now by some ruined towers. Probably originally these and the
larger Tekfur Sarayı farther along the Land Wall were part of
the same palace complex. For about four centuries (c. 1060 to
1453) Blachernae, instead of the Great Palace on the Seraglio
Point, was the imperial residence. It had started as a 5th century church founded by the Empress Pulcheria (could its name
be a corruption of hers?) to which Anastasius I added a summer house. Peter the Hermit (a revivalist preacher and one of
the instigators of the First Crusade) was received here by
Alexius I Comnenus in 1096 and given a financial contribution
(with the hope that he would not stay long) before he and
Walter the Pennyless went on to be confounded by the Turks in
Asia Minor. One of the towers of Blachernae, the **Prison of
Michael Anemas**, is named for a young revolutionary who
was imprisoned here for trying to overthrow that same Alexius
I (c.1100). He was released eventually, thanks to the interven-
tion of the emperor's daughter, Anna. Fate was not as kind to
later prisoners.

Boğaziçi
(Bosphorus)
The Turkish name is a geographic designation (*boğaz*: throat): it
means the strait; the English word harks back to the Greek
legend that says this is the body of water that Io, disguised as
a heifer, forded in her wanderings to escape Juno's jealous
wrath. The first Turks to see it gave it the name Nehr-i Aziz —
"the sacred river." The Bosphorus separates Europe from Asia
at Istanbul.
It is a little more than thirty kilometers long from north to
south, and between a half a kilometer and five kilometers wide.
The narrowest point is between Anadolu Hisar and Rumeli
Hisar; the widest is at the mouth of the Black Sea, with the
Büyükdere bay being almost three and a half kilometers across.
The greatest depth is 66 fathoms, both off the Kandilli point
and at the Black Sea mouth. Generally the surface current
flows south from the Black Sea to the Sea of Marmara, but
when a strong south wind blows (known locally as a *lodos*)

even supertankers have rough sailing. The average speed of the current is about one meter a second, but the direction changes frequently, and the costal indentations create many eddies. (The mythical crashing rocks which legendary Jason had to run are firmly fixed; however, the entrance to the Black Sea, and that Sea itself still have a reputation for being stormy.) Turkey controls the use of the Bosphorus, but those ships that do not cut their engines are considered to be in international waters while in the strait. Most of the several thousand ships that ply the waters daily are from the countries that border the Black Sea.

Commuter ferries sail on regular schedules up and down and across the Bosphorus. There is also a special ferry run designed for tourists that goes for lunch or early supper up to Sarıyer, the fishing village (consult hotel's reception for schedules). The return ferries are timed to accommodate the diners.

Boğaziçi Köprüsü
(Bosphorus Bridge)
The effort to establish a bridge between Europe and Asia goes back to the sixth century BC. The Persian Emperor Darius the Great ordered his engineer Mandrokles of Samos to build a bridge of boats across the Bosphorus in 590 BC.

The first of the two suspension bridges in Istanbul built to cross the Bosphorus, the Bosphorus Bridge, stretches 1,074 meters from Ortaköy to Beylerbeyi. Its builders were a British-German consortium of the Cleveland Bridge Engineering Company and Hochtief. The fifth longest suspension bridge in the world, it was opened for the celebration of the 50th anniversary of the Turkish Republic on October 29, 1973.

Boğaziçi Üniversitesi
in Rumelihisarı; tel. (212) 263 1500.
The Bosphorus University, located in two almost-adjacent campuses, is on the hill above Bebek and overlooking the Fortress of Rumeli Hisar and the Bosphorus.

It is one of the most beautiful campuses in the world. Established in 1971, it inherited the traditions and buildings of Robert College which had been founded in 1863 on the same grounds. Most of the instruction is in English and many of its faculty have degrees from prestigious foreign institutions. Universities in Turkey are state-supported and are under the control of an inter-university council (YÖK).

Bosphorus
(see Boğaziçi)

Bosphorus Bridge
(see Boğaziçi Köprüsü)

British Crimean Cemetery
in Haydarpaşa
Just south of the Selimiye Barracks is the cemetery where many of the British soldiers who died in the Crimean War are

buried, along with a few of Florence Nightingale's nurses, some British expatriates, and a few British soldiers who died at Gallipoli in World War I.

Burgaz Adası ☀
(Antigone)

It is one of the nine Princes' Islands in the Sea of Marmara near Istanbul. Burgaz figures in the last of the church squabbles over iconoclasm (image-smashing): A churchman, Methodius, was tortured and imprisoned on Burgaz in the early 9th century for championing the veneration of religious art. When the Empress Theodora became the regent in 843, she restored the images and Methodius became Patriarch of Constantinople. (It was during this period that the monks, particularly Abbot Theodore, of the Monastery of St.John of Studion, were leaders in religious scholarship and hymnology, both fields of which were threatened by the iconoclasts.) Scheduled ferries start from Sirkeci to the islands.

Büyük Ada ☀
(Prinkipo)

Büyük Ada is the largest of the Princes' Islands and has long been a favorite summer resort. In Byzantine times it and the others of the archipelago were the places of exîle (often also misery) for members of the royal family who were out of favor. Well into the 20th century the population was mainly Christian; several unoccupied monasteries and churches reflect the history of past years. The gardens on Büyük Ada, the grand old wooden houses, and the absence of cars give the island a relaxed atmosphere during the summer months. On the top of Yüce Tepe, the highest point on Büyük Ada, is the monastery of St. George, an inactive convent with chapels, tombs, a spring, and a belfry. The convent may date back to the 6th century. There are scheduled ferries from the Galata Bridge and hydrofoils from Kabataş and Bostancı. From spring to fall it is a very pleasant site for walking and relaxing under the pine trees. The island boasts of good fish restaurants.

Büyük Valide Han
(Valide Kösem Sultan Caravansary in Mercan)

The Büyük Valide Han is the largest of the commercial *hans* in Istanbul. It was built about 1650 by the grandmother of the reigning sultan. In the Ottoman city the hans served as a hotel for travelling merchants, and a place of business — buying and selling, discussing business deals, a place for safe storage of their items, and a stable for their animals. The entrance to the hans was high enough to admit the heavily loaded camels and horses that were stabled on the ground floor. On the second floor the rooms for travellers opened onto a covered gallery which looked out above the courtyard. For years the Büyük Valide Han was the location of the Persian merchants in the city; it is now occupied largely by brass foundries and textile looms. Its roof is used sometimes by weavers who wash and dry their rugs to age them in the sun. The stump of the

Tower of Eirene is located in the northeast corner of the Han; perhaps it was once one of many gloomy Byzantine prisons.

Byzantium

The city's ancient name comes from its supposed founder, Byzas, the leader of a colony of settlers from Megara. Following the advice of the Oracle of Delphi, Byzas is credited with establishing his city in 667 BC on the land "opposite the people who were blind." Byzas decided that the residents of Asian Chalcedon (Kadıköy) were blind because they had not settled on the more promising European coast. Constantine wanted to change the name of his capital to "New Rome" in 330, but while the city took his name instead, the term "Byzantine" has continued to characterize the behavior of its citizens.

C-C-C

Cafer Ağa El Sanatları Çarşısı

(Applied Handcrafts Market) just off a street west of St. Sophia
A small center making and selling handcraft items is located in the Cafer Ağa Medresesi. Open in summer months only. The original school was founded by Süleyman's Chief Black Eunuch, Cafer Ağa, and was built by Sinan in 1559/60.

Cağaloğlu Hamamı

(Cağaloğlu Baths)
Tel.212-522-2424; open: men every day 07:00 am to 09:00 pm; women every day 08:00 am to 08:00 pm.
The Cağaloğlu Baths are among the best known and largest of the public baths of the city. Built in 1741 by Sultan Mahmut I, they follow the pattern of the old Roman baths. The areas are divided between the men's and the women's sections.You enter a large hall with stalls where you may undress, put on wooden clogs, and wrap yourself in a towel. From there you go into a"cool room" (*soğukluk* in Turkish) where you perform the first part of the bath yourself, again in private cubicles. In the third,"hot room" (*hararet*), there is a marble platform (*göbek taşı*) where you may lie down and be massaged. This room also has marble basins along the wall from which you dip water and pour it over yourself repeatedly as you soap yourself and rub the dirt and the dead skin off. As few homes until the establishment of the Republic had their own bathrooms, let alone running water, there were over a hundred public baths (*hamams*) scattered throughout the city. For the women, the hamam was a social center where they regularly spent the day visiting with their friends.

Cathedral of St. Esprit

in Elmadağı
Built in 1846, this church since 1876 has been the seat of the Bishop of Istanbul; it is the second largest Roman Catholic church in the city. Angelo Guissepe Roncalli was Papal Nuncio here during World War II before he became Pope John

XXIII in 1958. Both Pope Paul VI (in 1965) and Pope John Paul
II (in 1979) have officiated at masses observed here.

Cemal Reşit Rey Konser Salonu
in Harbiye; Tel. (212) 240 5012.
A concert hall named after one of Turkey's best known com-
posers and the founder of Istanbul Symphony Orchestra, the
building hosts a wide variety of musical events throughout the
year. It is within walking distance from the Istanbul Hilton
hotel.

Church of ...
(see also listings under the name of the building: i.e.. Dutch
Chapel, Surp Astvadzadzin, etc.)
There are at least 32 Armenian Orthodox churches in Istanbul,
16 Roman Catholic, 80 Greek Orthodox, 2 Bulgarian Orthodox,
and 4 Protestant, in addition to Greek Catholic and Syrian
Orthodox churches. The following listing is therefore obvious-
ly incomplete and yet provides information on the most used
ones.

Church of St. Andrew in Krisei
(see Koca Mustafa Paşa Camii)

Church of St. Antoine
(Church of St. Anthony of Padua); in Galatasaray
The largest Roman Catholic church in Istanbul, this handsome
Italianate building was built in 1913. It is occasionally used as
a concert hall for organ music.

Church of Fishes
(Zoodochus Pege) (see Balıklı Kilisesi)

Church of St. George
(see Rum Ortodoks Patrikhanesi) in Fener

Church of St. George
in Galata
The records of this Church of St. George in Karaköy suggest
that the present building is on the site of a church possibly
older than the founding of Constantinople. The holy spring
(*ayazma*) of St. Irene is in the choir.

Church of St. Louis
in Beyoğlu
This is the chapel built for members of the French legation in
1847. The community associated with it had been active in
other buildings (destroyed by fires) since the early 17th century

Among the gravestones preserved in the wall of this 19th century building is one commemorating Louis Jean Henry, Comte de Vaujany, an army captain who died during the siege of Rhodes in 1522.

Church of St. Mary Draperis
in Galata

Records of the picture of the Virgin Mary above the altar of the church begin in 1584 when Clara Bartolda Draperis offered a chapel in Galata to monks of the Franciscan order. Saved from a fire by a member of the Draperis family in 1660, the picture barely escaped the frequent fires and an earthquake before it was mounted in the present building in 1769.

Church of St. Savior in Chora
(see Kariye Müzesi)

Church of SS Sergius and Bacchus
(see Küçük Ayasoya Camii)

Church of St. Stephen of the Bulgars
in Fener

Erected in 1871 the church is constructed of iron sections that were cast in Vienna, shipped down the Danube, and assembled here within one week's time. Painted gray on the outside, it stands alone in the park along the Golden Horn, a strikingly different church than the usual stone and brick Byzantine buildings. (Its double was in Vienna until it was destroyed in World War II).

Church of the Pantocrator
(see Zeyrek Camii)

Church of the Theotokos Pammakaristos
(see Fethiye Camii)

Cisterns of Aetios, Aspar and Mocius
Aetios (Sixth Hill), Aspar (Fifth Hill) and Mocius (Seventh Hill)

These three open cisterns were part of the 5th century city water system. They later fell into disuse as such, and became vegetable gardens. Aspar is a car park now. Aetios is a soccer field.

City Museum
(see Şehir Müzesi)

Column of Constantine
(see Çemberlitaş)

Column of Marcian
(Kız Taşı) in Fatih

Erected about 452 for the Emperor Marcian whose seated figure was on top, this is a granite column resting on a high carved marble pedestal and topped by a Corinthian capital. A chipped representation of winged Victory on the base suggests the reason why this has been confused with another Byzantine column (now one of those in Süleymaniye) that reputedly distinguished between girls who were virgins and those who weren't. (The historical records are unclear about the precise method.)

Covered Market
(see Kapalı Çarşı)

Crimean Memorial Church
Serdari Ekrem Sok., Tünel, Beyoğlu

A striking Gothic building, the Crimean Memorial Church was dedicated in 1868 to commemorate the British who struggled in the Crimean War. Unused for several years, Sunday services are again held here regularly for the Anglican community.

Cumhuriyet Caddesi
It is one of the main thoroughfares of the newer part of Istanbul. It runs from Taksim Square north past Radio Istanbul to Harbiye. The Istanbul Hilton is on this street.

Ç-Ç-Ç

Çamlıca
It is the double hill rising 267 meters above Üsküdar, each peak crowned by a small pine (çam) grove from which they get their name. It is the ideal place to have a bird's eye view of the Bosphorus. In Byzantine times the taller of the two was the peak from which important military signals were sent throughout the empire. When the outskirts of Üsküdar were still rural, it was a favorite place for outings in the spring: Young couples hoping to be serenaded by nightingales came by horse-drawn carriages from Üsküdar and Kadıköy. Now its visitors have followed international routes: ornithologists from around the world gather on Çamlıca to watch the migrating birds and the Touring and Automobile Association of Turkey runs a delightful coffee house and a tea garden.

Çatalca
(50 km west of Istanbul)

The region around Çatalca offers a variety of places of historic interest to explore. At the village of İnceğiz are a number of caves used by the Thracians in the 4th century BC. These caves are similar to those found in Ürgüp, and probably have a similar story. Eighteen km west of Çatalca can be found parts of the Long Wall of Anastasius which he built between 507 and 512 as an outer defense of the city. A bridge of twenty-eight arches spans the draw at Büyük Çekmece; it was built by Sinan in 1567/8, and carries the name of its architect. During the Balkan Wars, Bulgarian invaders advanced into Thrace as far as the Çatalca Fortified Line which ran from Büyük Çekmece through Çatalca to Terkoz Lake. The European section of Turkey, including Edirne, was regained in the Treaty of Bucharest the next year (1913).

Çemberlitaş

(Burnt Column, Column of Constantine)

Constantine considered that his column and his Forum around it were the heart of his city. The Forum was a large oval space encircled with columned porticoes, the senate building, the praetorium, temples, and churches. His statue, representing himself as the God Apollo, stood on the top; his crown was supposed to include pieces of the nails from the Cross. At the bottom was a small chapel. Constantine's statue fell in a storm in 1106; the chapel that he had built at the base of the column perhaps had disappeared before that. The large dark red porphyry drums had been bound together with iron hoops as early as 416; the hoops have had to be replaced several times since.

Çemberlitaş Hamamı

(Baths at Çemberlitaş)

These baths were built by the Queen Mother Nur Banu Sultan in 1583. Classical in style, only the men's section is still left. See Cağaloğlu Hamamı for a description of a Turkish bath.

Çırağan Saray

(Çırağan Palace)Tel. (212) 258 3377.

Can be visited upon appointment with the public relations manager. North of Beşiktaş is the now handsomely restored Çırağan Palace. It was built first in 1874 for Sultan Abdül Aziz. Sultan Murat V was kept here as a prisoner by his brother, Abdül Hamit II. It was used as the parliament building during the Constitution Period at the turn of this century until it was gutted in an electrical fire in 1910. Now it is an entertainment complex including a casino and convention center for the next-door Çırağan Palace Hotel Kempinski Istanbul.

Çiçek Pasajı

(Flower Market) in Beyoğlu

Çiçek Pasaji meaning Flower Passage, originally was a service alley for apartment houses which were built in 1860 in what was then the most fashionable part of town. The first vendors to come in were the flower sellers, hence the name given to the passage. A semi-covered alley off İstiklâl Caddesi once sheltered one of the more boisterous, colorful collection of small taverns in the city. Still an informal eating place, it has been

discovered by the tourist crowd. Next to it is the **Balık Pazarı**, a
street largely of outdoor fruit, vegetable, flower, and fish sellers. In addition there are shops selling turkeys (a few in time
for the American holiday, but more for New Year's), pork,
game animals, herbs and spices. A walk on İstiklâl Caddesi
offers window shopping and gives a chance to see the recently
restored old buildings of Beyoğlu and gets one easily to Çiçek
Pasajı for drinks and snacks.

Çinili Camii
(Tiled Mosque) in Üsküdar
A small building with tiles lining the inside walls, this mosque
was built about 1640 by the Queen Mother Kösem Sultan, one
of the most influential and intriguing wives of the sultans. The
dependencies include two schools and a bath.

Çinili Köşk
(see Arkeoloji Müzeleri)

D-D-D

Darüşşafaka Lisesi
in Fatih, Tel. (212) 524 1813.
Darüşşafaka was founded in 1855 as an orphanage and
school. It was part of the imperial decree of 1846 that
encouraged an educational system separate from that of the
mosques. It is still run by its foundation. The graduates are
often very successful.

Deniz Müzesi
(Naval Museum) in Beşiktaş. Tel. (212) 261 0040; open 09:00 am
to 05:00 pm, closed Monday, Tuesday; entrance fee 15,000TL.
The Naval Museum displays a number of pictures of naval
battles and some of the equipment of the Ottoman ships in the
section that faces on the main street. In the second building,
between the Beşiktaş and Hayreddin Paşa ferry landings
(named after the famous Ottoman admiral known to the foreigners as Barbarossa) are a number of the sultans' caiques
and part of the Byzantine chain that closed the Golden Horn.
One of the caiques, a galley belonging to Mehmet IV in the 17th
century, was propelled by 144 rowers with three men to an oar.
Other ships belonged to 19th century sultans.

Divan Edebiyatı Müzesi
or Galip Dede Tekkesi (Mevlevi Dervish Museum and Classical
Turkish Literature Museum); at the end of İstiklâl Caddesi, off
Tünel square on Galip Dede Caddesi , Tel. (212) 245 4141; open
daily 09:30 am to 04:30 pm. except Mondays; entrance fee
10,000TL.

The museum of the Mevlevi Dervishes contains a number of
documents and instruments used by the dervish order in their

religious ceremonies. The *tekke* was built about 1492. (Mevlana, the greatest mystical poet of any age, lived in the 13th century and died in Konya. He wrote poems calling for peace, for love of man and love of God. His greatest book, the **Mesnevi**, has been translated into all major languages. He expressed his feelings best in the following quatrain: " Come, come again whoever, whatever you may be, come:/ Heathen, fire-worshiper, sinful of idolatry, come./ Come even if you broke your penitence a hundred times,/ Ours is not the portal of despair or misery, come." After his death his followers initiated the Mevlevi Sect, commonly referred to in the West as "The Whirling Dervishes". Mevlana described the soaring spirit of the dervish in the act of the '*sema*' (the whirling dance) as the falcon flying towards God.

There is a chance to attend a sema (the whirling) session here only once a month. It takes place every last Sunday each month from 05:00 pm to 07:00pm. Galip Dede Tekkesi has a 200-seat capacity and tickets can be bought after the 15th of the month.

Divan Yolu
(known in history as the "Council Road")
It is the main street between the Hippodrome and Istanbul University. Now used mostly by the Metro trolleys, it follows the main street (Mese) of old Constantinople. Concubines from Topkapı were taken up this road when they went into exile in the Old Palace (near the Bayezit square) upon the death of their master. The Mese (Middle Way) was the beginning of the Via Egnatia.

Dolmabahçe Camii
Dolmabahçe Mosque
At entrance to Dolmabahçe Palace
It was founded by Bezmiâlem Sultan, mother of Abdül Mecit who completed the building in 1853. The architect was an Armenian, Nikogos Balyan, who also built the clock tower.

Dolmabahçe Sarayı
(Dolmabahçe Palace) Tel.(212) 258 5544. Open 09:00 am to 03:00 pm except Mondays and Thursdays; entrance fee 100,000TL. Dolmabahçe was built for Sultan Abdül Mecit in 1853 because he no longer wanted to live in Topkapı. Statistically alone Dolmabahçe Palace is staggering. The palace contains 285 rooms, plus 43 major salons, six large balconies and six Turkish baths, all richly and heavily decorated. Almost 5,000 m^2 of handloomed silk and wool Turkish and Persian carpets cover floors inlaid in mosaic-like patterns of mahagony. Fourteen tons of gold leaf adorn columns, walls, doors, furniture - even radiators! Bohemian and Baccarat crystal chandeliers as well as fireplaces tinkle and glisten at every turn. All pale, however, alongside the four-and-a-half-ton chandelier of the Reception Hall, a gift of England's Queen Victoria and the largest in the world. Ornate in the style popular in France at the time, the palace is important in Turkish Republican history as the place where Mustafa Kemal Atatürk died on November 10, 1938.

Recently the apartments of the sultan's concubines have been opened to the public. Part of the main building, the entrance to them is from the garden on the west side. A second, adjacent building was the home of the crown prince.

Dutch Chapel ⛪

Postacılar Sok., Beyoğlu; Tel. (212) 244-5212. Located on the grounds of the Netherlands consulate.
The Dutch Chapel was built about 1705 as a private chapel for legation members. The building belongs to the Netherlands Ministry of Antiquities. With the permission of the royal family, it has been the church building of an English-speaking Protestant community since 1857.

E-E-E

Eminönü

The square at the foot of the Galata Bridge in the Old City
In Ottoman times the customs house (emin) was here and the square was in front of it (ön); today it is a major transfer point between busses, dolmuşes (shared taxis that follow a given route when they are full) and boats. Until the new Galata Bridge and its connecting roads are complete, Eminönü will be unforgettable for its rubble, noise, confusion and discomfort. Eminönü is the location of the New Mosque and the Spice Bazaar. A few streets to the west is the Mosque of Rüstem Paşa; the Mosque of Süleyman is on the skyline. On the east side of the Spice Bazaar is a colorful flower market. A famous Turkish restaurant, Pandeli, is located in the entrance to the Spice Bazaar. Several streets in the area are full of people selling small clothing items from squares of cloth spread on the ground. (A short whistle will send the hawkers scurrying to grab up the ends of their display and escape with it from the police.) Depending on the season, other peddlers have hot braziers where they're roasting chestnuts or open carts of peeled cucumbers for quick snacks. Just before a holiday the square is crowded with people selling picture postcards.

Emirgân

It is one of the villages on the European side of the Bosphorus. Its name comes from the title (mir, meaning lord) of Prince Revan, Khan of Erivan who was allowed to live here briefly after Murat IV captured that city in 1635. For several weeks in the spring the park above the village is a tulip garden, recalling the Tulip Period (1703-1739, the reign of Ahmet III) when a passion for tulips and other extravagances claimed the attention of many in the court. Every year in May the Tulip Festival takes place here with a great variety of tulips exhibited in the garden. The Touring and Automobile Association of Turkey has restored the gardens and several old kiosks in the park. The **Beyaz** (White) **Köşk**, the **Pembe** (Pink) **Köşk** and the **Sarı** (Yellow) **Köşk** are now cafes and tea houses, used sometimes for concerts or special entertainment.

Ermeni Patrikhanesi

(Armenian Orthodox — Gregorian — Patriarchate) in Kumkapı. Tel.(212) 5277 0323.

The Armenian Orthodox Patriarch was recognized as the head of his *millet* (national/religious identity) by Mehmet the Conqueror in 1461. This recognition legalized the position of the church and its followers throughout the Ottoman Empire. Full citizens of the Republic, the members now are under the spiritual leadership of their patriarch. His offices are on Şarapnel Sokak where they have been since 1641. The patriarchal church of the Armenian community is Surp Astvadzadzin; it is just across the street from the patriarchate. The building is recent, dating only from 1913.

European Fortres

(see Rumeli Hisar)

Eyüp

It is a village at the far end of the Golden Horn

It is named for Ebu Eyüp Ensari, the man who was the close friend and standard bearer of the Prophet Mohammed. Eyüp died during the Arab assault on the walls of Constantinople in about 677. His close relation to Mohammed has sanctified this place for Muslims. Many Muslims have chosen to be buried in the Eyüp cemetery within hearing of the call to prayer from his mosque. Among the better known of these are members of the royal family and grand viziers, including Sokollu Mehmet Paşa and Melek Ahmet Paşa.

Eyüp Camii

(Mosque of Eyüp Sultan)

Mehmet the Conqueror built the first Mosque of Eyüp at his grave in 1458. By tradition each Ottoman sultan was girded here with the sword of Osman on his accession to the throne. Time and earthquakes had taken their toll on the building by the late 18th century. Except for the minarets which had been built by Ahmet III (1703-1730), the mosque which is now standing was completed in 1800. Many of the royal family made the gifts which they presented to the mosque: İbrahim made the large silver candlesticks at the head and foot of the casket, Mahmut II worked the embroidery on a cover for the casket, and Selim III made the brass railing that is on the window of the *türbe* (small mausoleum). People believe that Eyüp loved children, so parent brings them here to mark the important events in their lives such as circumcision and weddings.

F-F-F

Fatih Sultan Mehmet Camii

(Mosque of Fatih Sultan Mehmet)

One of the landmarks of the city, the Mosque of Mehmet the Conqueror is on the top of the Fourth Hill. The complex was first built between 1463 and 1470. It occupies the site of the ruined Church of the Holy Apostles which furnished some of its building materials.

The present mosque dates from 1771: the earlier building was destroyed by an earthquake. The building sits in a large open square, high above the streets of the neighborhood. Originally the complex included a number of schools and a hospital that are no longer standing.

Fatih Sultan Mehmet Köprüsü
(Fatih Sultan Mehmet Bridge)

Completed in 1988, the second Bosphorus bridge is the fourth longest suspension bridge in the world. It spans the strait between Rumeli Hisar and Kavacık, the narrowest point of the Bosphorus. This is approximately the place where Darius built his bridge of boats in 512 BC. The planning, financing, and construction of the bridge had an international aspect. It was built under the auspices of the Turkish General Directorate of Highways. Freeman Fox of London and Botek of Istanbul were the consulting engineers. Its contractors were the Ishikawajima-Hariman Heavy Industries with Mitsubishi Heavy Industries and Nippon Kokan (all of Japan), Sezai Türkeş-Feyzi Akkaya (STFA) İnşaat (Turkey), and Impreglio (Italy) consortium.

Feriköy Cemeteries

Twin cemeteries for the foreign Catholic and Protestant communities are located in the Feriköy section of Istanbul. Each has a small chapel; the dead are buried according to their nationality.

Fethiye Camii
(Church of the Theotokos Pammakaristos) in Fatih

A twelfth century building, it was the Greek Orthodox Patriarchate from 1456 to 1568. In 1591 the main interior area was converted into a mosque. The side chapel, probably the mortuary chapel, has been sealed off from the rest of the building. Its walls and ceiling are decorated with priceless early fourteenth century mosaics similar to those in Kariye Camii. (It is rarely open.).

Fildamı
(Elephant Shed) in Bakırköy

An open cistern probably dating from the eighth century, Fildamı was part of the complex of the Palace of Hebdomon outside the city walls. The Byzantines gathered their armies here before they marched off to war. From Valens in 364 to Nicephorus II Phocae in 963 the soldiers proclaimed whom they had chosen emperor here. Then the emperor rode triumphal through the Golden Gate into his city.

The race course close by Fildamı was a military parade ground for the Byzantines and the Ottomans also. At one time the Ottomans used the cistern as a stable for elephants (*fil* in Turkish).

Forums

Four of the forums or public squares of Constantinople still affect the patterns of the city streets. The Augustaeum was between St. Sophia and the Hippodrome, now the Sultanahmet square. (Constantine named it for his mother, the Augusta St. Helena.) The oval Forum of Constantine around Çemberlitaş was where the wall built by Septimius Severus crossed the Mese. Beyond, the Forum of Theodosius I (Bayezit Square) was the biggest square in the city. Today's intersection of streets and overpasses at Aksaray was the Forum Bovis which had a statue of a large brass bull.

Flea Markets
(See Bit Pazarları)

Florence Nightingale Museum
(See Selimiye Kışlası)

Flower Market
(see Çiçek Pasajı)

Fountain of Kaiser Wilhelm II
at Hippodrome

Built in 1898, the fountain was a gift of Kaiser Wilhelm II during his visit to Sultan Abdül Hamit II. It marks the approximate entrance to the Byzantine Hippodrome.

G-G-G

Galata

Galata at first was the strip of land between the two bridges on the north side of the Golden Horn.

It started as a Genoese concession in the mid-12th century. Its population grew when the emperor moved the Genoese from near Eminönü to Galata to prevent their frequent quarrels with the Venetians who had been their western neighbors. After the Venetians sacked their village in 1296 they were allowed to fortify it with stone walls and a moat. At its greatest expansion it included the region just north of Tophane up to the Galata Tower and back down to the present Atatürk Bridge. Its residents managed their own affairs (with oversight from Genoa), including accepting only coins minted in Genoa. While today it is rarely called Galata, that name persists for the bridge between it and Eminönü. Part of the wall and the one remaining gate can be seen not far from the Azap Kapı Mosque. Into the 19th century its gates were locked at night, and woe to the errant youth caught outside. The residents of Galata remained non-Turkish long after Constantinople had become an Ottoman city.

Galata Köprüsü
(Galata Bridge).

The first bridge across the Golden Horn was built in 1845 by

the mother of the reigning sultan, Bezmiâlem Sultan. Before
that, the crossing had been only by boat. It was a wooden
structure and a toll bridge which was closed at night. The later
1910 floating bridge, which threatened many times in the 1970s
to sink, was replaced by the present one in 1992. The center of
both the Galata and the Atatürk bridges can be lifted to allow
large ships entrance into the Horn for repair at the dry docks.
 The 489 meters long and 42 meters wide Galata Bridge rests on
114 steel piles. It is the world's largest bascule bridge with 1700
ton steel platforms on each side. The platforms (each 40 meters
long) can be lifted in three minutes. Almost as soon as the
bridge was opened it was damaged by a burning ferry which
bumped into it.

Galata Kulesi
Galata Tower

Galata Tower foundations date from the 6th century; the main
structure was built by Genoese residents about 1350. The
Ottoman sultans used it for their prisoners of war and as a fire
tower. A short section of the inner wall of the moat that protected Galata is just east of the tower. It has been restored and
an elevator carries the public to the top where one may enjoy
the view, a drink or an evening meal in the restaurant,
enlivened by a belly dancer.

Galatasaray Hamamı
(Galatasaray Bath)Tel.(212) 249 4342; open 08:00 am to 08:00 pm.
The Turkish bath was built in the late 18th century as part of
the Galatasaray school next door. It now does a lively business
among the public, both local and foreign. Note its proximity to
the Istanbul and Parksa Hilton hotels.

Galatasaray Lisesi
in Galatasaray; Tel. (212) 249 1100

Galatasaray Lycée (high school) was started by Sultan Bayezit
II in the sixteenth century to augment the palace school system
already in operation at Topkapı. Sultan Abdül Aziz reorga-
nized it in 1868 and modelled it on the French system.
Instruction is in Turkish and French. Its graduates have
become important statesmen, politicians and writers.

Golden Gate
(at Yedi Kule)

About 380 a triumphal arch was built over the main Via
Egnatia some distance outside Constantine's city walls so that
the emperor could ride through it proudly announcing his victories to the inhabitants of the city. When Theodosius came to
enlarge the city soon after, he incorporated the arch into the
new walls. In time it was decorated with bas-reliefs, with
statues (including four brass elephants), and highlighted
with gold. The last Byzantine emperor to ride through the
gate was Michael Paleologus whose victory in 1261 marked the
end of the Latin kingdom of Constantinople.

Golden Horn
(see Haliç)

Got Sütunu
(Goth's Column) at Gülhane Park
The Goth's Column is said to be a tribute to the Emperor
Claudius II for his victory over the Goths in Nish in 259 AD.
Perhaps the oldest monument in Istanbul, it is sometimes identi-
fied as part of a theater built by Septimius Severus after he had
razed the city in 196 AD and then decided he had made a mistake.

Goth's Column
(see Got Sütunu)

Göksu Kasrı
or Küçüksu Palace (Pavilion of Göksu)
This ornate palace on the Asian shore was built by Abdül Mecit
in 1856 and used by the sultans as a hunting lodge. In the park
near by is the picturesque marble fountain built by Selim III in
1806. The fountain was once part of a *namazgâh* (open-air place
of prayer); it was the place for the men's ablutions before they
performed their *namaz* (prayers). Under restoration.

Grand Bazaar
(see Kapalı Çarşı)

Great Palace of Byzantium
(Seraglio Point)
Constantine and his successors built a complex of buildings —
residences, administrative offices, and churches — on the slope
of the First Hill (now occupied in part by the Blue Mosque).
The Point was the lookout for ships approaching from the Sea
of Marmara and the Bosphorus, and for signals from Çamlıca
with news of the Empire in Asia.
 By the sixth century the richness of the main palace had
reached fabled proportions. Gilt lions guarded the throne, and
gilt birds perched in trees around it. When visiting dignitaries
approached, the lions roared, the birds twittered and the
emperor's throne (reported to have belonged to Solomon) was
raised - apparently miraculously - by mechanical contraptions.
The complex was walled, but communicated with the
Hippodrome through several gates. When Mehmet the
Conqueror took the city he commented ruefully on the spi-
ders'curtains that hung at the ruined Great Palace windows.
 Mosaics that decorated the floor of one of the courts of the
Great Palace of Byzantium have been rescued and are now displayed in the **Mozaik Müzesi** (Mosaic Museum; Tel. (212) 518
1205; open 09:30 am to 05:00 pm except Tuesdays; entrance fee
20,000 TL) about the same place where they were found.They
are mostly hunting scenes (lions and elephants and hunters);
they are Roman in style and spirit, possibly from the time of
Constantine.

Greek Orthodox Patriarchate
(see Rum Ortodoks Patrikhanesi)

Gülhane Parkı
Once the gardens of the Fifth Court of Topkapı Palace, Gülhane Park is now a shady amusement center with fast food concessions, a small outdoor theater and a small, shabby zoo. Near the entrance to the park is the **Alay Köşkü** (rarely open), the pavilion from which sultans watched the parades.

H-H-H

Haliç
(Golden Horn)
A deep, narrow estuary of two small streams, the Golden Horn divides Old Istanbul on its south bank from Karaköy on its north.
Its shape of a cornucopia is sometimes given as a reason for the name. A more romantic reason is the glitter of the water during a golden sunset. It has long been a major commercial highway for the city. A point of interest is **Pierre Loti Coffee House** in Eyüp overlooking the Golden Horn, a peaceful place to rest after touring the area.

Harbiye
It is the section of the city where Cumhuriyet Caddesi divides into Halâskârgazi Caddesi and Vali Konağı Caddesi..
The complex of buildings of the Ottoman Ministry of Defence (Harbiye) that used to be here are now largely devoted to the Military Museum and its Cultural Center. (Tel.233 27 20) located next door to the Istanbul Hilton.

Haseki Hürrem Camii
(Mosque of Hürrem Sultan)
The first of Sinan's imperial works in Istanbul, the Haseki Hürrem complex (completed in 1539) is the third largest mosque complex in the city.
It was commissioned for Süleyman's wife, Hürrem Sultan who is called Roxelana in English. The restrictions that were imposed by the small size of the property that was available are obvious in the sense of confinement that the complex gives. (The *imaret*, although part of the complex, is not one of Sinan's buildings.)

Haydarpaşa
It is a section of Üsküdar, a ferry stop, and the place of the Asian terminal of the Berlin-to-Baghdad railroad. The Selimiye mosque and barracks stand out above its skyline.

Heybeliada
(Chalki in Byzantine times)
Second largest of the Princes' Islands, Heybeli is a popular summer resort. It is the location of the Turkish Naval College, and the former Theological Seminary of the Greek Orthodox Church.

G
O
L
–
H
E
Y

Hıdiv Kasrı
(Khedive's Pavilion) in Çubuklu. Tel.(216) 331 2651
This palace of the Ottoman Governor (Khedive) of Egypt was
built about 1906 by Abbas Hilmi Paşa, the last of the Ottoman
governors of Egypt, as his summer residence. It was built on a
large estate which extends over the most thickly wooded areas
on the slopes of Çubuklu overlooking the Bosphorus, offering
a different world, a soothing place with fresh air, relaxing
greenery, a beautiful view of the Bosphorus and the nostalgic
grandeur of old days. It is only half an hour drive from the
Istanbul Hilton. Recently restored by the Touring and
Automobile Association of Turkey in the original Art Nouveau
style, it is now an exclusive luxury hotel overlooking the
Bosphorus with a good restaurant, a coffee house and a beautiful garden. It is a popular outing place over the weekends. Tea
is served under the trees in the park around the pavilion.

Hippodrome
(see At Meydanı)

Hünkâr İskelesi
It is located north of Beykoz
Once a summer residence of the sultans, Hünkâr İskelesi is
known as the place where a treaty between the Ottoman
Empire and Russia was signed in 1833. In effect only briefly,
that treaty gave Russia the power to control shipping on the
Bosphorus and Dardanelles straits.

I-I-I

Ihlamur Kasrı
(Linden Pavilion) in Beşiktaş; Tel.(212) 259 5086; open 09:30 am
to 04:30 pm except Mondays and Thursdays; entrance fee
20,000 TL.
A linden (*ihlamur*) grove here was a pleasure park for the 18th
and 19th century sultans. Two small pavilions were built
between 1849 and 1855 and furnished in the style of 19th century Europe.

i-i-i

İbrahim Paşa Sarayı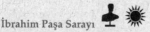
(Museum of Turkish and Islamic Arts) in Sultanahmet;
Tel.(212) 518 1805-6; open 09:30 am to 04:30 pm except
Mondays, entrance fee 30,000TL.
Moved in 1983 from the *imaret* of the Mosque of Süleyman, the
museum has seven distinct sections, the most famous of which
is the priceless collection of rugs. Calligraphy, ceramics,
stonework, and ethnography from the 9th century onwards are
richly represented. There are chased bronze candlesticks,
carved wooden doors, illuminated Korans, and inscribed
stones, gold inlay, sultan's *tuğras* (stylized signatures), and mar-

quetry.The building has had a complicated history. It probably started as army barracks, but the date of its first construction is unknown. Süleyman had it renovated and gave it to his Grand Vizier İbrahim when İbrahim married Süleyman's sister in 1524. İbrahim at that time was Süleyman's closest friend, having grown up with him and even shared his tent when they were on campaign. Twelve years later İbrahim was executed on suspicion of treason and the palace reverted to the throne. It was used for official functions because its rooms were larger than any at Topkapı. A number of miniatures show the sultan sitting in the small balcony overlooking the festivities in the Hippodrome. One of the sultan's concubines in the mid-17th century is remembered for having squandered his money covering the walls of its 200 rooms with furs. That sultan was deposed, and the palace then went back to being army barracks for a while. It was a hotel for a delegation from Poland, a prison, and a land registry office. By the time of the Republic the building, still identified by the Grand Vizier's name, was falling apart from neglect. When the Anatolian Civilizations Exhibition was being mounted in 1983 İbrahim Paşa's palace was chosen as one of the places for the displays.

The museum has a charming coffee house where one would enjoy a Turkish coffee or tea and Turkish cookies. Refurbished, in 1985 it was given the award of "Museum of the Year" by the Council of Europe.

İnönü Football Stadium
in Dolmabahçe
Named after İsmet İnönü, second president of Turkey, the İnönü Football Stadium is frequently full of fans watching the soccer (*futbol*) matches between their favorite teams. Fenerbahçe, Galatasaray, Beşiktaş, Trabzonspor and a host of other teams compete to the loud shouts of their supporters. In summer months world-renowned stars like Michael Jackson and Madonna give concerts to an audience of 50,000.

İskele Camii
İskele Mosque in Üsküdar
Built in 1547/8 by Sinan and commissioned by Süleyman for his daughter Mihrimah, İskele Camii dominates the Üsküdar square directly across from the ferry landing (*iskele*). The general impression of the mosque interior is shaded and somber partly because of the wide porch on the west side. Other buildings of the complex are used for a clinic and a children's library.

İstanbul Büyükşehir Belediyesi Nejat Eczacıbaşı Çağdaş Sanat Müzesi
(Municipality of Greater İstanbul Nejat Eczacıbaşı Contemporary Art Museum) in Eyüp; currently closed.
Used once as a factory for fezzes and then as a cloth factory, a large one-story building on the Golden Horn in Eyüp is being renovated to house exhibits of the İstanbul Biennal arts exhibition.

İstanbul Sanatlar Çarşısı
(İstanbul Handicraft Center) Tel.(212) 517 6782-4; open 09:00 am to 05:00 pm. Located in the Cedid Mehmet Efendi Medresesi.
This handicrafts workshop was renovated by the Touring and Automobile Association of Turkey in 1987 together with the adjacent **Yeşil Ev Hotel** which is very popular among elite foreigners. Each of the rooms of the *medrese* is devoted to a particular art: jewelry, bookbinding, calligraphy, embroidery, miniature, glasswork, porcelainwork, doll making, or painting on cloth.

İstiklâl Caddesi
in Beyoğlu
Once known as the Grand rue de Pera, the avenue now called İstiklâl Caddesi runs from the head of the *tünel*, Turkey's only and the world's second underground system, to Taksim. Now shut off to all traffic except the electric trolleys, it is a popular promenade spruced with stores, restaurants and schools. Most of the old stone buildings lining the street have recently been restored to recreate the glorious impression of former times.

K-K-K

Kabataş
It is a landing for regular ferries to Üsküdar. It also is the landing for the *deniz otobüsleri* (hydrofoils) to Bostancı and the Princes' Islands. The hydrofoils have connecting bus service from Kabataş to Taksim.

Kadıköy
(Chalcedon in Byzantine times)
Kadıköy claims to have been founded ten years before Byzas settled his colony across the strait. However, archaeologists uncovered a fishing village in the region of Fikirtepe that seems to date back to the Early Bronze Age (c. 5000 BC). The Fourth Ecumenical Council (also known as the Council of Chalcedon) convened in 451 in the Church of St. Euphemia; all traces of it here are gone, but it was located probably not far from Altı Yol. Kadıköy has grown in population and business activity as well as in good shopping since the 1970s.

Kalenderhane Camii
(Church of the Kyriotissa) is located between the Şehzade and Süleymaniye mosques)
Kalenderhane Mosque is a Byzantine structure adjacent to the Valens Aqueduct. The ruins of a Roman bath and a basilica are visible between the present twelfth century building and the aqueduct. Scholars studying the building in the 1970s uncovered a fresco cycle depicting the life of St. Francis of Assisi. These were painted, probably about 1250, when the

church was in the hands of the Latins; they predate the Giotto frescoes in Assisi. The building has been a mosque since 1453. The frescoes are on display in the Archaeological Museum.

Kandilli

One of the villages on the Asian shore, Kandilli was the site of several royal palaces, long since destroyed. In the 6th century the Empress Theodora built a Convent of Repentance in Kandilli for girls of dubious reputation. Procopius, the author of the "Anecdotes" and an historian who despised Theodora, added that some of those girls whom she tried to reform threw themselves into the Bosphorus.

Kanlıca

on the Asian side north of the Fatih Sultan Mehmet Bridge

It is a charming village with a ferry landing, a square dotted with coffee houses, restaurants, street sellers of some Turkish delicacies, a gift shop and a pastry shop. Kanlıca is famous for its yoghurt. Every day tourists come here by boats or buses to enjoy the peaceful atmosphere. Mehrabad is a national park on the hills of Kanlıca where one can picnic and enjoy the view of the Bosphorus. An interesting spot next to the delightful Kanlıca Mosque, one of the early works of great master Sinan, is **İskender Baba's** *türbesi* (a local folk saint). When one makes a wish, one promises to light a candle at İskender Baba's *türbe* if the wish is granted.

Kapalı Çarşı

(Covered Market, Grand Bazaar) Open 09:00 am to 19:00 pm except Sundays.

A maze of streets crowded with tourists of every nation and peddlers of every kind of merchandise, the Grand Bazaar is both a working market selling everyday items and a kind of museum where the most unlikely bargains can be found by the smart shopper. The market was established by Mehmet the Conqueror, perhaps where informal markets had been located in Byzantine times. Its interior streets reflect the names of the ancient guilds such as the makers of fezzes (Fesçiler Sokağı) and the makers of saddle girths (Kolancılar Sokağı). Jewelry, furniture, rugs and carpets, foam rubber, ceramics, leather, trinkets, comforters — everything from junk to items worth a king's ransom are for sale. The bazaar houses under one roof 50 streets, 4,400 shops, the **İç Bedesten** (Inner Bazaar), the Sandal Bedesten (New Bazaar), 40 hans (office buildings with 2,200 rooms), warehouses, one mosque, ten *mescids* (little mosques), 19 fountains and eight wells.

The center of the market is the **İç Bedesten,** a domed, self-enclosed rectangle devoted mostly to jewelry, copper and brass, and antiques (more or less authentic). Originally the bedesten was the place where fine silk cloth was sold; as it became a storehouse for other valuables its merchandise diversified.

The **Bakırcılar Çarşısı** (copper sellers' market) is located on the west side of the Grand Bazaar. It's a good place to start looking for characteristic hand-made (new or old) copper or brass trays, pitchers, braziers, buckets and ladles.

Karacaahmet Mezarlığı
(Karacaahmet Cemetery) in Üsküdar in Asia

Most of the old tombstones with their graceful Ottoman inscriptions, beautifully carved decorations and historic head-dresses are quickly disappearing because the places of the old graves are being reused.

Karaköy

Karaköy is the area of the city on the northeast shore of the Golden Horn. It covers the area previously known as Galata.

Karikatür ve Mizah Müzesi
(Museum of Caricatures) at Gazanferağa Medresesi, Saraçhane; Tel. (212) 521 1264; open 09:00 am to 05:30 pm, closed between 12:00 noon to 01:00 pm except Sundays; no entrance fee. The current display of caricatures is in a small *medrese* that was founded in 1599 by Gazanfer Ağa, Chief White Eunuch under Mehmet III.

Kariye Müzesi

Kariye Museum (Church of St. Savior in Chora) Tel. (212) 631 9241 open 09:30 am to 16:30 pm except Tuesdays; entrance fee 30,000 TL.

Kariye Camii ranks next only to St. Sophia as important in the history of Byzantine art. The building is a late eleventh century church that was greatly remodelled about thirty years later. The frescoes and the mosaics that give it its unique value were added between 1315 and 1321. A benefactor and an artist are responsible for the quality of the work. The artist's name is unknown; although he followed many of the contemporary church conventions, his works are among the masterpieces of the world.

 The benefactor was Theodore Metochites; his portrait with the soaring hat, the symbol of his position as the prime minister, is in the lunette over the door to the nave. He is the one who worked out the theological meaning and the relationships of the scenes to be represented in the church. Among the striking qualities is the prominence of women: where other contemporary paintings of the apocalypse show Jesus raising only Adam from the dead, in the parecclesion here Eve is of equal size to Adam. Much of the story in the mosaics of the inner and outer narthexes is taken from the early life of Mary. This is confusing for Westerners who know only the events in the Bible.These events are from the Apocryphal Gospel of St. James: Mary's parents, Joachim and Anne are each pictured praying for a child. Then Mary's birth is shown, as are her first steps and her parents' fondness for her. She is presented to the Temple where she is taught and fed by an angel. By lot Mary is chosen to weave the royal colors for the new Temple veil. (Notice the dismay and jealousy on the faces of the girls with her.) Her husband is decided by the one whose dead branch placed on the altar sprouts green leaves — and in the subsequent pictures Mary is accompanied by that sprouting twig. Joseph hurries her home, his neck almost out of joint from looking back at her. From here the scenes are biblical except for the death of Mary above the door inside the nave. The frescoes of the parecclesion represent Jesus' resurrection, the Last Judgment, and the symbolism of Mary, the Mother of God, "the dwelling place of the uncontainable."

Kılıç Ali Paşa Camii
in Tophane

the Mosque of Kılıç Ali Paşa (1580), sometimes attributed to Sinan, is reminiscent of a small St. Sophia. Kılıç Ali Paşa was the admiral of Sultan Selim II's navy; he participated in the Battle of Lepanto in 1571 when the Ottomans were badly defeated.

Kız Kulesi
(Leander's Tower)

Said to have been originally constructed in the 330's A.D. during the time of Emperor Constantine, an eighteenth century lighthouse that has been repaired many times is there now. The tower is on a tiny bit of land close to the Üsküdar shore. Some scenes of the famous movie called "Topkapı" took place in this lighthouse.

The English name is misleading: legend says that Leander swam the Hellespont (Dardanelles), not the Bosphorus, to see his lover Hero and died while swimming. The origin of the Turkish name (the Girl's Tower) is of equally dubious authenticity, but either name makes a romantic story. It is now open to the public.

Kilyos
(European Black Sea port) 30 km from central Istanbul

Kilyos and the adjacent villages of Gümüşdere and Kısırkaya are Istanbul's closest seaside resorts. The long stretches of sandy beaches and the clean water make them most popular during the summer.

Koca Mustafa Paşa Camii
(Church of St. Andrew in Krisei) at Yedi Kule

While the early history of this building is unclear (was it dedicated to the Apostle Andrew?), parts of it are from the 6th century. Mustafa Paşa, who converted it to a mosque in 1520, was Süleyman's grand vizier.

Ahmet I saw the minaret illuminated on a religious festival and ordered similar illuminations (*mahya*) to be hung between the minarets of his mosque. The custom continues to today for all mosques on each night of Ramazan (the month of fasting). A large dead tree in the courtyard has a heavy iron chain hanging from the trunk. The chain was supposed to indicate whether a person standing under it was telling the truth about his debts: It fell on the heads of liars.

K
A
R
–
K
O
C

Kuleli Askeri Lisesi
in Çengelköy

A well-known naval training school, the building on the water with its striking towers was built in 1860 by Sultan Abdül Mecit.

Kumkapı

A region on the Sea of Marmara in the valley between the Second and Third Hills.

It is known for the excellent restaurants which serve a variety of fish dishes in a joyful atmosphere. It has become one of the most favorite eating places at night for the tourists. In and around the main square you can still find traces of old Istanbul in the buildings, small shops, and the life of the residents.

Küçük Ayasofya Camii
(Church of SS Sergius and Bacchus) behind Hippodrome

A mosque since the beginning of the sixteenth century, the Church of SS Sergius and Bacchus was built in 527 by Justinian and Theodora in honor of two saints whom he credited with saving his life. The building is interesting because it shows the development of church architecture just prior to St. Sophia being built. It is a slightly irregular octagon; its dome rises above the piers in sixteen undulating ribs. The poetic inscription on the frieze around the nave honors St. Sergius and mentions Justinian's pious intentions and Theodora's social service. The reference to St. Bacchus perhaps is in vines and grapes that separate the lines of the poem.

L-L-L

Laleli Camii
Laleli Mosque in Laleli

The influence of the 18th century Tulip Period which started in the Ottoman Empire with Ahmet III is seen in this baroque mosque which was built by his son, Mustafa III between 1759 and 1763. The interior decoration includes marbles of many colors and medallions with the designs picked out in onyx, jasper and lapis lazuli.

Libraries

Istanbul is rich in the variety of libraries and in the rare collections of some of them. The following is only a partial list.

Among the libraries emphasizing English language books are the **British Council** (Cumhuriyet Cad. 22-24, Elmadağ) and the **USIS** (Meşrutiyet Cad. 108, Tepebaşı). Other non-Turkish language libraries are at the **American Research Institute in Turkey** (Çitlenbik Sok. 18/2, Beşiktaş), the **Armenian Patriarchate** (Şarapnel Sok. 20, Kumkapı), the **Austrian Cultural Office** (Silâhhane Cad. 101/2, Teşvikiye), the **Casa d'Italia** (Meşrutiyet Cad. 161, Tepebaşı), the **French Cultural Center** (İstiklâl Cad. 8, Taksim), the **French Institute** (Nuruziya Sok. 22, Beyoğlu), the **German Archaeological Institute**

(Sıraselviler Cad. 123), the **Greek Patriarchate** (Sadrazam Ali Paşa Cad. 35, Fener), and the **Netherlands Historical and Archaeological Institute** (İstiklâl Cad. 393, Beyoğlu).

The major newspapers have their own archives: **Cumhuriyet** has been publishing for over 70 years; **Hürriyet** and **Milliyet** for almost 50; and the **Daily News** (main office in Ankara) for more than 30.

Some of the Turkish language libraries are at the **Archaeological Museum** (Topkapı Palace), the **Devlet Kütüphanesi** (State Library) at the Mosque of Bayezit II, at **Boğaziçi University** (Bebek, tel. 212-263 1500), at the İstanbul Kitaplığı (Soğuk Çeşme Sok., Sultanahmet), at **İstanbul University** (Bayezit), at Süleymaniye, and at the **Topkapı Palace**.

For each of these libraries you should check before you go to find out if you need special permission to use their facilities.

M-M-M

Mahmut Paşa Hamamı
Mahmut Paşa Bath on Mahmut Paşa Yokuşu
Possibly the oldest public bath in the city, it was built in 1476. Mahmut Paşa was born a Byzantine; his grandfather was Caesar Philaninos, ruler of Greece, and his mother was from Trabzon. Having fought with Mehmet the Conqueror before Constantinople, he rose to become Grand Vizier. When Mehmet was provoked to capture the last Byzantine stronghold of Trabzon, Mahmut Paşa negotiated the terms of the surrender of the Emperor of Trabzon through one of his cousins who was adviser to the emperor. (Later he angered Sultan Mehmet and was executed by him.) See Cağaloğlu Hamamı for a description of the Turkish batih.

Mahmut Paşa Yokuşu
It is the street that leads down the hill from the Mahmut Paşa gate of the Covered Market.
Now closed to cars, it is full of people looking for cheap clothing, including those produced in Turkey with internationally fashionable name brands.

Marmara Üniversitesi
Most of the buildings of Marmara University are located in İçerenköy in Asia and some faculties are scattered all over the city; the administrative offices of the president are in a building at the southern end of the Hippodrome. Teaching in certain departments is in English.

Maslak Kasırları
(Maslak Pavilions) Tel. (212) 276 1022; open 09:30 am to 04:30 pm except Mondays and Thursdays; entrance fee: 10,000TL. on Fridays, Saturdays and Sundays, 20,000TL other days.
Three examples of 19th century Ottoman architecture that were once part of the sultan's recreation facilities outside the city

have been restored by the Turkish Grand National Assembly Foundation. They include the **Kasr-i Hümayun**, the **Mağbeyn-i Hümayun** and the **Çadır Köşkü**. The glassed-in greenhouse of the Mağbein-i Hümayun is a delightful place to have tea, particularly when the spring flowers are in bloom.

Mausoleum of Barbarossa
(see Barbaros Hayreddin Paşa Türbesi)

Mevlevi Dervish Museum
(see Divan Edebiyatı Müzesi) (Museum of Classical Turkish Literature)

Mısır Çarşısı
(Egyptian Bazaar, Spice Market) Open 08:00 am to 07:00 pm except Sundays.
The Spice Market in Eminönü is the second biggest covered market in Istanbul.
 An ell-shaped building, it contains a number of shops selling spices and herbs, in addition to those selling jewelry, baskets, embroidery, cloth, and Turkish Delight. At one entrance there is the **Pandeli Restaurant**; at another there is a newspaper stand.
 It's also a good place to look for freshly roasted nuts, for henna, and for dried fruit. Its name comes from the fact that the taxes that came from Egypt contributed to its upkeep when it was built in the 1660s.

Mihrimah Camii
Mosque of Mihrimah in Edirnekapı
One of Sinan's buildings, this mosque was founded by Süleyman's daughter and completed before 1569 when its first administrator was appointed. It sits on the crest of the Sixth Hill just inside the city walls. Relative to the area of the floor, the dome appears to be unusually high, partly because the sides of the building are not masked by semidomes.
 Instead, each side of the upper stone canopy under the dome is a great arch with 19 windows like lacy cutwork flooding the interior with light.

Military Museum
(see Askeri Müze)

Mimar Sinan'ın Türbesi
(see Süleymaniye Camii)

Modern Mausoleum for Adnan Menderes
A mausoleum for Adnan Menderes, prime minister of Turkey from 1950 to 1960, has been built at the junction of the Menderes Caddesi and the Topkapı-Edirnekapı Caddesi. Turgut Özal, the eighth president is buried in close vicinity.

Monastery of Constantine Lips
(Fenari Isa Camii) in Fatih
One of the most important church complexes in the city during
the latter years of the Byzantine Empire, today the church of
Constantine Lips is in ruins. The founder was a high official in
the court of Leo the Wise; along with the first church built in
907, he also founded a hospital. Many of the royal family were
buried here.

Mosaic Museum
(see Great Palace of Byzantium)

Mosque of ... (see listing under the name of the founder)

Muhsin Ertuğrul Şehir Tiyatrosu
(City Theater) in Harbiye. Tel. (212) 240 7720
The theater is named after the man who started theater perfor-
mances in Istanbul in Tepebaşı. It is supported by the city.
This theater hosts a variety of entertainments including
plays, ballet, school performances, and musical events.

Museum of Painting and Sculpture
(see Resim ve Heykel Müzesi)

Museum of the Ancient Orient
(see Arkeoloji Müzeleri)

Museum of the Reform Period
(see Tanzimat Müzesi)

Museum of Turkish and Islamic Arts
(see İbrahim Paşa Sarayı)

N-N-N

Naval Museum
(see Deniz Müzesi)

Neve Shalom
in Şişhane
It is a small synagogue for some of the Sefardic Jews of
Istanbul. Other synagogues in the city are the Beth Israel in
Şişli, the Ashkenaz and the Italian in Karaköy, and the Hemdat
Israel in Kadıköy.

Nuruosmaniye Camii
It is one of the landmarks on the Second Hill. Its name means
the Sacred Light of Osman. It was begun by Mahmut I in 1748;
his brother Osman III finished it in 1755. There are several
odd structural details in the building: The *mihrab* is semi-circu-

lar and is flanked by two side chambers almost like the transepts of a church. The inner court is horseshoe in shape rather than the usual rectangle. A long covered incline — the sultan's entrance to the imperial gallery — leads from the east side of the outer courtyard. People entering the Covered Market frequently walk through the courtyard of Nuruosmaniye.

Nusretiye Camii
in Tophane

Mahmut II named his mosque not for himself but for his victory (*nusret* means God's help in war) over the Janissary Corps which he had liquidated in 1826, the year that the mosque was finished. Its onion-domed weight towers and thin minarets distinguish its baroque style from the classic style of the Kılıç Ali Paşa Mosque just south of it. The Nusretiye marks a change in emphasis in mosque architecture. In the place of a courtyard surrounded by the mosque dependencies of schools and caravansaries and *hamams*, this building has a large sultan's apartment across the whole of the west side. This was the time when the sultan used the mosque both as a place of prayer and as a kind of office building.

O-O-O

Open Air Theater
(see Açık Hava Müzesi)

Ortaköy
It is one of the areas (formerly a village) about 4 km north up the Bosphorus from Karaköy.
On Sundays when the weather is good there is a lively outdoor market of books and artists' work in the square around the ferry landing and the streets nearby. There are exciting little eating places in the square.

Ortaköy Camii
The Ortaköy Mosque was built in 1854 by Abdül Mecit. Its architect was the same Nikogos Balyan who built the Dolmabahçe Mosque. Perhaps because you usually see this mosque from a distance, its lines and proportions are more satisfying than his other. It has recently had to be extensively repaired because the currents of the Bosphorus were undermining the foundation.

P-P-P

Palace of the Porphyrogenitus
(see Tekfur Sarayı)

Pera
(see Beyoğlu)

Pera Palas Otel
Pera Palas Hotel in Tepebaşı; Tel. (212) 251 4560.

Almost a museum piece in itself, the Pera Palas is a four-star hotel with several handsome nineteenth century reception rooms and a congenial bar in which to relax in fin de siecle splendor.

Room 101 is kept as a museum to Mustafa Kemal Atatürk who used it when he was in Istanbul. Room 411 was Agatha Christie's when she was here.

Piyerloti Çayevi
(Pierre Loti Teahouse) in Eyüp

The 19th century French novelist Pierre Loti sat at a table in this teahouse in Eyüp overlooking the cemetery, the Golden Horn and the distant view of the Seraglio Point when he was writing his sweetly sad romances of Istanbul. Loti must have visited Istanbul several times in his career as a naval officer, as *Aziyade* was published in 1876 and *Les Désenchantées* appeared in 1906.

Piyale Paşa Camii
Piyale Paşa Mosque in Kasımpaşa

Piyale Paşa was one of Süleyman's admirals. His mosque, built in 1573, is unusual for the time because it has six equal domes rather than a single central dome. (This was the style of the much earlier Great Mosques such as Ulu Cami in Bursa.) The tiles around the *mihrab* are from the best period of İznik ceramics. The approach to Piyale Paşa's mosque was up the Dolapdere stream which he ordered to be dredged so he could sail his ship to its courtyard. (The stream bed has since silted up again.)

Polonezköy
Polish Village, 25 km west of Beykoz

The village was settled in 1842 by Poles whose support of the Allies and the Ottoman Empire during the Crimean War won them tax-free rights to own the land. Once a community known for its agricultural products (including forbidden pork and wonderful cherries in the spring), it is now a popular week-end resort.

Princes' Islands
(see also Büyük Ada and Heybeli)

Nine islands near Istanbul in the Sea of Marmara are summer resorts. In the order of the nearest to the farthest from Istanbul they are Kınalı (Proti in Greek), Burgaz (Antigone), Kaşık, Sivri (Oxya), Yassı (Plate), Heybeli (Chalki), Büyük Ada (Prinkipo), Sedef (Antherovitos), and Martı (Neandros).

The history of the islands is that of places either of exile or refuge. More than one unlucky Byzantine ruler suffered here; more than one Greek Orthodox monastery has crumbled away. In more recent times Leon Trotsky was a refugee on Büyük Ada early in this century.

N
U
S
–
P
R
I

R-R-R

Resim ve Heykel Müzesi

(Museum of Painting and Sculpture) in Beşiktaş; Tel.(212) 261 4299; open 12:30 am to 16:30 pm except Mondays and Tuesdays; no entrance fee.

Located in the Dolmabahçe apartments of the crown prince (Veliaht Dairesi), the museum contains a collection of important works beginning with the 19th century. Every now and then exhibits by Turkish painters take place here. Recently, Turks started to invest in paintings, hence encouraging Turkish painters to produce more works.

Riva

It is a small resort on the Asian shore of the Black Sea, about a two-hour drive from central Istanbul. A small Genoese castle overlooks the sandy beach.

Robert College

in Arnavutköy; Tel(212) 265 3430.

An American lycée, Robert College was founded by Christopher Robert in 1863; its first president was Cyrus Hamlin. One of the more prestigious schools in Istanbul, it is part of the Turkish educational system with a student body of almost 950 Turkish youngsters.

Rumeli Hisar

(European Fortress)

The fortress, now a museum (Tel. (212) 263 5305) open 09:30 am to 05:00 pm except Mondays; entrance fee: 20,000TL

The village of Rumeli Hisar takes its name from the fortress on the cape that was built by Mehmet the Conqueror in 1452. It consists of three large towers and fourteen smaller ones joined together by the curtain walls. The Black Tower is to the north, the Rose Tower to the south, and the Tower of Çandarlı Halil Paşa with its barbican is close to the water. The building of the towers was delegated to Mehmet's generals with the command to compete in finishing them quickly. Mehmet made himself responsible for the curtain wall. They completed the work in four months. With Anadolu Hisar directly across the Bosphorus, Mehmet controlled the passage of ships through the strait. He sank a Venetian ship almost at once that was trying to run the blockade and the fortress was never again challenged. Since the restoration of the fortress in 1953, it has become a museum and an open-air theater for summer productions and concerts.

Rumeli Kavağı

It is the northernmost ferry stop on the European side of the Bosphorus.

A fishing village, there are a number of good, inexpensive restaurants in and around the landing. The beach at Altınkum, just north, is open for swimming in the summer.

Rum Ortodoks Patrikhanesi
(Greek Orthodox Patriarchate) in Fener. Tel (212) 527 0323.
The Greek Orthodox community considers that it was established by the Apostle Andrew. Located first in St. Sophia, the Patriarchate moved to several different churches until it settled in Fener in 1601. The black Central Gate is welded shut in memory of Patriarch Gregory V who was hanged here for treason in 1821. The patriarchal office building was rebuilt in 1991. The Church of St. George on the grounds of the Patriarchate was built in 1720. It is a small basilica rich in relics from past centuries. Among these are an icon of the Virgin Mary, the bodies of several saints, and the partiarchal throne. Pilgrims from around the world congregate in the church and in its courtyard at Easter.

Rüstem Paşa Camii
Rüstempaşa Mosque in Eminönü
Rüstem Paşa was the husband of Süleyman's daughter Mihrimah and his Grand Vizier two different times. His mosque, built in 1561, sits above the shops that support it. (Rüstem Paşa was known for keeping a tight control over his finances.) In addition to the building being one of Sinan's works, its walls are famous for the beautiful sixteenth century İznik tiles.

Rüstem Paşa Hanı
Rüstempaşa Caravansary in Karaköy
Built in 1550 by Sinan for Rüstem Paşa, this *han* (inn) has an unusual arching double staircase that leads to either side of the upper floor from the center of the courtyard.

S-S-S

Sadberk Hanım Müzesi
at Piyasa Caddesi 27/29, Büyükdere Tel. (212) 242 3813-14
open 10:00 am to 5:00 pm except Wednesdays; entrance fee 30,000TL.
Sadberk Hanım, the wife of Vehbi Koç, Turkey's foremost industrialist, was a collector of ethnological items that are displayed in one of the two houses of this museum. That house has been restored as the nineteenth century mansion that it was.
The newly renovated building next door has been modernized and holds the archaeological collection of Hüseyin Kocabaş. Both the Ottoman items and those of ancient Anatolia are choice.

Sahaflar (Çarşısı)
(see Bayezit Camii)

Saint Irene

(Aya Irini) just inside the walls of Topkapı Palace

It is a small building in relation to its neighbor, Saint Sophia. However, it was the first cathedral of Constantinople before Saint Sophia was built. It was the cathedral again between 404 and 415 because St. Sophia had been destroyed in a riot. Throughout the years these two buildings — connected by passageways — were thought of as one institution, the Megale Ekklesia (the Great Church). They shared the same bishop, they suffered in the same disasters. In the 9th century their combined staff numbered 688, of whom 525 were clergy. The foundations of St. Irene may be earlier than the 6th century work; and there were repairs following an earthquake in 740, but the building is essentially the one Justinian built and consecrated in 537. Architecturally it represents a transition from the basilica to the domed cruciform church, and in that it is as interesting as St. Sophia, but it lacks the details and the decorations of the larger building. Perhaps the subdued interior hints of the early Byzantine attitude that because Christ never laughed Christians shouldn't either. St. Irene is open during the Istanbul Festival for classical music concerts.

Saint John the Baptist of Studius

in Yedikule

The Studion is the oldest church building in Istanbul. From the founding of the monastery by Studius in 462 until the end of the 15th century (well after the Conquest) its monks were spirritual and intellectual leaders in the Eastern Roman Empire. Walls, some columns, and some of the mosaic floor are still in place.

Saint Sophia

(Haghia Sophia, Ayasofya Müzesi) Tel. (212) 522 1750; the museum and the gallery open 09:30 am to 16:30 pm except Mondays; entrance fee 60,000 TL.

St. Sophia was built between 532 and 537 to be the patriarchal church of the Eastern Roman Empire. Sultan Mehmet II converted it to a mosque (Ayasofya Camii) upon his conquest of the city in 1453. It is now a museum. The present building replaced one that had burned during the Nika Riots of January 532. Wishing to atone for the wide-spread destruction of his capital, Emperor Justinian ordered Anthemius of Tralles and Isadore of Miletus to build without regard for expense.

Their work was completed in less than six years. Writing about twenty years later, Procopius remarked that the effect of the church on the people, no matter how familiar they were with it, was to lift their thoughts to God.

St. Sophia is outstanding architecturally because Anthemius and Isadore were able to build a large dome on top of a very large square. They engineered it so that the outward thrust of the dome is carried down to the four huge columns of the square room through the graceful sweep of the pendentives. Thus they created an uninterrupted covered space for religious ceremony and pageant, and in so doing influenced the science of architecture ever after.The building and its prelates have been important in both Eastern Orthodox and Ottoman history. Two Ecumenical Councils were held here before the Eastern Orthodox and the Roman Catholic Churches became divided.

So great was Sultan Mehmet's regard for this church that he ordered it not to be defaced when he converted it into a mosque. Under the Turkish Republic its universal importance was recognized when it was declared a museum in 1935.

While the exterior of the building may impress you from its bulk more than from its elegance, when you enter the nave your reaction probably, like the contemporaries of Procopius, will be to look up to the dome that seems, as he said, "to be suspended from heaven." In fact, it is so high that not until you look down at the floor and then up at it again from the gallery do you have some perspective to judge its height of 180 feet.

The complexity of the building (architecture, art, history, trivia, personalities) could occupy you for many years. To mention only a few superficial points, you might notice the distortion of the walls when you are in the gallery.

In the floors you may make out the stonemasons' signatures on the slabs. If you enjoy puzzles you can decipher the wording in the monograms on the capitals of the columns in the nave. A hint: the inscription on a red porphry column in the southwest corner identifies it as the first one to be raised. Read Villehardouin's "Memoirs of the Crusades" for information about Henrico Dandalus who was buried in the gallery. Five sultans chose to be buried on the grounds. And feel yourself privileged: the general public had to crane their necks to see into the nave through most of the church ceremony, and women were allowed only in the gallery. At the height of the Empire the building was richly decorated with gold, silver, ivory, silks, jewels, and icons. Procopius likens the effect to that of a meadow in bloom with flowers. Today a few of those colors are to be seen in the several mosaics. Most are conventional representations: the Madonna and Child, churchmen, emperors and empresses. However, the 14th century panel in the gallery portraying Mary, Jesus and St. John the Baptist (a grouping known as the Deisis) is both realistic and, in its truth, timeless. St. Sophia is the transcendent embodiment of Byzantine architecture. A stately, majestic building, it has inspired respect for more than fourteen hundred years.

Sarayburnu
(Seraglio Point)

The First Hill of the city is called Sarayburnu in Turkish, which means the palace cape

Probably the walls of the city built by Septimius Severus in about 200 enclosed little more than the First Hill, but that was double the size of the previous city which was on just the acropolis.

Both the Byzantines and the Ottomans had their palaces here. Many of the museums and places of historical interest are located on or near this cape.

Sarıyer

is about 15 km as the crow flies north up the Bosphorus

A number of good fish restaurants and very good bakeries are located around the harbor.

Schools

(see also Galatasaray Lisesi, Robert College, Üsküdar Amerikan Lisesi)

Public education in Turkey is secular; it is controlled by the Ministry of Education. School attendance is required for all citizens through the fifth grade. Public schooling is free; however parents are responsible for furnishing the required school uniforms. Entrance to middle school (*orta*) is through examination. It includes the 6th through the 8th grade. Lycée (*lise*) is from the 9th through the 11th grade. Entrance to any of the private middle and lycée schools is through a competitive national examination. Graduation from lycée is a prerequisite for being able to take the university entrance examination. Performance on it determines the field of study.

During the Ottoman Empire education had been provided by the mosque (and was theoretically open to all males), by the minority groups for their own people, or by the palace. The best mosque education, such as was available at Süleymaniye, prepared a man for a career in Islamic law, in Islamic theology, or in medicine. Education among the minority groups followed similar lines, with the emphasis on Christianity or Judaism rather than Islam.

The Palace School (*Enderun Mektebi*) was founded by Mehmet the Conqueror and lasted into the 19th century. A branch of it, the Galatasaray Lisesi, continues much of its role. When it was functioning, it trained conscripted boys (*devşirme*) in Turkish, Arabic and Persian languages and literature, Islamic beliefs, military sciences, mathematics, etiquette, politics, diplomacy, and a vocation. Graduates became members of the military and political services of the sultan; they might rise to be a governor of a province, an admiral, a head agha of the janissaries, or eventually a grand vizier.

The first attempts at a public education system were made in the 19th century. These bore fruit as the Turkish Republic instituted the remarkable liberalizing reforms of the 1920s. Three in particular have affected the levels of education: 1) public education in the primary grades is compulsory for all, boys and girls alike; 2) since 1928 the language has been written in a modified Latin script, making it much easier to read than the previous Osmanlıca (modified Arabic); and 3) the status of women has continued to improve, encouraged in part by Atatürk's speeches in 1923 on the need for men and women to share in the social, cultural and economic life of the country.

Students from several private schools founded and/or administered by foreigners have achieved considerable distinction. Besides those listed here, the following should be noted: the **Avusturya** (Austrian) **Lisesi** (Karaköy), the **Alman** (German) **Lisesi** (Tünelbaşı), the **Koç Lisesi** (Kurtköy), **Notre Dame de Sion** (French) **Lisesi** (Elmadağ), **St. Benoit** (French)**Lisesi** (Karaköy), **St. Joseph** (French) **Lisesi** (Moda), **St. Michel** (French) **Lisesi (Feriköy)**, **St Pulcherie** (French) **Lisesi (**Taksim) and the **Italyan Lisesi (**Tophane).

These of course are in addition to the public schools. In 1990 there were a total of 1,082 primary, 439 middle, 292 lycée and 134 trade schools in the city.

Selimiye Camii 🕌
Selimiye Mosque in Haydarpaşa

The Mosque of Selim III was built in 1803-04 to honor his mother, Mihrişah Sultan.

It is the last of the baroque style mosques. Among its details are the bird houses built into the façade of the building and the huge plane tree in the courtyard.

Selimiye Kışlası
(Selimiye Barracks) in Haydarpaşa

A rectangular building with a large central courtyard and towers on each of the four corners, the Selimiye Barracks was the hospital during the Crimean War (1853-1856). A room in the north tower has been set aside as a **Florence Nightingale Museum** (open every day except Saturdays and Sundays) honoring the English lady who established the profession of nursing here.

Sirkeci

It is the area of the old city where the trains from Europe arrive. Car ferries to Harem in Asia leave from Sirkeci, as do passenger ferries for Heybeli, Büyük Ada, Yalova and Çınarcık, Üsküdar and the Bosphorus. Ships to the island of Marmara and to İzmir are found at the dock farther east. The city wall built by Septimius Severus about 200 AD probably followed the line of the street (Ankara Caddesi) that goes up the hill.

Soğuk Çeşme Sokağı
(Ayasofya Pensions) between Topkapı Palace and Saint Sophia

Adjacent to the walls of Topkapı, the entire block of brightly painted, Turkish-style wooden houses, which was restored by Touring and Automobile Association of Turkey, offer sleeping accommodations and a simple breakfast, in the tradition of the European pension. The rooms (each with private bath) are furnished in old-fashioned style. The real bonus here is the breathtaking view of the domes and minarets of Saint Sophia. Another Touring and Automobile Association establishment on this street is the **Sarnıç** (Turkish word for cistern) **Taverna**. The building was originally a Roman water reservoir. It impresses people with its cavernous walls, trestle tables, and mammoth fireplace.

Sokollu Mehmet Paşa Camii
Mosque of Sokollu Mehmet Paşa in Akbıyık

Founded by Esmahan Sultan (daughter of Selim II and wife of Mehmet Paşa), the Sokollu Mehmet Paşa Mosque is a Sinan building. It was built in 1571/2; the dramatic entrance to its courtyard is up through a covered flight of stairs. Inside, the *mihrab* is decorated with İznik tiles as are the pendentives. Above the *mihrab* and the *minber* are pieces of the black stone from the Kaaba.

Sound and Light
in Sultanahmet

Throughout the summer a Sound-and-Light show of the history of the city is presented to people sitting on benches in the open area next to the Blue Mosque. The languages rotate each night from Turkish to English to French to German.

Spice Market
(see Mısır Çarşısı)

Sublime Porte
This English name for the Ottoman Government is said to have come from the flamboyant ornamental gateway to the offices of the Grand Vizier which stand across the street and a bit below the entrance to Gülhane Park. In addition to being given his seal of office by the sultan, he also had a key to the inconconspicuous door in the palace wall just across the street from the gateway.

Sultanahmet Camii
(Mosque of Ahmet I, Blue Mosque)

Named for the blue İznik tiles (21,043 of them) that face the lower walls of the mosque and those of the balcony, the Blue Mosque is one of the symbols of Istanbul. Sultan Ahmet built his mosque on a small section of the land of the Great Palace of Constantinople. The architect was Mehmet Ağa, a pupil of the great Sinan. Its graceful silhouette with the six well-proportioned minarets and the huge interior prayer space lighted with 260 windows have made it the most admired mosque of the city. Sultan Ahmet hoped that the light diffused by the blue tiles would suggest a celestial garden. The mosque was dedicated in 1617 by Ahmet who had been so eager to see his building completed that he often spent Fridays working on it himself.

Well into the 19th century a new green covering for the Kaaba was woven each year in Istanbul. Following the service in the Blue Mosque, it was started on its way by camel caravan on the 12th of the Muslim month of Recep in time to be in Mecca for Kurban Bayramı (the Festival of Sacrifice). In addition to Ahmet I himself, his favorite Kösem Sultan, his sons Bayezit, Osman II and Murat IV and a number of other family members are buried in his *türbe* on the northwest corner of the complex.

Sultan Selim Camii
on the Fifth Hill
Sultan Selim I ruled from 1512 to 1520; during those years his campaigns into the Persian and Arabic lands doubled the size of the Ottoman Empire. Upon his conquest of Cairo in 1517 he acquired the title of Caliph (which all subsequent sultans held) and brought home a number of trophies including the sword and the mantle of the Prophet Mohammed. His mosque and its dependencies which crown the Fifth Hill were completed in 1522 by his son, Sultan Süleyman.

Surlar
(Walls)
The walls surrounding the Seven Hills of Constantinople were built in three main sections, the sea walls first by Constantine in 330, the land walls by Theodosius II by 447, and the walls along the Golden Horn which Constantine started and which were extended by Theodosius II and repaired by most of the subsequent emperors. Two gates are still preserved in the Golden Horn walls, one at Cibali and the other at Aya Kapı. In the land walls, there are several of the old gates that are little changed: the Edirne and the Fifth Military (just south of the Mosque of Mihrimah) are a squeeze even for pedestrians today.

The Topkapı Gate has been rebuilt to commemorate Mehmet the Conqueror's soldiers who penetrated the city defenses here. Between it and Yedi Kule parts of the old wall are now new. Clean, pretty stone has been cemented into place, imposing defense towers have been engineered, and Theodosius' wall looks just as it was when the city was threatened by Atilla the Hun.

Süleymaniye Camii
(Mosque of Süleyman the Magnificent) in Süleymaniye
Sultan Süleyman's mosque (dedicated in 1557) dominates the skyline of the Old City above the Golden Horn. Magnificent in itself, it was intended to be Süleyman's statement of both the political splendor of the Ottoman Empire and the religious power of Islam. There is elegance here in the grace and restraint of its lines, yet they combine to give a sense of awe and grandeur as you enter the building.

When first built, besides the mosque the Süleymaniye complex included school buildings of several levels, a bath, a hospital, an *imaret*, a caravansary, markets and a cemetery. All were arranged on the hill so that the mosque was the culminating point. While most of the dependencies are no longer used for their original purposes, some of the school buildings are now libraries.

The four minarets have been thought to symbolize the fact that Süleyman was the fourth sultan after the conquest of the city; their ten balconies therefore showed that he was the tenth after Sultan Osman. Inside, Süleymaniye displays many priceless treasures of the sixteenth century, among them İznik tiles,

S
O
K
–
S
Ü
L

exquisite marble and wood carvings and mother-of-pearl
inlays. *Sarhoş* (drunken) İbrahim (who was masterful only
when inebriated) made the stained glass which is considered
the best of its kind. Ahmet Karahisarî, the greatest Ottoman
calligrapher, wrote the many inscriptions on the walls.

In the adjacent cemetery to the south are found the *türbes*
(mausoleums) of Süleyman and of his wife Hürrem. That of
Süleyman is decorated with beautiful İznik tiles; its ceiling is
painted red, black and gold and studded with sparkling gems.
Süleyman, known in Turkish as "Kanunî" -- the law-giver --
requested that a copy of his laws be buried with him.

Across the street from the north corner of the complex is the
small, open *türbe* of Süleyman's Chief Court Architect. So outstanding was this man's work that his profession has become
almost inseparable from his given name: Mimar Sinan. During
his 50 years in office (1538-1588) he was involved in the construction or repair of 477 buildings: mosques, schools, mausoleums, dervish lodges, caravansaries, soup kitchens, bridges,
palaces, pavilions, warehouses, and baths. These spread geo-
graphically from his restoration of the Grand Mosque in Mecca
to the bridge across the Drina River in old Yugoslavia. One
hundred and seven mosques are attributed to him; 62 are still
in good repair. However, Sinan's work was concentrated on
the buildings in Istanbul.

Of the 136 still standing, a number are identified in this listing.
Sinan considered the Şehzade Mosque (1548) to be the work
sealing his apprenticeship. With the Süleymaniye in Istanbul
and the Selimiye (1574/75) in Edirne, Sinan created a universal
statement of classical Ottoman architecture in the clarity and
monumentality of those buildings. Sinan's genius continues to
be recognized throughout the world.

Sweet Waters of Asia

Two short streams a couple hundred meters apart make up the
Sweet Waters of Asia. Göksu which empties into the
Bosphorus at Anadolu Hisar, and Küçüksu which empties near
the Küçüksu Palace frame a small meadow. The streams and
the meadow were favorite excursion spots on Fridays for members of the Ottoman palace and their hangers-on.

Sweet Waters of Europe

The Alibey Suyu to the west, and the Kâğıthane Suyu, streams
that rise in the Belgrade Forest and empty into the Golden
Horn, were known in Ottoman days as the Sweet Waters of
Europe. With the meadows in between they were once pleasant picnic spots.

Ş-Ş-Ş

Şehir Müzesi

(City Museum of Istanbul) in Yıldız Park, Beşiktaş; Tel. (212)
258 5344; open 09:00 am to 04:30 pm except Thursdays; no
entrance fee.

The Museum houses a collection of objects --paintings, ceramics, embroidery, calligraphy, and jewelry-- relating to the history of the city since 1453.

Şehzade Camii
(Mosque of Prince Mehmet) on Şehzadebaşı Caddesi

The mosque founded by Süleyman in memory of his oldest son, Mehmet, was completed in 1548/9. Mehmet had died of smallpox in 1544.

Sinan called this his work as an apprentice; it established his reputation in the capital. Mehmet's *türbe* is in the mosque yard. In it is also buried his crippled brother Cihangir; Grand Vizier Rüstem Pasha is buried near by.

Şemsi Paşa Camii
(Mosque of Şemsi Ahmet Pasha) in Üsküdar

Another of Sinan's mosques, this one was built in 1580 for one of Selim II's grand viziers.

Best seen as you approach the Üsküdar ferry landing, it stands out almost as an icon of Sinan's work. The medrese of the complex is now a public library.

Şile
An Asian Black Sea port 72 km from Üsküdar

It is world famous for its coarsely woven cloth (*Şile bezi*). Şile attracts many people in summer because of its long stretch of golden sandy beach. A small Genoese castle, now ruined, sits on the rocks a short distance off the shore.

T-T-T

Tahtakale
It is the name of a short street and an area behind the Mısır Çarşısı (the Spice Bazaar). It became the identification of illegal trafficking in the city in the 1970s. There the daily price of a pack of Marlboro cigarettes reflected the health of the Turkish economy. Today it is one of the few surviving areas of small craftsmen (woodworkers, bookbinders) who have kept their trades alive for hundreds of years.

Takkeci İhrahim Ağa Camii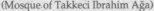
(Mosque of Takkeci İbrahim Ağa)

Located just outside the city walls at Topkapı, and visible from the E-5 highway south of the Adnan Menderes interchange. The mosque has several interesting features: It's old. It was built in 1592, and is one of the few surviving wooden mosques with a wooden roof. Its founder, a maker of tall, conical felt hats (*takke*), managed to get some İznik tiles (available only to royalty) to face the inside walls.

Taksim
It is the main square in Beyoğlu where a number of streets converge, among them İstiklâl Caddesi, Cumhuriyet Caddesi and Sıraserviler.

Distribution (*taksim*) of water to parts of Beyoğlu is made from the large reservoir on the west side of the circle. The statue in the center of the circle was created by an Italian sculpture, Pietro Canonica, in 1928 to honor the founding of the Turkish Republic.

Tanzimat Müzesi
(Museum of the Reform Period) in Gülhane Parkı
It is not far from the outdoor theater in the Gülhane Park. Tel. (202) 512 6384; open every day 08:30 am to 05:00 pm; no entrance fee.
The museum contains pictures, official papers and medallions of the years from 1839 to 1871 when the government tried to limit the sultan's power and institute Western reforms with the hope of maintaining the Ottoman Empire.

Tekfur Sarayı
(Palace of the Porphyrogenitus)
This three-story shell of a building is wedged into the land walls not far from Kariye Camii. It may have been built before the 13th century; perhaps it was enlarged after the Byzantines regained the city from the Latins in 1261. It probably was part of the palace complex that included Blachernae. For a while the Ottomans used it as a stable for their elephants.

Telli Baba
It is a shrine of ancient memory near the road that winds up the hill between Sarıyer and Rumeli Kavağı.
The current reputation of this folk saint (*baba*) is that he will help girls find the right husband. Those who are newly married and made a wish to him visit the spot to leave him a strand of their silver ribbon (*tel*) in thanks to his response.

Tophane
It is the site of the Ottoman cannon foundry.
According to the 17th century raconteur Evliya Çelebi, there is a legend that Alexander the Great tied up a number of witches from the magical land of Gog and Magog here, commanding them to protect the city during the depths of winter, but they were drowned in a storm that came down from the Black Sea. Mehmet the Conqueror built the first foundry; the present deserted building is of more recent date : 1803.

Tophane Çeşmesi
(Tophane Fountain)
Baroque in design and decoration, the large marble fountain in Tophane was built by Sultan Mahmut I in 1732.

Topkapı
It is the place of one of the gates in the city's land walls.
In Byzantine times it was called the Gate of St. Romanus (the Church of St.Romanus stood nearby). Its Turkish name (*top*=canon; *kapı*=gate) comes from the battering it took from Mehmet the Conqueror's big Orban cannon during the siege of the city. The noisy city bus terminal was across the avenue.

International Istanbul bus terminal, the most modern in Europe, has been moved to its new place outside the city in Esenler.

Topkapı Palace Museum
(see Topkapı Sarayı)

Topkapı Sarayı
(Palace of Topkapı) Tel. (212) 512 0480; open 09:30 am to 05:00 pm; Harem open 10:00 am to 04:00 pm except Tuesdays; entrance fee 60,000 TL.
The residence and administrative center for the sultans for four hundred years, Topkapı Sarayı has been the symbol of the power, the magnificence and the statecraft of the Empire for both Ottomans and foreigners. Begun by Mehmet the Conqueror in 1459, it was identified as the New Palace to distinguish it from the first residence he built at the old Forum of Theodosius (now the grounds of Istanbul University). A twin-towered, heavily armed sea gate and an 18th century pretty marble summer palace next to it (lost in a 19th century fire) gave the palace its present name.

The palace grounds, open areas with relatively small buildings hidden behind crenellated walls, are divided into five courts, each with its separate functions. The First Court, beyond the Imperial Gate, is now mostly park. It encloses the Church of St. Irene. The Second Court, entered through the Middle Gate, includes the kitchens (now the Chinese porcelain display) the Council Chambers (Divan), and the Tower of Justice. Around the Third Court are the Reception or Throne Pavilion (*Arz Odası*), the library of Ahmet III, the former school and dormitories of the pages (*Enderun Mektebi*), the treasury, the Pavilion of the Holy Mantle, and the Harem. The Fourth Court, an extension of the Third, has both the Revan and the Baghdad Kiosks. The Fifth Court is mostly the Gülhane Park; it had included hanging gardens, a zoo, a fruit orchard and vegetable garden, and several pretty kiosks. Towards the end of the 19th century the railroad bed was cut through it.

The Divan was the collection of rooms in which the sultan's council of state met. It is also the name given to that council. Above the council seats a small curtained window gave into an alcove from which the sultan could monitor his ministers' judgements. The tower, which this is part of, is called the **Tower of Justice**; it was one of Mehmet the Conqueror's buildings.

On the stone wall close to where you buy tickets to enter the Topkapı Palace is a small, nondescript **executioners' fountain** where those functionaries cleaned their hands and their sword after they had carried out the sultan's order.

Just west of the Divan is one of the entrances to the **Harem**, the private living quarters of the sultans, his women and their servants.

The sultans' table service, the third richest and most varied collection of Chinese porcelains in the world, is found in the former **kitchens** of the palace.

TAN - TOP

The **Revan** (1635) and **Bağdat** (1638) **Kiosks** were built by Murat IV to celebrate his victories over those cities.

The Holy Mantle of the Prophet (*Hırka-i Saadet*) and other similar relics are kept in the **Pavilion of the Holy Mantle.** Long displayed briefly only by the sultan in solemn ceremonies, the Pavilion has been open to the public since 1962.

Hundreds of jeweled items that are on view in the **Treasury** were the personal possessions of one or more members of the royal family. A small emerald-encrusted sword from this collection was popularized by the movie "Topkapı" and the famous spoonmaker's diamond is worth seeing.

Besides the areas and displays already listed, there are also the following (but note that the displays are constantly being changed and not all are always on view): miniatures and manuscripts, weaponry, clocks, royal tents, costumes and fabrics.

Tünel

It is a very short subway running up the hill from near the Galata Bridge to the beginning of Istiklâl Caddesi.
It was built in 1877 and used first to carry horses and cows. Later its two carriages had curtained sections to shield its lady passengers. It was last renovated in the 1970s. It is supposed to be the world's second underground transportation the first being the London tube.

U-U-U

Universities

Istanbul boasts its collection of six universities: **Boğaziçi** University inherited the campus and the tradition of Robert College. **Istanbul** University dates its foundation from the time of Mehmet the Conqueror. **Istanbul Technical** University specializes in the sciences and engineering. **Marmara** University is located largely in Kadıköy; it has a faculty of Islamic studies in addition to those of sciences. **Mimar Sinan** University on the Bosphorus shore includes faculties of architecture and fine arts. Yıldız University is located in some of the buildings of Abdül Hamit's palace.

Uzunçarşı

Long shopping street near the Grand Bazaar
A street that slopes from the Golden Horn up almost to one of the entrances to the Grand Bazaar is the colorful market for hand-turned wooden objects, quality leather pocket books, brass coffee grinders and mosque finials, hunting supplies and used clothing.

Ü-Ü-Ü

Üçüncü Ahmet Çeşmesi
(Fountain of Ahmet III)

Standing between St. Sophia and the imperial gate of Topkapı, the Fountain of Ahmet III was built in 1728. The white, red and pink marble is intricately carved with floral designs and inscriptions.

Üsküdar
(ancient Chrysopolis)

Üsküdar was once the Asian port for the city. The name apparently is an adaptation of a word for the shield-bearing soldiers (skoutari) who were quartered here in the 11the century. All the Asian trade routes converged here until the Bosphorus Bridge was opened in 1973. The five imperial mosques of Üsküdar (plus one in Beylerbeyi) were all built either for or by women. At the ferry landing are the İskele Camii, the Yeni Valide Camii, and the Şemsi Paşa Camii; 3 km southeast is the green area of cypress trees in the Karacaahmet cemetery; about 5 km up the hill above the landing are the two peaks of the Çamlıca hill.

Üsküdar Amerikan Lisesi
at Bağlarbaşı; Tel. (216) 310 6823

It is a coeducational junior and senior high school for Turkish students. It was founded in 1876 by missionaries under the American Board of Commissioners for Foreign Missions.

V-V-V

Valens Aqueduct
It was built by the Roman Emperor Valens in about 375 as part of the system bringing water to Constantinople from the small streams west of the city. Originally it stretched almost a kilometer over the valley between the Fourth and the Third Hills. Where it crosses Atatürk Caddesi it is 20 meters high.

Via Egnatia
It was the Roman road that began at the Golden Milestone near St. Sophia in Constantinople and led through Thrace and Macedonia to present-day Durres in Albania.

From there the traffic sailed across the Adriatic Sea to the Italian port of Egnatia (Gnatia, near today's Fasano). It linked the Eastern to the Western Roman Empire. (The highway that replaced it is called the London Asphalt, and the "new" road has been replaced by two superhighways.)

W-W-W

Walls
(see Surlar)

Y-Y-Y

Yalı
It is the term for the wooden summer mansions on the waterfront. Most of the famous ones have met their fate through

time, taxes and fires. The remaining ones, mostly restored in their original looks, are worth seeing during a Bosphorus cruise either by regular ferries going from Beşiktaş or Sirkeci to the end of the Bosphorus or by floating restaurant boats mostly starting from Kabataş for dinner. The hotel reception can arrange reservations on such boats.

Yalova
(about 50 km across the Sea of Marmara)
The town of Yalova is part of greater Istanbul. Its tourist attraction is the forested Thermal spa (hotels, baths, museum) 12 km into the hills southwest of the port. The facilities are administered now by the Tourism Bank. Ferry boats to Yalova start from Karaköy. At Yalova a shared taxi (*dolmuş*) takes you to the spa.

Yedi Kule
(Seven Tower) Tel. (212) 585 8933; open 09:30 am to 05:00pm except Mondays; entrance fee 20,000 TL.
The enclosure at the southwest corner of the city where the sea wall meets Theodosius' land wall dates as a fortress only from the 15th century when Mehmet the Conqueror added three inner towers and their curtain walls to the four previous towers. Yedi Kule was used by the Ottomans as a dungeon. Its most famous prisoner was Sultan Osman II who was assassinated by his soldiers here in May of 1622 when he was 18 years old. He had ruled four years.

Yeni Cami
(New Mosque) the prominent mosque in Eminönü
It was started by the Queen Mother Safiye Sultan in 1597. She died before it was built, and it was left to the later Queen Mother, Türkhan Sultan, to complete it in 1663. One of the architects responsible for the work earned his nickname *dalgıç* (diver) because he solved the problem of the water from the Golden Horn which kept seeping into the site. Dalgıç Ahmet Ağa built a series of arching stone bridges reinforced with iron on which the foundations of Yeni Cami have stood securely ever since.
The long ramp that leads to the sultan's gallery was the first part of the mosque that was completed. It allowed Türkhan Sultan to watch the progress on her building. The north side of this ramp made use of part of the old sea wall of Constantinople.

Yeni Valide Camii
New Valide Mosque in Üsküdar
Built to honor the Queen Mother Gülnuş Sultan by Ahmet III in 1710, the mosque and its dependencies are somewhat hidden among the trees and other buildings to the south of the Üsküdar landing. Notice the bronze grillwork on the mausoleum and the fountain, and the small bird houses on the mosque walls.

Yer Altı Camii
(Underground Mosque) in Karaköy

The basement of the Castle of Galata, built during the reign of Tiberias II (578-82) is thought to be the building that was converted into the present Yer Altı Camii in the 17th or 18th century. The worship area is interrupted by a grid of fifty-four pillars to which one end of the iron chain blocking entrance to the Golden Horn was attached. (Part of that chain is in the Museum of the Sultans' caiques in Beşiktaş.)

Yerebatan Sarayı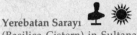
(Basilica Cistern) in Sultanahmet; Tel. (212) 522 1259; open everyday 09:00 am to 04:30 pm; entrance fee 30,000 TL.

Undoubtedly the most impressive of all the cisterns in the city, the Basilica Cistern was built by Constantine and enlarged by Justinian. Its name came from a law school that was housed in a basilica near by. Pierre Gilles, a traveller and writer who studied the city and recorded what he saw in the 16th century, reported that the people living above it were not aware of it even though they drew their water from it. He also described being rowed around the pillars, his way lit by torches. Into the early years of this century visitors were treated to the same circuit of the columns, a romantic or a spectral excursion depending on their mood. Since then the water has been drained, electric lights installed, and now strains of Beethoven symphonies echo against the dark walls.

Yeşilköy
It is the town on the Sea of Marmara closest to the Atatürk Airport. It is a fashionable residential area.

Into the early years of this century it was known as San Stefano. A treaty between Turkey and Russia was signed here in 1878 that gave independence to Rumania, Serbia and Montenegro, and that extended the border of Bulgaria in Thrace, including what is now Edirne. (The Congress of Berlin a few months later reworked the terms of that agreement, including changing the Bulgarian border.)

Yıldız Sarayı
(Palace and Park of Yıldız) Tel. (212) 258 3080 (5 lines); open 09:00 am to 04:00 pm except Mondays.

The grounds of Yıldız apparently became part of the sultan's holding in the early 17th century. Evliya Çelebi reports that Murat IV gave the property to his daughter Kaya Sultan who married Melek Ahmet Paşa (Evliya Çelebi's maternal uncle). The park and its seaside palace were famous in the 18th century for the pretty illuminations (çırağan) in lanterns and crystal lamps in the spring tulip gardens. When Abdül Hamit II (1876-1909) wanted to distance himself from his subjects he chose this large area, encircled it with a double wall, and hid himself among its trees. The Şale, named for its exterior resemblance to a Swiss chalet, consists of two adjacent buildings that

Y
A
L
_
Y
I
L

were part of Abdül Hamit's palace. In true Ottoman style, it had both its men's and women's sections. The floor of the great reception room is covered with a 400 m^2 Hereke rug. Other furnishings indicate the sophisticated European taste of the late 19th century. Four buildings in the park have recently been restored by the Touring and Automobile Association of Turkey: the **Malta Köşkü**, the **Çadır Köşkü**, the **Pembe** (Pink) **Sera** and the **Yeşil** (Green) **Sera**. These are places to sit for a quiet cup of tea and enjoy the view of the city.

Yıldız Sarayı Müzesi

Yıldız Palace Museum in Beşiktaş. Tel. (212) 258 3080; open 09:30 am to 4:00 pm except Mondays and Thursdays; entrance fee 20.000 TL. The museum displays woodworks and Turkish porcelains.

Yuşa Nebi Türbesi
(Mausoleum of the Prophet Joshua) in Anadolu Kavağı

The grave of the person buried here is remarkably large. One legend says that God gave Joshua the privilege of dying and being buried on the Bosphorus. Whoever it was, the memory of the saint is much revered among people today.

Z-Z-Z

Zal Mahmut Paşa Camii
(Mosque of Zal Mahmut Pasha) in Eyüp

Zal Mahmut Paşa was the husband of Selim II's daughter Şah Sultan. His soubriquet, Zal, which means both "old hag" and "hero" was his because he had been the one to strangle Prince Mustafa in 1553, opening the way for Selim to inherit the throne. With Sinan as the architect he built the mosque and its complex in Eyüp probably between 1575 and 1580. The complex includes school buildings and the *türbe* of Zal Mahmut Paşa and Şah Sultan.

Zeyrek Camii
(Church of the Pantocrator) in Unkapanı

The large, red brick Byzantine building that is part of the skyline above Atatürk Caddesi was one of the early 12th century religious establishments. This building is a chapel flanked by two churches, of which the southern church is now used as a mosque. The rest of the complex included a monastery, an insane asylum, a hospice for old men and a hospital.

Zindan Kapı
(Dungeon Gate)

It was one of the gates of the Byzantine city wall. It took its name from the prison (*zindan*) which was in the tower of the gate. That crumbling tower is still there, somewhat more visible now than for many years because most of the buildings in the area were demolished in an attempt in the 1980s to clean up the Golden Horn and its shores.

Further Reading

Ambler, Eric: **The Light of Day** (1963) (basis of the movie "Topkapı")

Atıl, Esin: **The Age of Süleyman the Magnificent** (1987) (prepared for the museum exhibits)

Berlitz Travellers Guide To Turkey 1993 (see chapter on Istanbul)

Blanch, Lesley: **The Wilder Shores of Love** (1954) (particularly the chapter on Aimée Dubucq de Rivery)

Comnena, Anna: **The Alexiad** (12th century account of the reign of Anna's father, Emperor Alexius I)

Davis, Fanny: **The Palace of Topkapı in Istanbul** (1970)

Davison, Roderic: **Turkey** (1968) (short, concise general history)

Edip, Halide: **Memoirs of Halide Edip** (1926)

Forster, E. W. ed.: **The Turkish Letters of Ogier Chisholm de Busbecq, Imperial Ambassador at Constantinople** 1554-1562 (1968)

Gilles, Pierre: **The Antiquities of Constantinople** (1988) (Gilles was in Constantinople during the reign of Süleyman the Magnificent)

Goodwin, Godfrey: **A History of Ottoman Architecture** (1971)

Hotham, David: **The Turks** (1972) (general study of the people)

Kinross, Patrick Balfour: **Atatürk, A Biography of Mustafa Kemal, Father of Modern Turkey** (1964)

Krautheimer, Richard: **Early Christian and Byzantine Architecture** (1965)

Kuran, Abtullah: **Sinan, the Grand Old Master of Ottoman Architecture** (1987)

Lewis, Bernard: **Istanbul and the Civilization of the Ottoman Empire** ((1963)

Lewis, Raphaela: **Everyday Life in Ottoman Turkey** (1971)

Mamboury, Ernest: **The Tourist's Istanbul** (1953)

Miller, Barnette: **The Palace School of Muhammad the Conqueror** (1941)

Muallimoğlu, Nejat: **The Wit and Wisdom of Nasraddin Hodja**

Murphy, Dervla and Pick, Christopher, ed.: **Embassy to Constantinople, The Travels of Lady Mary Wortley Montagu** (1988) (Lady Mary was in Constantinople from 1716 to 1718)

Necipoğlu, Gülru: **Architecture, Ceremonial, and Power: The Topkapı Palace in the Fifteenth and Sixteenth Centuries** (1991)

Pallis, Alexander: **In the Days of the Janissaries** (1951) (selections of Evliya Çelebi's *Seyahatname* -- travel account -- written between 1611 and 1684)

Procopius: **Secret History** (all the dirt about Justinian and Theodora)

Sumner-Boyd, Hilary and Freely, John: **Strolling Through Istanbul** (1989)

Taşkıran, Tezer: **Women in Turkey** (1976)

Underwood, Paul et al.: **The Kariye Djami** (1966)

Men's &Women's Wear

Atalar 99-106
Beymen 99-104
Beymen Club 101
Daks 106
Endican 103
Fibula 100
IGS 99-104
Kip 101-104
Mac Renzi 106
Mudo 101 - 106
Mudo Collection 102
New Men 101
Park Bravo 106
Pollini-Teodem 106
Polo 104
Polo-Ralph Lauren 106
R.Country Store 100
Silk & Cahsmere 106
Sisley 101-106
Show Off 106
Stefenal 101
Sümerbank 99
Tiffani Tomato 101-106
Titiz 101
Vakko 103 - 104
Vakkoroma 101
Yargıcı 106

Men's Wear

Abbate 99 - 106
Adam's 103
Ali Alta Moda 99
Asım Barlas 99
Ermenegildo
Zegna 101
Jentilmen 101
Kip 106
Newmen 106
Trussardi 106

Music Shop
Uzelli Müzik 106

Optician
Fahri Kuz
Optik 106
Şişli Optik 106

Photo Service
Vakkoroma 101

Shirts & Neckties
Abbate 99
Bisse 106
Cotton Bar 101 - 102
Pancaldi & B 106

Think Pink 106
Vakko Kravat 102

Shirts (for women)
Netay 106

Shoes
Bata 106
Beymen Club 101
Divaresse 101
Erol Odabaşı 101
Goya 104
Gucci 102
Hotiç 102
Karaca 99
Mondi 102
Pierre Cardin 106
Shoe and Me 106
Timberland 102 - 106
Vetrina Discarpe 102

Shopping Arcades
Lale Pasajı 99
Gizer Çarşısı 99
Pilavcı Pasajı 99
Polat Pasajı 99
Site Pasajı 99
Yılmazlar Pasajı 99

Silk Scarves
Ipek 105
Pierre Cardin 106
Vakko 103 - 104

Silk Yardage
Hacı Resul İpekçi 105
İpeker 105

Socks
Berk 106

Sports Outfit
Fred & Perry 101
Sport Service 99

Sportswear
Kappa 106

Sweaters & Slacks
Denver 106
Karaca 101-106

Swim Wear
Fiorucci 101 - 106
Gottex 106
Gruppa La Perla 106
Zeki 100-106

Toys
Elit 106
Fatoş 106
Vakkoroma 101

Women's Wear
Adrtan 99
Ahmet Ozan 102
Arkline 103
Chipie 106
Derishow 102
Ecla 102
Escada 102
Faik Sönmez 100
Foli 102
Gazellini 102
Gusto 101
Handa &Hayat 103
Infinity 101
İpek Kramer 106
İpekyolu 101
Laurel Boutique 102
Onna 102
Rachel's 103
S & Villa 101
Tierry Mugler 102
Vepa 101

Youthful Sportswear
Benetton 99-101-104
Hey 101
Kookai 103
Lacoste 101
Limon 101
Mudo 101
Vakkorama 101-104
Yargıcı 99-102

Watches
Fahri Kuz Optik 106

Plan for Walkable Shopping
from the Hiltons

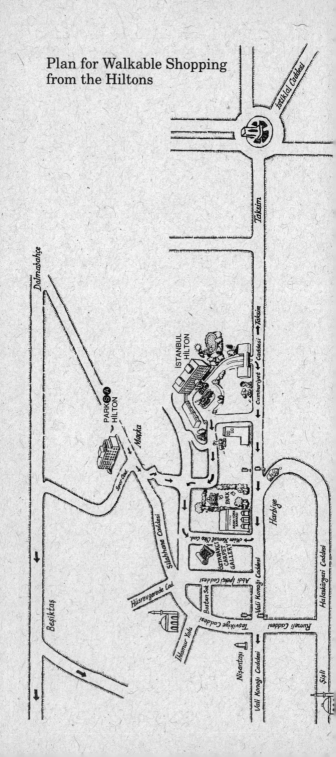

STROLLING

WHILE

SHOPPING

There are worlds within worlds in Istanbul. That is part of the city's long history and mystique. Everything is here. Everyone passes through. The ability of the city to offer something for everyone is legend. Istanbul and its shopping pleasures are laid out for you in this section. Enjoy them.

Shoppers will have no difficulty finding that special something. Istanbul abounds with delights - from standard tourist fare like copper accessories and meerschaum pipes to fine clothing and leather goods and export quality glassware.

The Hilton is its own world within a world. The Hilton shops sell merchandise of high standards covering the gamut of the city's choices. The boutiques in the hotel and in its two arcades offer convenience and quality.

For the traveller with more time wishing to wander further afield, this section provides guides to the city's top shopping districts: Harbiye/Şişli, Rumeli Caddesi/Nişantaş, Teşvikiye/Maçka (these sections of the city as seen on the shopping plan are within walking distance both from the Istanbul and Parksa Hiltons) and İstiklâl Caddesi. Shopping Malls such as Ak-Merkez, (Nisbetiye Caddesi, Etiler - see page 106) Galleria Ataköy), Capitol (Tophanelioğlu Caddesi, Altunizade - on the Asian side), Çarşı in Maslak, Pabetland (Büyükdere Caddesi 57/1, Maslak), Yeni Karamürsel (Halâskârgazi Caddesi, Şişli) and ' man Çarşısı (Şakayık Sokak 47, Nişantaş) offer a great variety of goods under one roof. Ak Merkez Shopping Center offers everything -best of its kind and internationally renowned labels- a traveller would need to buy. Outside rush hours it can be reached by car within fifteen minutes. The city's top stores have their shops there. Best of all, is the **Beymen Mega Store** selling a wide range of products.

Istanbul's first elegant fashion house **Vakko** (İstiklâl Caddesi 123-125, Beyoğlu) and **Vakkorama** (Osmanlı Sokak 13, Taksim and Rumeli Caddesi, 80, Nişantaş), Vakko's outlet for younger set should also be on top of the list for shopping outlets.

SHOPPING IN OLD ISTANBUL. Needless to say the Covered Bazaar is the focal point of shopping where one can find antiques, typical Turkish handicraft and everything that one would need to buy. It is a city within a city and must be enjoyed leisurely on one's own. The shop keepers are very hospitable and helpful. (See Kapalı Çarşı "Covered Bazaar" on page 67).

SHOPPING

The shopping hints for gifts and souvenirs which are Turkish handicrafts are as follows: Brassware, copperware, onyx chess figures, cups, vases and boxes, meerschaum pipes, dervish dolls in permanent pose, embroideries in special Turkish designs on blouses, scarves, purses and eyeglass covers, Kütahya ceramicware, Yıldız porcelain, gold chains and bracelets, water pipes, mother-of-pearl inlaid wooden boxes for cigarettes and knick knacks, jewelry of all types and periods, carpets and kilims (flat woven colorful rugs - light to carry), leather wear and accessories, evil eye beads, turn-up toe slippers, shish kebab skewers, Turkish Delight and pistachios just to name of a few suggestions. They can be purchased from the Covered Bazaar or from the Istanbul Hilton shops.

Mahmutpaşa Yokuşu (Mahmutpaşa Hill Street) offers action and history as does so much of the old city. Connecting the Egyptian, or Spice Market with the Kapalı Çarşı, or Covered Bazaar, it bisects the heart of Ottoman Istanbul. The street reverbates with vendors' cries as it has for hundreds of years. Mahmutpaşa is fun and it is Turkish. It has the flavor for which visitors come to Istanbul. This is where the people shop. They come for reasonably-priced clothes, yard goods and notions. They find them in the shops and with the kerbside hawkers who spread their wares on the same plastic sheet which will be used to wrap up the merchandise at the end of the day when the load is carried off on the man's back. Much is transported by back in this neighborhood of narrow lanes.

Ambling is the name of the game. Poke into any intersecting lane. Explore any corridor. Here are things the intrepid shopper might look for: inexpensive denims—pants, jackets, boots, purses; brass cymbals from a street seller—traditionally used by belly dancers, tablecloth sized pieces of white cotton, hand block-printed in black with Hittite designs. This area is ripe with shops selling inexpensive costume jewelry. Temptation might be a piece with turquoise-colored stones. Such stones are often incorporated into jewelry as they are believed to ward off the evil eye. Mahmutpaşa Yokuşu downhill leads to the Spice Market which should not be missed. (See Mısır Çarşısı "Spice Market" on page 72). Such an enterprizing shopping expedition can be crowned with a delicious Turkish meal at famous Pandeli Restaurant at the entrance of the Spice Market.

Harbiye/Şişli

Just beyond the Hilton to the north is a large military complex including museum, offices and hotel. It is from this presence that the neighborhood, Harbiye (harp-military), takes its name. To Istanbullus, Harbiye means home-furnishing textiles. But it and its companion district, Şişli, just beyond, also offer convenient, walkable shopping for the Hilton's guests. Although Halâskârgazi Caddesi's ambiance is ruled more by its double lane bus traffic than softer distinctions, this is one of the city's major shopping areas. Retailers recognize this and Istanbul's top clothing stores all have branches here or on adjacent

Rumeli Caddesi (Istanbul's Fifth Avenue). In addition to clothing, one will also find a good selection of leather product
shops, two galleries of contemporary ceramics and an outlet for
world-famous **Paşabahçe** glass.

Our purview of the area starts at the meeting place of
Halâskârgazi Caddesi and Rumeli Caddesi. At Istanbul
Hilton's main entrance to the street, turn right and walk
straight for 15 minutes. (For the street that breaks off to the
right at the end of the military complex, see the section "Rumeli
Caddesi/Nişantaş").

Moving up the right side of the street, in the first block is **İGS**,
198, carrying men's and women's ready-to-wear. In the next
block at 202 is **Atalar** for family clothing. **Sümerbank** at 204 is a
reasonably priced family shop. Further along is **Desa**, 218, with
leather goods ranging from backgammon sets to luggage. At
222, **Derimod** offers quality leatherwear and shoes. Across the
street, on the corner, is **Yargıcı**, youthful sportswear. The same
block contains **Beymen**, 230, one of the city's most elegant specialty shops. This main store has frequent art exhibits, a trend
among Istanbul's best clothiers. **Güral Porselen**, 236, has a
large collection of Turkish chinaware. **Benetton** has a shop for
sportswear at 246. Benetton line is locally manufactured by
leading textile company Beymen. Beyond is the Atatürk Müzesi
(museum). **Polat Pasajı** at 274 is a must for the bargain seeker.
The small shops in this arcade specialize in seconds. It's a great
place to pick up inexpensive sportswear. Check carefully for
flaws, though. The stick-on size notation, for example, may
cover a hole. **Abbate** shirts are available at 286. **Asım Barlas**, at
288, offers quality men's wear. At the corner of the next block,
stop in at **Ali Alta Moda** for high-styled Italian sportswear.
One block further is **Odam**, 336, which specializes in fine bath
and bed linens. **Sport Service** at 366, offers equipment, clothing
and shoes for a variety of sports. Further on make a turn to the
right where there is **Migros**, Istanbul's foremost supermarket
chain, worth a look. To head back, continue on up past the
mosque for a pedestrian overpass. Returning toward the
Istanbul Hilton now, on the westhand side of the street, stop
for **Gorbon Sanat Seramik** at 345. Here one will find useful
kitchen and household ceramic pieces from spice sets to coffee
services, but there is also a wide selection of unusual art pieces
and vases. Just beyond the bus stop is the large, walled garden
and *köşk* (wood summer house) belonging to the Bulgarian
Orthodox Church. **Ancien** at 315 is a small antique shop deal-
ing primarily in crystal, porcelain and silver. Check for Art
Deco objects. Further down comes a series of shopping arcades:
Yılmazlar Pasajı, 304, **Lale Pasajı**, 307, **Gizer Çarşısı**, 299,
Pilavcı Pasajı, 295 and **Site Pasajı**, 291 has many costume jewelry and clothing boutiques. In the last block before Rumeli
Caddesi do not miss **Paşabahçe** at 287. This company exports
its glass and crystal worldwide including to Crate & Barrel in
the US. Its designs are pleasing and the prices are conducive to

buying. Bowls, vases and decanters all make excellent gifts. A long line of jewelry and clothing stores lead up to **Karaca**, 259, shoe store. The merchandise here provides great fun for those who dream of decking their feet in rhinestones, lamé or sequined plastic. Be sure to send your teens here. Also along this stretch is **Sörmen**, 269, which carries a good selection of inexpensive luggage should your shopping necessitate another bag. At the corner, **Adnan** and **Fibula**, 251, both carry attractive women's wear; the latter also caters to men. If you are interested in unique upholstry and drapery fabrics in pure cotton, make a detour to Abidei Hürriyet Caddesi 13 to find **Aykut Hamzagil**'s showroom.

Rumeli Caddesi/Nişantaş

The Ottomans were great archers. Competitions were held to see which sportsman could set his arrow sailing the greatest distance. In those times, when the hills surrounding the Hiltons were all forest and hunting lands, these matches were held nearby. Nişantaş (stone target), Istanbul's district adjacent to the Hiltons, commemorates those days. Two of these markers can be seen in these excursions. The first is at the intersection of Teşvikiye and Vali Konağı (governor's mansion) Caddesi. Today this area is known for fine shopping. Turning right from the main street entrance of the hotel, Vali Konağı begins just a 10-minute walk away. It is the road which angles off to the right. You will want to position yourself on the left-hand side of the street where most of the shops are. (For the streets leading off to the right and down the hill see "Teşvikiye/Maçka".) At 23/1 **Zeki** specializes in bathing suits of international reputation. At the end of the block on the corner is one of Istanbul's top boutique for ladies, **Faik Sönmez**. **Mothercare**, 45, caters to children in 0-8 age group. **Desa** at 85 has another impressive shop offering leather wear, bags, luggage and accessories. As you are walking, keep an eye cocked upward. Often in this part of town second floor shops differ from those at street level.

At the intersection cross to the other side of the street and walk back towards the Istanbul Hilton. On the corner is another outlet of **Yargıcı**, the sportswear and modern outfits emporium. At 28 you will find a charming shop called **Replay Country Shop** offering top quality clothing for men and women, blue jeans, pants, shirts, shoes and accessories. **Concitta** at 26, **Fox Fun** at 20 and **Premo** at 6 caters to children. Turkey produces wonderful baby clothes, lavish with smocking, embroidery and quilting.

Rumeli Caddesi (a street within walking distance from the Hilton hotels and should not be missed by those wishing to buy quality clothing and accessories. Standing at the Nişantaş stone facing the Istanbul Hilton, the street running off to the left is Teşvikiye Caddesi (see "Teşvikiye/Maçka").

On the other side of the intersection this same street is called Rumeli Caddesi. It is our next destination. Here is an avenue

dedicated chiefly to clothing and accessories. Shoe stores and
jewelry shops are interspersed with apparel. For the age
groups between 0-12 **Sevim Bebe** at 2/1 has a great choice.For
jewels stop at **Mücevher** at 4/6. **Gusto** at 10, is a women's boutique with reasonable prices.The gowned mannequins in the
windows of **Faize Sevim**, 14, keep one current on bridal fashion and flamboyant evening wear. Underneath Faize Sevim
Lee sells jeans and shirts which are locally manufactured. At
16/A **Benetton** sportswear are sold. Next door, **Fred & Perry**
sells top quality sports outfits. At 26-28 **Limon** offers modern
sportswear for youth. **S & Villa** at 32 is a quality boutique for
ladies' wear. **Hey** at 38 has good quality sportswear for
younger set. **Lacoste** at 52/A is the branch of Lacoste in France.
Mudo, 44, offers youthful sportswear. **Sisley**, 54, has womens's
and mens's wear.

  Further along **Titiz**, 62, have interesting fashions and accessories. **Disney**, 66, is a popular children's orthopedic shoe
shop. At 64/1, **Stefanal** carries Italian style sportswear for
women and men. One of Istanbul's top women's store is **Vepa**,
70, with cosmetics, accessories, costume jewelry and fine clothing. The wide selection of specialty shops continues to the end
of the street including **Karaca** at 78 for quality knits for men
and women. The impressive **Vakkorama** at 80, in the recently
renovated historical building brings a new concept for shopping offering a wide range of services from gift items to bookstore, cosmetics, toys, clothing for the family, accessories, jeans,
photo service, home decoration and tickets to major art events and
a pleasant snack bar. **Lingerie Pelin**, 86, features ladies' underwear. Next to Pelin is **Senem** offering a rich collection of quality costume jewelry which they export to Europe and the US.

  Cross the street. Now we can begin to work our way back in
the direction from which we came. **Cotton Bar** in the same
compound offers very good quality men's cotton shirts and
neckties. **Divaresse**, also at 81, is the place for imported shoes
for both sexes. **Beymen Club** and **Beymen Kids** also at 81
offers best quality Turkish-made clothing and shoes for the
family. **Tiffany Tomato** at 63 sells sportswear for men and
women. At 47 **İpekyol** has elegant dressy ladies' wear. **Kip**, 47 A,
displays classical women's and men's wear. **Infinity** at 35/37
has women's wear. At 25/27 **Jentilmen** specializes in men's
wear. Evening shoes extraordinaire are commonplace at **Erol
Odabaşı**, 21-23. Sequins, rhinestones and glitter abound. At 13 A
Fiorucci offers a good selection of swimwear and accessories.
At 9 there is a shop that interests elegant gentlemen. The
imported Italian men's wear from **Ermenegildo Zegna** are sold
in the shop bearing his name. **New Men** at 3/B has a selection
of clothing for women and men. Continuing along, do poke
into the side lanes. Wind your way back to the hotel or, fortified with a pastry, continue on to Teşvikiye.

Teşvikiye/Maçka

  There are some of us to whom the districts of Teşvikiye and
Maçka speak immediately. This is a land of lap dogs, birds of

paradise and the first strawberries of the season. There are art galleries and antique shops, boutiques and more boutiques. It is the upper Madison Avenue of Istanbul. With its graceful apartment buildings, it is a pleasure to meander—except as school is letting out in the late afternoon. Several major high schools have their campuses here.

Begin this exploration at the Nişantaş stone walking away from Rumeli Caddesi along Teşvikiye Caddesi. Taking the left-hand side of the road, one first encounters **Diamond** Jewelry Shop and then **Defile Çanta**, 180, with reasonably-priced purses and bags. Adjacent to it on Vali Konağı Caddesi is **Vakko Kravat**, a delightlful little shop offering world quality neckties. The shopping arcade at 172 on Teşvikiye Caddesi has a shop specializing in slippers and several other attractive clothing stores. Alluring baby clothes fill **Prenses**, 170, and in the adjacent mall are additional infantwear outlets. **Cotton Bar** at 168 offers high quality cotton shirts and neckties for men. Beyond the mosque, shops start up again. At the bend in the road after the mosque, one will find Hüsrev Gerede Caddesi. Back at the intersection, **Koşar** specializes in men's and women's leather outerwear. Cross the street and head back toward Nişantaş. Or continue downhill towards Parksa Hilton.

Coming back toward Nişantaş look for shoes at **Vetrina Discarpe**, 69, **Timberland**, 115/B and **Hotiç**, 135/1. Before the end of the street do not miss the elegant clothing shop **Mudo Collection**. Now it's time to explore the sloping side streets which spring off from Nişantaş leading down toward green valley parks and the Bosphorus. In addition to galleries and boutiques, one will find a number of impressive fabric and home furnishing shops and the showrooms of some of the city's top interior designers. Turn left at Yargıcı, head back toward the Istanbul Hilton for one block, turn left again. On the corner is **Derishow** selling genuine leatherwear and high fashion for ladies. Formerly Emlak Caddesi, this lovely passage has been renamed in honor of the famous Turkish UPI journalist, Abdi Ipekçi, known for his espousal of rapprochement between Turkey and Greece; he was assassinated in 1979.

Abdi İpekçi Caddesi is lined with the city's most elegant and top name boutiques. Working our way down the hill on its right-hand side comes **Gazellini Boutique** 2, **Laurel Boutique** 6/8, **Thierry Mugler**, 10. **Home Store** is at 12. **Beymen Home** decoration is at 16. **Nursan**, 18/1, sells quality imported chinaware and gift items. **Onna** is a modern boutique for ladies at 20. On the left-hand side, first comes **İpek Kramer**, 7, with fine lingerie and night clothes. Close by are **Gucci**, 11, and **Mondi** ,13, both selling top quality accessories, shoes and bags for ladies. The **Urart Sanat Galerisi** (art gallery) and **Urart** jewelry showroom is at 21 and should not be missed. Urart recreates designs of old Anatolian civilizations which yield to very smart jewelry unmatched in its own style. **Acqua Kids**, 17, for 0-12 age group. **Ahmet Ozan**, 19, a very elgant boutique. **Ecla**, 21, women's wea. **İpeker**, 25, assorted good quality clothing material.

Escada, 25, German high fashion. **Foli** 55, outsize women's clothes. Before reaching Vali Konağı Caddesi turn to the left alley called Altın Sokak where you will find at 2/5 **Kookai**, young fashion from France. At the end of Abdi İpekçi turn left to get on Teşvikiye Bostanı Sokak. **Endican**, 7, mostly Italian fashion for men and women. **Adam's**, 4, creations by internationally renowned designers. Where Bostan Sokak meets Teşvikiye Caddesi you will see on the corner **Handan & Hayat**, (Teşvikiye Cad. 113/1) women's wear and knitwear. Cross Teşvikiye Caddesi to get on Nişantaşı Ihlamur Yolu to get to **Arkline**, 5, a very smart boutique.

Mim Kemal Öke Caddesi. Back at Valikonağı Caddesi, Nişantaşı's heartline, turn left, walk one block further, and turn left again onto Mim Kemal Öke Caddesi. On the corner you will admire the beautiful gift shop **Fiyonk Sanat Galerisi**. Look for **Güneş Öztarakçı Carpet Gallery**, 5, which has a spacious showroom for its new and used carpets, a small rear garden and another showroom in the back and a basement. Istanbul's best and most reliable carpet gallery with a wide range of selections and excellent service. Güneş Öztarakçı, the first woman carpet dealer in Turkey with twenty years of experience, has one of the richest collections of carpets and kilims and copies of museum pieces which she gets woven on her own looms using natural dyes. For varying interests, the choices are different and wide-ranging in each category. She happily shares her valuable knowledge with her clients by briefing them in detail and answering all the questions. At the end of the visit the customers become quite knowledgeable about Turkish carpets and kilims. **Rachel's** at 13, offers imported women's fashion. At 19A is **Raffi Portakal**, antiquaire. Portakals have been in the antique trade for generations. Besides the large shop, be sure to ask to see the treasures in the house-annex across the street.

İstiklâl Caddesi. İstiklâl (Independence) Caddesi is a daguerreotype of 19th century European Istanbul. It is the city's Shanghai—its most Westernized quarter. Here the traveller feels transported to the western side of the continent, miles and years from minarets and harems. One can almost see the twirl of parasols, hear carriage wheels and hooves on cobblestones. At night, when the street and its side lanes are lit like so many mini Times Squares with the neon of nightclubs and reviews, (not recommendable) it's difficult to imagine that this was once the city's countryside, its summer resort, its vineyards. But it was this freshness which attracted the foreigners. Up from the shores of the Golden Horn they came, moving beyond the Genoese community's Galata Tower to the top of the plain, creating a boulevard of their monuments. As one peeks through the gates of embassies, now consulates, or into the dim interiors of ornate Catholic and Orthodox churches, an image of the lavish life of the late 19th century emerges.

Although today there are residents of İstiklâl who are of European descent, the diplomats at those foreign consulates, like their ambassadorial predecessors, have moved up and out, preferring to live in communities along the suburban Bosphorus. They, like all of us, return to İstiklâl, however, for its bookstores, fine fabric shops, beguiling fish market and fur salons. Along its stretch every priced apparel is available, from haute couture to inexpensive synthetics.

Begin at the top of the Tünel, the 19th century funicular which was burrowed beneath the hill leading down to the Galata Bridge. With the entrance of the Tünel at your back, İstiklâl is to your left and right. It commences at this bend in the road. Before setting out, however, take a quick side trip down the lane to the right. Here are located the Mevlâna Müzesi (Whirling Dervish Museum) and numerous music shops carrying both contemporary and classical instruments. There is also a sprinkling of bookstores.

Back out on İstiklâl itself, walking on the right-hand side one encounters more book stores, including **Dünya,** 469, **ABC** and the Swedish Consulate. Possibly the best bookstore for scholars is **Eren**, Tünel Sok., 34, run by personable and knowledgeable Muhittin Salih Eren. Beginning at 415 with **Süper Süet** the line-up switches to leather and silver. Be sure to admire the handsome copper façade of **Panter Kürk Evi**, fur salon, at 363. At **Hacı Salih Restaurant**, 201, try authentic Turkish cuisine and buy Turkish Delight from **Hacı Bekir**, 127. If you are in a hurry, eat at Turkey's first fast food chain **Borsa**, 89. If you wish to taste traditional Ottoman dishes stop over at **Hacı Baba** at 47.There are then several more jewelry shops before the clothing begins with **Kip**, 195, and **İGS**. **Vakko**, 125, an enviable institution, handles first quality clothing, fabric, an art gallery and tea room replete with live classical music. On its other side is **Goya**, 117, also for shoes and bags. Further on is **Benetton**'s shop. From here on to the square at Taksim there is a good assortment of lingerie, cosmetic and gift shops. One spot to note further on, for the teenagers in your tour, is the youth world of **Vakkorama**. This emporium is down the stepped sidewalk on the right on the road just before the The Marmara Hotel. Getting back to Istiklâl, the return swing starts in front of the French Cultural Center and Consulate. At **Olgunlaşma Enstitüsü** (Technical School for Girls), 48, exqusite clothing and accessories with Turkish embroiry can be purchased. **Beymen**, 68, outfits men and women as does the smaller **Polo**, sportswear boutique, 78. **Europhila Pul Evi** at 152 is interesting for philatelists. At 170 you will reach Balık Pazarı (fish market) (see *Çiçek Pasajı* on page 54) where you will find some of the city's gayest restaurants and beer halls. The covered lane leading through these establishments also opens into the fish market.

Do make the diversion. Balık Pazarı is one of Istanbul's special places. Before the fish come the flowers, plastic and real. These are followed by the kitchenware shops close on the heels of the vegetable vendors. Here it is essential to sample two of the city's special taste treats: fried mussels on a stick and a grilled sheep's intestine sandwich. No judgement should be offered on the latter until it has passed the palate. It is guaranteed you will want another. To reach the beer halls from this side, pass through the massive wrought iron gateway to the right guarding the building Cite de Pera. Continuing straight through the market, without a restaurant diversion, one finds a doorway on the right leading to the local Armenian church, just before the T-intersection. Straight ahead the fish vendors begin in earnest with their wonderfully fresh samplings from the Black Sea and Sea of Marmara. In addition to the newly caught, one can also find smoked fish in abundance. Several mongers carry different varieties as do the food emporiums behind the street-side stalls.

Turn left at the T-intersection and the butchers and poultry shops begin. **Şütte,** on the right, is famous for its pork and ham. Up a little on the left, in the Aslıhan building, is another institution, **Bünsa**, purveyor of herbs, spices, oils and natural teas. The fascinating assemblage is decoded in Turkish and Latin. Botanists take note! At the corner, turn left to return to İstiklâl. Across the way is the famed Galatasaray High School. Turn right and continue back toward the Tünel. Shops in this section answer sewing, knitting and crocheting needs. There are vendors of wool, threads, yardage and notions. Walk down the lane just after the Şanzelize Nightclub for a variety of small costume jewelry outlets, custom-made hats and notion stalls. **İpek** has silk scarves and **Dekor**, 238 fabrics. **Eren Triko,** 244, and **Kuşam** produce bridal finery and gala evening outfits. There is more silk yardage at **Hacı Resul İpekçi** and **İpeker**, 264. The last major one that should not be cut, is **Paşabahçe**'s three-floor store at 314. The top floor is crystal; street floor has glassware, china and the basement has kitchenware, less expensive glassware and overproduced special orders. This Paşabahçe outlet is a dream.

Closing the gap between here and the Tünel are two more fur salons, **Mink Kürk, 350** and **Oslo Kürk Evi**, 366. While in this area a coffee break at Lebon, the Richmond Hotel's cafe, is worthwhile. Lebon was one of the two fashionable cafes of Istanbul until forty years ago. Get on Istanbul's only nostalgic street car to get to Taksim.

Akmerkez Shopping Center

In Etiler, easy to reach off rush hours, one can find a great variety of family shops of great reputation as well as a wide range of eatery under one roof. Both local makes and imported goods are available. It is convenient and time saving.

THE GROUND FLOOR HAS THE FOLLOWING SHOPS: **Remzi Bookstore**: Nazlım: Florist; **Euromode**: Accessories, costume jewelry; **Şişli Optik**: optician; **Home Store**: Home accessories, upholstery, curtain material, furniture; **Fahri Kuz Optik**: deluxe foreign brand eye glasses, watches, cuff links, lighters (Ceruti, Dupont, Dior, Raymond Weil); **Benetton**: 0-12 years age group clothing; **Fatoş**: toys; **L.C.Waikiki**: 3-15 years age group sportswear; **Fox Fun**: 3-12 years age group clothing; **Kid's Story**: Children's wear; **Panço**: Children's wear; **Kebo-Land**: Children's wear; **Kids Only**: Children's wear; **Elit**: Toys, gifts; **Ceylan**: Children's wear; **Beymen**: Children's wear; **Beymen**: Home Store; **Uzelli Müzik Sarayı**: Music shop; **VIP Seyahat: Travel Agent.**

SECOND FLOOR SHOPS ARE: **Abbate**: men's wear; **Nectar**: herbal creams, shampoo, soap; **Beymen Club**: Women's and men's wear, perfumes, cosmetics (Clarins, Givenchy, Sothys); **Pırıltı**: Jewelry, silverware; **Silk & Cashmere**: 100% silk and cashmir women's and men's wear; **G. Franko-Ferre**: Handbags, luggage, ties, umbrellas, accessories; **Pancaldi & B**: men's shirts (La Coste, Stefanel, Ellesse); **Tiffany Tomato**: Sportswear for women and men; **Bisse**: Men's shirts and ties; **Trussardi**: Italian fashion for men; **Mola**: Handbags; **Makro**: Supermarket of international standards; **Lee**: Jeans; **Original Levis**: Jeans; **Blue Family**: Jeans, **Sisley**: Women's and men's wear; **Timberland**: Shoes; **Pierre Cardin**: Accessories, bags, shoes and scarves; **Yargıcı**: Women's and men's wear; **Pollini-Teodem**: Leather clothing and shoes; **Daks**: Women's and men's wear, accessories; **Polo-Ralph Lauren**: Women's and men's wear; **Bata**: Shoes; **Kip**: Men's wear; **Park Bravo**: Women's and men's wear; **Fendi**: Handbags, luggage; **Sanfa Square**: Leatherwear; **Mudo**: Women's and men's wear; **Oxxo's** (to be opened soon) assorted inexpensive clothing; **Ten**: Women's underwear; **Gruppa La Perla**: Very smart women's and men's underwear, swim suits; **Atalar**: women's and men's wear; **Ipek Kramer**: women's wear.

THIRD FLOOR PRESENTS: **Kappa**: sportswear; **Ertuğrul**: Shoes, handbags; **Netay**: specialist in women's smart shirts; **Denver**: Sweaters, slacks; **Show Off**: Women's and men's wear; **Mac Renzi**: women's and men's wear; **Futuro**: jean-type men's wear; **Matraş**: handbags and luggage; **Bisse**: men's shirts and neckties; **Berk**: Socks; **Karaca**: Women's and men's knitwear; **Zeki Triko**: ladies' bathing suits; **Gottex**: bathing suits and underwear; **Pelin**: Women's and men's underwear; **Sevil**: ladies' knitwear; **Fiorucci**: Swim suits, accessories; **Rifle**: jeans; **Newmen**: Men's wear, jeans; **Think Pink**: men's shirts; **Wrangler**: jeans; **Chipie**: Ladies' boutique; **Shoe and Me**: Shoes; **Lee Cooper**: Jeans.

Flea Markets

Istanbul is an exciting and ideal place to hunt for antiques. Different districts, both on the Asian and European sides, have a series of shops, either grouped under one roof or lined on one or more streets. Quite often each shop specializes in given wares and shopkeepers willingly help the customers find their preferred items in neighboring shops. This group of shops are flea markets and can be found at the following addresses:

ON THE ASIAN SIDE
Üsküdar Bit Pazarı at 30, Büyükhamam Sokak, İnkilâp Mahallesi
Kadıköy Antikacılar Çarşısı at Çakıroğlu İşhani, Moda Caddesi Tellalzade Sokak, Kadıköy

ON THE EUROPEAN SIDE
Çukurcuma is spread on the back streets of Beyoğlu.
Horhor Bit Pazarı is in a block of buildings at 13/22 Kırık Tulumba Sokak, Aksaray.
Sadabat Antikacılar Çarşısı at Dolapdere Kaşkaval Sokak, Martı Sitesi 5, Yenişehir

Antique Shops

Antique shops offer valuable antiques from Ottoman days and from Europe ranging from carpets, silver, furniture, porcelain, calligraphy, old jewelry, books, maps, old prints, manuscripts, paintings, furnishing accessories, icons, ceramics, glass, bronze items to lamps, miniatures and textiles. The Covered Bazaar has many reputable antique shops waiting to be discovered. Reliable antique shops within easy reach from the Hilton hotels are as follows:

Abdül Antik
Kalıkçı Sokak 119/2, Teşvikiye
Tel. 231 7470 - 247 7196

Antik A.Ş.
Eytam Caddesi 16/1,Nişantaş
Tel. 241 4776

Ahmet Keskiner
Abdi İpekçi Caddesi,Deniz Apt., 20, Nişantaş
Tel. 246 5833

Mecidiyeköy Antikacılar Çarşısı
Located in a large building at 1-7, Tomurcuk Sokak. Most antique shops have branches there.

Artisan
Şakayık Sokak 54/1, Nişantaş
Tel. 247 9081

Chalabi Antik
Mim Kemal Öke Caddesi 17
Nişantaş
Tel. 225 0185
Chalabi has another shop in the Covered Bazaar at Sandal Bedesten Sokak 6, Nuruosmaniye
Tel. 522 8171

Raffi Portakal
Mim Kemal Öke Caddesi 19
Nişantaş
Tel. 225 4637

━━━━ Selected Auction Houses ━━━━

Antik A.Ş.
Eytam Caddesi 16/1, Nişantaş
Tel. 241 4776

Küsav Müzayede
Hasfırın Caddesi, Sinanpaşa İş Merkezi Kat 3, No. 304, Beşiktaş
Tel. 227 3485-86   260 7700
260 5266

Maçka Mezat
Mecidiyeköy Antikacılar Çarşısı
Tomurcuk Sokak
Tel. 259 4513

Raffi Portakal
Mim Kemal Öke Caddesi 19
Nişantaş
Tel. 225 4637

AKM Sergi Salonu
Taksim Square
Tel. 251 5600

Aksanat
İstiklâl Cad., 16
Zambak Sok., Beyoğlu
Tel. 252 3500

Artisan
Sanat Galerisi
Şakayık Sok., 54/1
Nişantaş
Tel. 247 7191

Art Gallery
Şakayık Sok., 62/5
Nişantaş
Tel. 247 4746

Art Frame
Kalıpçı Sok., 132
Teşvikiye
Tel. 230 2007

Ayşe Takı
Şakayık Sok., 62/5
Nişantaş
Tel. 247 4746

Cemal Reşit Rey
Sergi Salonu
Darülbedai Cad.,
Harbiye
Tel. 240 5012

Cumalı Sanat Galerisi
Şakayık Sok., 45/3
Teşvikiye
Tel. 248 3165

Destek Reassürans
Sanat Galerisi
Abdi İpekçi Cad., 75
Maçka, Tel. 231 2832

Emar Sanat Galerisi
Abdi İpekçi Cad., 79/1
Maçka
Tel. 231 2837

Fransız Kültür Merkezi
İstiklâl Cad., 8
Taksim
Tel. 249 0776

Galeri Baraz
Istanbul Hilton &
Kurtuluş Cad., 191
Kurtuluş
Tel. 240 4783

Lebriz Sanat Galerisi
Eytam Cad., 16/2
Nişantaş
Tel. 240 2282

Galeri Oda
Hüsrev Gerede Cad.,
102/B, Teşvikiye
Tel. 259 2208

Galeri Remzi
Sıraserviler Cad., 109
Taksim
Tel. 249 4770

Galeri Vinci
Ihlamur Yolu
Günol Apt., 1,Teşvikiye
Tel. 248 3986

Garanti Bankası
Sanat Galerisi
Vali Konağı Cad.,117/2
Nişantaş
Tel. 230 3980

Hobi Sanat Galerisi
Vali Konağı Pasajı 73
Nişantaş
Tel. 225 2337

Kare Sanat Galerisi
Atiye Sok., 12,Teşvikiye
Tel. 247 48878

Maçka Sanat Galerisi
Eytam Cad., 31
Maçka
Tel. 240 8023

Nüans Sanat Merkezi
Şakayık Sok., 40/5
Nişantaş
Tel. 246 0178

Opera Sanat Galerisi
Hariciye Konağı Sok.,
Sağlık Apt., 1, Taksim
Tel. 240 9202

Ramko Sanat Merkezi
Atiye Sok., 8/2
Teşvikiye
Tel. 236 1538

Rönesans Sanat
Galerisi
Teşvikiye Ihlamur
Yolu 3/1
Nişantaş
Tel. 232 9664

Salih Zeki
Resim Atölyesi
Kalıpçı Sok.,
Büyükbayraktar Apt.
112/124, Teşvikiye
Tel. 230 1745

Sandoz Sanat Galerisi
Barbaros Bulvarı 83
Beşiktaş
Tel. 259 7208

Studio Peinture
Kalıpçı Sok., 148/1
Teşvikiye
Tel. 232 2319

Taksim Sanat Galerisi
Cumhuriyet Cad., 23
Taksim
Tel. 245 2068

Tem Sanat Galerisi
Vali Konağı Cad.,
Prof. Orhan Ersek
Sok., 44/2, Nişantaş
Tel. 347 0899

Teşvikiye Sanat
Galerisi
Abdi İpekçi Cad.,
48/1, Teşvikiye
Tel. 241 0458

Urart Sanat Galerisi
Abdi İpekçi Cad.,
18/2
Nişantaş
Tel. 241 2183

Vakko Sanat Galerisi
Vakko Binası, Beyoğlu
Tel. 251 4092

Vakıflar Bankası
Sanat Galerisi
İnönü Cad.,
Vakıf İş Hanı 6
Taksim
Tel. 252 5900

Yapı-Kredi Beyoğlu
Sanat Galerisi
İstiklâl Cad., 141
Beyoğlu
Tel. 245 2041

Yurt & Dünya
Mete Cad., 38/1
Taksim
Tel. 293 2209

A BRIEF LOOK

AT THE

TURKISH CUISINE

If you haven't tasted the Turkish cuisine, you have been seriously deprived.

You have missed the kebabs and the meat stews, the forty different ways that eggplant can be cooked, the subtle flavors of Turkish soups. From the most elegant restaurants to the tiny holes in a wall, here you can find both exceptionally delicious and healthy meals.

The splendid mix in the Turkish cuisine is due in part to the influence of many cultures through which the Turkish tribes migrated on their journey to Anatolia.

As nomads on the Central Asian steppes they had little variety in their foods other than root vegetables, grains, milk products, and meat.

As they moved west that began to change. In the 10th century they came into contact with the Islamic cuisine of Persia and Arabia. They were introduced to rice pilaf by the Persians and spices and condiments by the Arabs. In return they taught the Persians how to cook *bulgur* (cracked wheat).

Börek (fluffy pastry stuffed with cheese or meat) they brought from eastern Turkistan, and *güveç* (vegetable stew cooked in small earthenware pots) they found before they arrived in Anatolia. By the time of the Seljuks, the earliest Moslem Turks in Anatolia, their eating habits had become sophisticated: They were cooking a variety of kebabs, pilafs, *zerde* (rice pudding with saffron), *kalye* (meatless vegetables), leafy vegetables such as spinach served with yoghurt and garlic, eggplant, pickles, and halva.

Having migrated into a temperate region, they gained access to a great variety of vegetables, fruits, and olives with which they were able to create new dishes. Anatolia is a fruit paradise, and fresh fruit has become the Turks' favorite dessert. Here also herbs and spices grow in abundance. Through their contacts with Greeks, Turks learned about seafood. Fish -- grilled, stewed, fried, baked -- is now a top culinary delight.

The Ottoman period saw an elaborate development of the Turkish cuisine which has remained popular throughout the regions once ruled by the sultans. A cuisine that appeals to many different tastes, it can be combined with many other national dishes.

From birth to death, food helps mark the important events in a family. A sweet drink called *lohusa şerbeti* (sugar syrup spiced with cinnamon) is served to guests when a child is born. At a boy's circumcision a special *zerde* is served, as it also is when a couple is married. During Ramazan *güllaç* (wafers filled with nuts, syrup and rose water) is the preferred dessert.

A lamb is sacrificed and the meat distributed to neighbors and the needy during Kurban Bayramı.

Aşure (Noah's Pudding) is made during the month of Muharrem in remembrance of the food left over when the great Flood receded: Traditionally forty different ingredients are used including chick peas, beans, wheat, rice, raisins, nuts, and dried fruits.

The Turkish cuisine is considered one of the three great cuisines in the world, the others being Chinese and French. Both Chinese and French cuisines originated in their own countries. As the Turkish cuisine exchanged culinary habits and recipes with other civilizations it became rich in variety and tasty to different palates. Not only that, it is a balanced, healthy cuisine.

Food is more than mere sustenance for Turks; it is a celebration.

SELECTED TURKISH RECIPES

Circassian Chicken
Çerkez Tavuk

3 1/2 lbs (1575 gr) stewing chicken
1 large onion quartered
salt and pepper to taste
8 cups (2 liters) water
WALNUT SAUCE
3 1/2 cups (350 gr) walnuts, shelled and chopped
4 slices day-old white bread, torn into small pieces
salt to taste
1 tablespoon minced onion
1 clove garlic, crushed (optional)
1 teaspoon paprika
1 cup (250 ml) chicken broth
DRESSING
1 tablespoon salad oil
1 teaspoon paprika

Wash and place chicken, onion, salt and pepper into a saucepan with water. Bring to a boil. Cook over medium heat until chicken is tender. Remove chicken from saucepan and cool. Remove skin and bones and cut it into small strips. Set aside, reserve the stock.

Grind the walnuts through a meat grinder. Remove the crust from the bread, soak in water and squeeze dry. Mix with ground walnuts in a bowl. Add salt, minced onion, garlic and paprika. Blender may also be used. Add chicken broth gradually until creamy consistency is obtained.

Place chicken on a serving platter, toss gently with half of walnut sauce. Spread the rest of sauce on top.

Place oil in a saucepan over low heat, add paprika and heat for 1 minute and trickle paprika dressing over the walnut sauce. Serve at room temperature as hors d'oeuvres.
8 servings.

Lamb with Lettuce
Kuzu Kapama

---

15 lettuce leaves
3 lbs (1350 gr) leg of lamb cut into 2 inch (5 cm) chunks
1/2 lemon(for rubbing the meat)
1 tablespoon butter
1 onion, sliced into rings
10 spring onions, thickly sliced
1 tablespoon sugar
salt and pepper to taste
1/2 cup (125 ml) water
1 cup (60 gr) dill, chopped

Separate lettuce leaves, wash and place them at the bottom of a large and heavy saucepan.

Rub meat with lemon. Place meat chunks over lettuce leaves. Add butter, onion, spring onions, sugar, salt, pepper and water. Cover. Cook over very low heat until meat is tender for about an hour. Add dill just before transferring to a serving platter. Serve hot as a main course with pilaf.
4 servings.

Green Beans in Olive Oil
Zeytinyağlı Taze Fasulye

---

2 lbs (900 gr) green beans
1/2 cup (100 ml) olive oil or salad oil
2 onions, grated
salt to taste
1 teaspoon sugar
2 medium tomatoes, cut into quarters
2 cups (1/2 liter) water

Top , tail and string the beans and wash. Place beans into a saucepan, add olive oil, onions, salt, sugar and tomatoes.

Cover the pan, cook over very high heat for 3 minutes. Lift the saucepan and hold it together with the lid by the hands and shake. Replace the pan on the stove. Repeat this process 3-4 times until the beans turn bright green. Add boiling water. Turn heat to medium and cook until beans are tender and the water is mostly absorbed. Pour the beans onto a serving platter and serve cold as a second course or as an appetizer or as a side dish.
6 servings.

Turkish Cookery
by Gülseren Ramazanoğlu

Turkey's best selling Turkish Cookbook
in English, French, German, Italian,
Spanish and Japanese

Pounded Wheat Pilaf
Bulgur Pilavı

1 cup (160gr) plain bulgur or
pounded wheat
2 tablespoons butter
1 large onion, grated
3 pepperones, seeded, chopped
salt and pepper to taste
1 cup (250 ml) meat stock or
chicken broth
l cup (250 ml) tomato juice
1/2 cup (30 gr) parsley,
chopped

Wash and drain bulgur. Place butter, onion, pepperones, salt and pepper into a saucepan, saute, stirring for 2 minutes; pour in chicken broth and tomato juice, bring to a boil. Add bulgur and stir once. Turn heat to very low and cook until bulgur absorbs all the liquid. Remove from heat and add parsley. Stir once with a wooden spoon. Cover saucepan with a clean paper or a napkin. Replace cover. Let it stand for an hour. Serve hot with any meat dish.
4 servings.

Pumpkin Dessert
Kabak Tatlısı

4 1/2 lbs (2 kg) pumpkin,
peeled
5 1/2 lbs (1kg) sugar
1 cup (100 gr) walnuts,
grated

Pare and cut pumpkins into slices. Wash. Cut each slice into 1-inch (2.5 cm) squares. Place them into a large saucepan, sprinkling sugar between layers. Cook over medium heat for more than an hour until pumpkin is very tender and syrup is formed.

Transfer to a serving plate with the syrup. Allow 2 hours before serving for pumpkin to absorb most of the syrup. When serving pour over a little syrup with a spoon from the serving plate.

Garnish with grated walnuts. It keeps for 2-3 days at room temperature. **16 servings.**

MOVEABLE FEAST
(Eating in the Streets)

Almost every major city in the world has churches, monuments and museums of varying interest to various people, and almost every major city has its street vendors. Only in Istanbul, however, is one treated to a daily moveable feast. Millions of people in Istanbul are constantly on the move so these sidewalk salesmen are a necessity as well as a joy. With tables of *baklava* balanced on their heads, they wind through the congested streets. From a push cart you can be treated to a strange concoction of pickled vegetables and juice called *turşu*. It is a refreshing and economical way to stock up on your vitamins. There is also the "nightclub cigarette girl" type carrying a tray from which one can grab the round soft bread called *pide*. It looks like, but is too delicious to be used as, a frisbee. It can be eaten by itself or used as an ingredient to the most favorite of all the street delights, *Lahmacun*, a southeastern Anatolian specialty is all that and more. It is hard to believe that any one thing can be as popular as the hamburger, eaten with the convenience of hot dog and taste something like pizza. Round flat bread is ladled with a tomato sauce and covered with ground beef and a hundreds of spices. When it is ready to go, it is sprinkled with freshly chopped parsley, onions and tomatoes and rolled up into a one-inch cone-shaped delight. If you do not want to sample it in the streets, go to Tatbak restaurant, at Akkavak Sokak, Nişantaş.

Simits (large, round, sesame topped pretzels) are favorite breakfast and tea time delights especially when accompanied by *kaşar* (yellow cheese) and freshly brewed tea. All of these things and many more bedazzling volumes of edibles are found on any street corner. Of course, to enjoy all this you've got to suppress any qualms you might have about sanitation aspects of buying and eating on the streets. Millions of people eat daily on the street and they survive!

Istanbul has many popular dishes which are not cooked at homes or served in international restaurants. Some are sold at street corners, and some small Turkish restaurants serve them. Such as *Kokoreç*: grilled sheep's intestine sandwich - see page 105. Besides the colorful, raffish Çiçek Pasajı at Galatasaray in Beyoğlu (where you should drink *rakı* - Turkish arrack - with it) you should try famous Vahap Usta's *Kokoreç* stand in Sirkeci around the corner of Konyalı Sirkeci Restaurant. It is open all day.

Fried mussels with *tarator* sauce and bread is another delight. You can find them in Balıkpazarı or in Sarıyer in the streets.

Unusual drinks: *Salep* is an interesting hot drink made from the powdered root of *sahlep* (orchis mascula). In winter months it is prepared and served at some cafes, pastry shops and *muhallebicis* (specialty restaurant). It is also sold from copper containers on the streets. *Turşu* (pickled juice) is drunk by old İstanbullus in the morning as a quick way to wake up.

Boza is a fermented drink made of *bulgur* (cracked wheat), water, sugar and yeast . It has always been a popular fermented drink, particularly in winter. The most famous boza place is Vefa, in the vicinity of the Covered Bazaar.

Muhallebici: It is a specialty restaurant of Albanian origin where traditionally chicken-related dishes and dairy desserts are served such as chicken soup with vermicelli, boiled chicken, fried eggs, rice pilav, yoghurt, milk pudding (*muhallebi*), *kazan dib*i (browned pudding), *sütlaç* (rice pudding), *aşure* (Noah's pudding). Moderately priced, clean with marble top tables, the Muhallebici's turnover is high and everything is freshly cooked and healthy. Now-a-days, their menus are enriched by *Döner* and Turkish sweets. Try Teşvikiye Saray Muhallebicisi which keeps its authenticity.

Restaurants: Istanbul, by all standards, can compete with any major capital in the world as far as the number of restaurants are concerned. There are more than 400 restaurants in town (the same number of mosques exist in Istanbul).

The restaurants can be categorized as follows: hotel restaurants, luxury restaurants serving both international and local dishes, Turkish restaurants, moderate restaurants, budget restaurants, specialty restaurants such as meat or fish, ethnic restaurants, cafes serving food, fast food, etc.

Almost every month one or two new restaurants, cafes or bars open in Istanbul. The sophisticated customers who frequent restaurants almost regularly desire to have novelty. This need pushes the enterprising restaurateurs to open new places or redecorate their existing locale. The food and beverage business in Istanbul is quite a lucrative business.

In the following pages you will find a selected and extensive list of restaurants, cafes, bars, discos and night clubs of Istanbul for your convenience.

Foreigner's Guide to Seafood

Anchovy	Hamsi	**Lobster**	Istakoz
Baby Bonito	Çingene palamutu	**Molanure**	Melanurya
		Mullet	Tekir
Blue Fish	Lüfer	**Mussels**	Midye
Bonito	Palamut	**Octopus**	Ahtapot
Chub Mackerel	Kolyos	**Oysters**	İstiridye
Clams	Tarak	**Red Mullet**	Barbunya
Coral Fish	Mercan	**Sardines**	Sardalya
Cuttle Fish	Mürekkep balığı	**Sea-bass**	Levrek
		Sea-bream	Karagöz,
Dentex	Sinarit	**varieties**	izmarit
Eel	Yılan Balığı	**Shrimps**	Karides
Guilt head bream	Çipura	**Squid**	Kalamar
Gurnard	Kırlangıç	**Sword Fish**	Kılıç
Horse Mackerel	İstavrit	**Turbot**	Kalkan
Large Bonito	Torik	**Umbra**	Minakop

Dictionary for the Names of Selected Turkish Recipes

Hors d'oeuvres
Cracked Wheat Salad
Mashed Broad Bean Salad
Eggplant Salad
Savory Rolls
Beans Pilaki
Circassian Chicken
Fried Mussels

Meze
Kısır
Fava
Patlıcan Salatası
Sigara Böreği
Fasulya Pilaki
Çerkes Tavuk
Midye Tava

Meats
Kebab with Eggplant
Meat Stew
Grilled Lamb Chops
Roast Leg of Lamb
Meatballs on Skewers
Grilled Meatballs
Kebab with Yoghurt

Etler
Patlıcanlı Kebap
Tas Kebap
Kuzu Pirzola
Kuzu Fırın
Şiş Köfte
Cızbız Köfte
Yoğurtlu Kebap

Fish
Poached Blue Fish
Swordfish on Skewers
Grilled Mackerel
Sea Bass Papillote
Fried Bonito
Grilled Turbot

Balık
Lüfer Buğulama
Kılıç Şiş
Uskumru Izgara
Levrek Kağıtta
Palamut Tava
Kalkan Izgara

Vegetables
Eggplant Purée
Eggplant with Minced Meat
Stuffed Tomatoes (Meat Dolma)
Stuffed Bell Peppers
Celery Root in Olive Oil
Green Beans in Olive Oil
Artichokes in Olive Oil
Stuffed Cabbage Leaves
   in Olive Oil (Rice Dolma)
Stuffed Vine Leaves
   in Olive Oil (Rice Dolma)

Sebzeler
Patlıcan Beğendi
Patlıcan Karnıyarık
Etli Domates Dolması
Etli Biber Dolması
Zeytinyağlı Kereviz
Zeytinyağlı Taze Fasulye
Zeytinyağlı Enginar
Zeytinyağlı Lahana Dolması

Zeytinyağlı Yaprak Dolması

Pilafs
White Pilaf
Oriental Rice
Pilaf with Tomatoes
Cracked Wheat Pilaf

Pilav
Beyaz Pilav
İç Pilav
Domatesli Pilav
Bulgur Pilavi

Böreks
Kebab in Pastry
Oriental Pie
Ravioli Alla Turca

Börek
Talaş Böreği
Su Böreği
Mantı

Desserts
Quince Dessert
Pumpkin Dessert
Cream-Stuffed Apricots
Noah's Pudding
Almond Pudding
Chicken Breast Pudding
Semolina Cake

Tatlılar
Ayva Tatlısı
Kabak Tatlısı
Kaymaklı Kuru Kaysı
Aşure
Keşkül
Tavuk Göğsü
Revani

HISTORY

OF

TURKISH WINE

Records dating back to 4000 BC of the first vineyards in the world have been found at the foot of Mt. Ararat, consistent with the story of Noah's drunkenness.

While the French may be better known for their wine, Asia Minor is where viniculture started. Residues of ancient wines have shown up in gigantic pottery jugs, some shaped like a bull's head, and a gold chalice came from the 2000 BC royal burial site of Alacahöyük. The very word "wine" apparently is related to the Hittite "wee-an" (the cuneiform spelling) or "weanes" (the hieroglyphic).

People thought that the dizzying and relaxing effects of wine were a kind of magic; red wine symbolizing the blood of deities held an important place in religious ceremonies. Wine was once poured on the sea to insure a smooth sailing (shades of today's ships' christenings?).

The inhabitants of Anatolia enjoyed wine with their meals until the eleventh century when they became Moslems: Islam prohibits intoxicating beverages.

During the time of the Ottoman Empire, however, the Jewish and Christian minorities were allowed to make wine for their own consumption and export. By the end of the 19th century their production was higher than it is in present-day Turkey.

After 1929, the new Turkish Republic modernized wine-making methods. Now the State Monopoly and the private sector own several wineries, capitalizing on different viniculture areas, each with their different characteristics.

European preference for Turkish wines leans to the varieties with a distinctive regional flavor. The best wines come from the Marmara, Thrace, and Central Anatolian regions. Since the farmers avoid using synthetic fertilizers as much as possible, Turkish wines retain a true natural flavor, and are famous for their bouquet and brilliant color.

Today Turkey is fifth in the world in grape production. The Turkish State Monopoly and the leading private companies such as Doluca and Kavaklıdere Wines have been awarded the highest prizes for premium quality wines in the international wine fairs.

Inheritors of the first wine growers and now leaders in international production, the Turks still recognize the ceremony of a glass of wine in their traditional toast, "Şerefinize" -- "To your honor!"

TURKISH DRINKS

Rakı

The national drink is rakı (a form of anisette). Rakı is a pleasant drink if you drink it with restraint. Diluted with a lot of water and ice, it turns smoky white. Sip it slowly while you enjoy the *meze* table (Turkish hors d'oeuvres). If you have it neat and gulp it down without some food at the same time, May God pity you! You will never forget your hangover the next morning.

Beer

Like wine, beer has been brewed in Anatolia for thousands of years. Today there are good Turkish beers. International brands are also available. *Kaşar* (yellow Turkish cheese) and Turkish bread make good accompaniments to beer.

Vodka

Turkish vodka (Binboğa) is worth trying as it can easily rival the Russian vodka Smirnoff. Mix it with freshly squeezed orange juice or, when oranges are out of season, try some tonic.

Liqueurs

Turkish liqueurs are very popular as they have a natural flavor and are available in a wide selection of flavors such as sour cherry, banana, strawberry, orange, coffee, mint, and lemon.

Hard liquors

The Turkish State Monopoly produces all kinds of hard liquors. Imported brands are also available in the market. Istanbul boasts a great number of bars with a pleasant ambience and tasty hors d'oeuvres to accompany the drinks. See the list of them which continues on the following pages.

Ayran (Yoghurt drink)

A mixture of yoghurt, water, salt, and ice, *ayran* goes very well with Turkish kebabs and bulgur. It is a great drink on a hot summer afternoon.

Turkish Coffee

You can order Turkish coffee to your taste: black (*sade*), medium (*orta*), or sweet (*şekerli*). Make sure not to drink (or eat) the thick dregs in the bottom of the cup. Instead, turn your cup upside down on the saucer, make a wish and let it cool, and look for someone to read your fortune in the grounds.

HOW TO MAKE TURKISH COFFEE. *1 heaped teaspoon ground coffee, 1/4 cup cold water, 1/2 teaspoon sugar (for medium-sweet coffee; no sugar for black coffee; 1/4 teaspoon sugar for coffee with little sugar.* Place coffee and sugar into a small pot with a long handle (*cezve* - you can obtain one while in Istanbul). Add water, mix them together. Cook on a very low heat stirring occasionally until the froth on the surface starts rising. Pour a small amount of froth into a demi-tasse. Return pot to the heat and bring to a boil. Pour remaining coffee into the demi-tasse until it reaches the brim. *1 serving*.

ISTANBUL HILTON
FOOD & BEVERAGE OUTLETS

Roof Rotisserie
Hotel's main restaurant
Open every day for dinner only except Sundays
from 7.00 p.m. to 1.00 a.m.
(last orders are taken at 11.30 p.m.)
Live music by Aysun Ercan and his Violins
(closed July and August)

Greenhouse
Coffee Shop
Open daily from 6.00 a.m. until midnight
Breakfast buffet from 6.30 a.m.-10.30 a.m.
Lunch buffet from noon to 3.00 p.m.
Dinner from 7.00 p.m. - 11.00 p.m.
Brunch (Sundays only) from noon to 3.00 p.m.
Special Evenings
Mondays - Turkish Night   Tuesdays - Italian Night
Fridays - Special Fish Buffet   Sundays - Brunch from noon to 3.00 p.m.

Lobby Lounge and Terrace
Open daily from 10.00 a.m. to 2.00 a.m.
Afternoon Tea with live music from 4.00p.m. to 6.00 p.m.

Lalezar Bar
Open daily from 10.00 a.m. to 2.00 a.m.
Live entertainment

DRAGON
Istanbul Hilton's Chinese Restaurant
Open daily for lunch and dinner except Mondays

Pool Restaurant
Open during summer for lunch only

PARKSA HILTON
FOOD & BEVERAGE OUTLETS

Korso Restaurant
Open daily from 6.00 a.m. to midnight
Open buffet service for breakfast, lunch and dinner
Turkish and international cuisine
Special evenings
Mondays - Chef's recommendation   Tuesdays - Mexican Night
Wednesdays - Fish and Seafood Night
Fridays - Italian Night   Saturdays - Spanish Night
Live music on Tuesdays, Wednesdays, Fridays and Saturdays
İlhan Gencer and Rafael Trio

Parksa Bar
Open daily from 11.00 a.m. to 2.00 a.m.
Live piano music (İlhan Gencer) except Sundays
Alpage Trio on Friday and Saturday evenings
from 11.00 p.m. to 2.00 a.m.

A La Turka
Hazine Sok.8, Ortaköy
Tel. 258 79 24
12.00 a.m.-10.30 p.m.
Simple restaurant, serving
mainly *mantı* (Turkish ravioli),
börek (cheese pie) and *köfte*
(meatballs), best of its kind.
No cards. $

Adil Restaurant
Kazım Özalp Cad. No.58
Şaşkınbakkal
Tel. (0216) 385 24 25 - 385 42 91
Reservations for dinner
12.00 a.m.-1.00 a.m.
Seafood restaurant. Along the
Sea of Marmara overlooking
the Princes' Islands.
Live music for dinner
All major cards.
Lunch $12.50 Dinner $22

Adres
Tamburi Ali Efendi Sok.11
Etiler
Tel. 263 14 04 - 263 66 98
Reservations necessary.
(Dinner for members.)
Only Saturdays and Sundays
for outsiders.
12.00 a.m.-3.00 p.m.
8.00 p.m. until early hours.
International cuisine, deluxe
atmosphere.
No cards. $$$$

Agora
Hyatt Regency Hotel
Taşkışla Cad.,Taksim
Tel. 225 70 00
7.00 a.m.-11.00 p.m.
Deluxe setting, Turkish and

Asian food (open buffet)
All major cards except Diners.
Lunch $20.- Dinner $22.

Akdeniz Balık Lokantası
Yeşilköy,Yat Limanı 3
Tel. 573 99 39 - 574 50 60
12.00 a.m.-12.00 p.m.
Fish restaurant with a speciali-
ty of fish cooked in steam
called '*Buğulama*'.
All cards except Diners. $$

Alageyik
Muallim Naci Cad. 120-A
Ortaköy
Tel. 258 87 35 - 260 51 07
Reservations suggested
8.00 p.m.-12.00 p.m.
Turkish atmosphere.
Live Turkish music
No cards. $$

Alem
Nisbetiye Cad., Etiler
Tel. 257 04 94
Reservations suggested
1.00 p.m. - 4.00 a.m.
Restaurant, Bar and Night
Club with live music, usually a
popular Turkish pop singer.
All cards except Diners. $$$$

Ali Baba Fish Restaurant
Kireçburnu Cad. 20, Sarıyer
Tel. 262 08 89 - 223 25 25
12.00 a.m. -12.00 p.m.
On the Bosphorus, serves *meze*
(Turkish hors d'oeuvres) and
fresh fish. Popular for week-
end lunches.
Visa, Mastercard, Eurocard.
$$

Allegria Ristorente Italiano
Nispetiye Cad. 27
Levent
Tel. 269 56 36
Reservations necessary on weekends
12.00 a.m. - 3.00 p.m.
  6.00 p.m.-11.00 p.m.
Italian cuisine, warm ambiance.
All cards except Diners. $ - $$

Ambassadeurs Restaurant
Cevdet Paşa Cad., 113-115
Bebek
Tel. 263 30 02
Reservations necessary
12.00 a.m. - 3.00 p.m.
  7.00 p.m.-12.00 p.m.
Bebek Hotel's deluxe restaurant along the Bosphorus.
French, Russian, Turkish cuisine.
All major cards. $$$

Antares & (Cafe Park)
Vali Konağı Cad.8
Işık Apt., Nişantaş
Tel. 224 97 24 - 224 96 66
Reservations necessary for dinner.
8.30 a.m.(breakfast) - 12.00 p.m.
A popular restaurant (only dinner). Exciting menu to be experienced. Nouvelle cuisine, antique decor.
Live music after 11.00 p.m.
(Coffee Shop operates as coffee shop/bar/ restaurant)
Live music after 10.30 p.m.
All major cards. $$ - $$$

Asithane Restaurant
Kariye Hotel, Kariye Camii Sok.
Edirnekapı
Tel. 534 84 14
Restaurant 12:00 a.m.-3:30 p.m.
6:30 p.m.-12:00 p.m.
Cafe 9:00 a.m.-6:30 p.m.
Located next to Kariye Museum famous for its Byzantine mosaics, serves Ottoman food.
Classical Turkish music.
 (Evenings live music)
Visa, Master Card, Eurocard, American Express. $

Ayazma Restaurant
Meserret Sok. 30, Çengelköy
Tel. 321 57 12 - 318 29 27
11.00 a.m.-1.00 a.m.
Spectacular view of the Bosphorus.
Live music (Turkish music, oriental belly dancer -weekends)
All major cards. $$

Baca Restaurant
Emirgân Yolu 58, Boyacıköy
Tel. 277 08 08
Reservations necessary
8.00 p.m.-4.00 a.m.
Overlooking the Bosphorus.
International cuisine.
Bar/Restaurant.
Live music and disco music on Fridays and Saturdays.
All major cards. $$$

Bellini
Çırağan Palace
Hotel Kempinski, Beşiktaş
Tel. 258 33 77
Reservations suggested
12.00 a.m.-3.00 p.m.
7.00 p.m.- 11.00 p.m.
Impressive decor, delicious Italian cuisine.
Live music (except Sundays)
All major cards. $$$

Beyoğlu Pub
İstiklâl Cad., Halep Çarşısı
140/17, Taksim
Tel. 252 38 42
Reservations suggested
12.00 a.m.-2.00 a.m.
Garden in summer, nicely decorated.
Live music on Wednesdays-Fridays.
All major cards. $$

Beyti
Orman Sok. 33
Florya
Tel. 663 29 90
12.00 a.m.-10.00 pm.
Closed Mondays
İstanbul's best meat restaurant near the airport.11 separate dining rooms. Turkish atmosphere.
Their guest book signed by

many international celebrities.
All major cards. $$$
Group Price $22.

Bilsak
Sıraselviler Cad.
Soğancı Sok. No.5
Cihangir
Tel. 243 28 79 - 99
10.00 a.m.-2.00 a.m.
French cuisine. Popular with
artists.
Major major cards. $$

Bizimtepe
Kireçhane Sok. 10/1
Kuruçeşme
Tel. 287 00 78
Reservations recommended
12.00 a.m. -12.00 p.m.
Open buffet on Tuesdays (din-
ner) and on Saturdays (lunch).
Club for Robert College Mem-
bers.
International cuisine.
Live music on Tuesdays,
Thursdays, Fridays, Saturdays.
All major cards. $$$
Fixed lunch menu $8.

Borsa
Halâskârgazi Cad., Şair Nigâr
Sok. 90/1, Osmanbey
Tel. 232 42 00
11.30 a.m.-12.00 pm
Popular at lunch time.
Traditional Turkish food, good
service. Entertains travel
groups in the evenings.
All major cards. $$ - $$$

Brasserie
Çırağan Palace
Hotel Kempinski, Beşiktaş
Tel. 258 33 77
7.00 a.m.-11.00 a.m. (Breakfast)
12.00 a.m.- 3.00 p.m. (Lunch)
7.00 p.m.-11.00 p.m. (Dinner)
Turkish and international cui-
sine. Saturday dinner : Seafood
buffet. Sunday: brunch buffet.
Other days of the week : Open
buffet.
All major cards.
$17 brunch, $22 for seafood
buffet, $ 17 for regular buffet.

Brasserie
The Marmara Istanbul, Taksim
Tel. 251 46 96
12.00 a.m.-3.00 p.m.
7.00 p.m.-11.00 p.m.
Open buffet. Turkish and inter-
national dishes.
All major cards. $$$

Bronz
Bronz sok. 5/A, Maçka
Tel. 232 76 31
Reservations suggested
12.00 a.m.- 3.00 p.m.
8.00 p.m.-12.00 p.m.
Closed Sundays
A popular restaurant with
good food.
Piano music for dinner
Visa, Amex, Mastercard. $$$

Çadır Köşk
Yıldız Park, Beşiktaş
Tel. 260 07 09
9.00 a.m.-6.00 p.m.
Breakfast, tea,coffee,snacks
(Reasonable prices)
Visa. $$

Çapari Restaurant
Çapari Sok. No. 22/24
Kumkapı
Tel. 517 22 75 - 517 75 30
Reservations for dinner
11.30 a.m.-1.00 a.m.
Fresh fish and seafood.
All major cards. $$

Çatı
Baro Han, İstiklâl Cad.,Beyoğlu
Tel. 251 00 00 - 251 51 05
Reservations suggested for
dinner
12.00 a.m.- 5.00 p.m. (lunch)
5.00 p.m.- 7.00 p.m.(bar/tea)
7.00 p.m.-12.00 p.m. (dinner)
A nostalgic roof-top restaurant.
Live music
Visa, Prestige. $$ - $$$
Fixed menu prices: $14 - $24

Çıpa Restaurant
Holiday Inn Corebrand
Ataköy
Tel. 560 41 10
7.00 a.m. -11.00 p.m.

International food.
All major cards. $$

Çırağan Restaurant
Çırağan Palace
Hotel Kempinski, Beşiktaş
Tel. 258 33 77
Reservations suggested
7.00 p.m.-11.00 p.m.
Splendid hotel restaurant with a
wonderful view of the Bosphorus.
All major cards. $$$

Çengelköy İskele Restaurant
Çengelköy
Tel. (0216) 321 55 05/6
12.00 a.m.- 3.00 p.m.(lunch)
 6.00 p.m.-12.00 p.m.(dinner)
12.00 a.m.-12.00 p.m.(Weekends)
Along the Asian shore and in
the heart of the village where
there are colorful vegetable
and fish markets.
Diners Club,Visa. $$$

Çiçek Pasajı (Flower Market)
İstiklâl Cad., Beyoğlu
11.00 a.m.-11.30 p.m.
Çiçek Pasajı (see page 54)
meaning Flower Passage, origi-
nally was a service alley for
apartment houses which were
built in 1860 in what was then
the most fashionable part of
town. The first vendors to
come in were the flower sell-
ers, hence the name given to
the passage.

Çiftnal
Ihlamur Yolu 6, Tarihi Süslü
Karakol Binası, Beşiktaş
Tel. 261 31 29
Reservations necessary
12.30 p.m. -12.00 p.m.
Closed Sundays
A Turkish restaurant specializ-
ing in kebabs and *mantı*
(Turkish ravioli).
All major cards. $$

Çizgi (Bar/Restaurant)
Bağdat Cad. Kasaplar Çarşısı
23/A, Bostancı
(0216) 366 08 47 - 336 34 86
Reservations necessary

12:00 a.m.-12:00 p.m.
Seafood, Turkish kitchen
Bar/ restaurant
Saturdays live music
All major cards. $$

Club 29 (Dodo)
Nisbetiye Cad. 29
Etiler
Tel. 263 54 11
Reservations necessary
8.30 p.m.- 4.00 a.m.
Bar/Restaurant/Disco
Smartly decorated.
Amex, Mastercard, Prestige,
Visa. $$$

Cuisine Restaurant (Alkent)
Tepecik Yolu, Hillside, Alkent
Etiler
Tel. 257 01 27
Reservations suggested
12.00 a.m.-12.00 p.m.
Pleasant restaurant in the
Hillside Club by the swimming
pool. International menu.
Buffet luncheons. Buffet din-
ners on Tuesdays. (Sundays
brunch $15).
All major cards. $$

Darülziyafe
Darülşifa Sok.
Bayezit
Süleymaniye Külliyesi
Tel. 511 84 14/5
12.00 a.m.-15.30 p.m.
 6.00 p.m.-11.00 p.m.
Conveniently located within
the Süleymaniye Mosque com-
plex serving authentic Otto-
man food. Unique in town.
Fasıl Heyeti (Turkish classical
music) on Saturdays
All major cards. $$

Deniz Park Gazinosu
Daire Sok.9
Yeniköy
Tel. 262 04 15
12.00 a.m. -12.00 pm.
Along the Bosphorus, pleasant
for summer outdoor eating.
Fish restaurant with good *meze*
selection.
No cards. $$

Deniz Restaurant
Kefeliköy 23
Kireçburnu
Tel. 262 04 07 - 262 67 77
Reservations for dinner
12.00 a.m.-2.00 a.m.
Fresh fish and tasty seafood
specialties.
All major cards. $$

Divan Pub
Divan Hotel
Elmadağ
Tel. 231 41 00
12.00 a.m. -11.00 p.m.
Popular restaurant for quick
meals. Good food.
All major cards. $$

Divan Restaurant
Divan Hotel
Elmadağ
Tel. 231 41 00
Reservations necessary
12.00 a.m.- 3.00 pm.
7.00 p.m -12.00 p.m.
Closed Sundays
Elegant hotel restaurant with
excellent Turkish and interna-
tional food, impeccable ser-
vice.
Live music in the evenings.
All major cards. $$$ - $$$$

Doğan
Ressam Hikmet Onat Sok. 2
İstinye
Tel. 277 80 30
Reservations necessary
12.00 a..m.-3.00 p.m.
8.00 p.m.-1.00 a.m.
A nice restaurant with deli-
cious food and Bosphorus
view. Excellent service.
All major cards. $$ - $$$

Doruk Restaurant
Holiday Inn - Crown Plaza
Ataköy
Tel. 560 81 00
12.00 a.m.- 3.00 p.m.
7.00 p.m.-12.00 p.m.
The roof restaurant of the
hotel
(24th floor).Splendid view of
the Sea of Marmara and the

Princes' Islands. Excellent
food. Brunch on Sundays.
All major cards. $$ - $$$

Dörtler Restaurant
Kasaplar Çarşısı No.8
Bostancı
Tel. 366 34 98
12.00 a.m.-12.00 p.m.
Meat Restaurant.
Visa. $

Dragon
Hilton Hotel
Elmadağ
Tel. 231 46 46
Reservations necessary
12.00 a.m.- 2.30 p.m.
7.00 p.m.-11.30 p.m.
Closed Mondays
Featuring mainly Hong Kong
specialties, Dragon is the best
Chinese restaurant in town.
Authentic decor.
All major cards. $$$$

Dynasty
Merit Antique Istanbul Hotel
Laleli
Tel. 513 93 00
Reservations necessary
Open 7.00 p.m.-11.00 p.m.
Closed Sundays
Hotel's Chinese restaurant serv-
ing tasty Chinese specialties.
Chinese music (tape)
All major cards. $$$$

Ece
Tramvay Cad. 104
Kuruçeşme
Tel. 265 79 40
Reservations suggested
12.00 a.m. -2.00 a.m.
Bar/restaurant. Brunch on
Sundays (no dinner service).
'Ece' is the first name of the
owner meaning 'Queen'.
Indeed she is the queen in her
kitchen where she cooks and
supervises other cooks. A very
popular restaurant with steady
local customers.Creative menu.
Live music on weekends at the
bar.
Visa, Amex. $$$

Escale
Meşeli Sok.3, Dördüncü Levent
Tel. 268 13 13 - 278 33 81
Reservations necessary
11.30 a.m.- 3.30 p.m.
7.30 p.m.-11.30 p.m.
Pool 10.00 a.m.- 6.00 p.m.
Restaurant/bar with outdoor
setting for summer months.
International cuisine, vegetari-
an food.
Tape music, jazz.
All major cards. $$$

Etiler Şamdan
Nisbetiye Cad. 30
Etiler
Tel. 263 48 98
Reservations necessary
9.00 p.m. - until morning
Stylish restaurant/bar/disco.
Excellent Turkish and French
cuisine.
Disco, tape music (restaurant)
All credit cards except Diners.
$$$$

Evim Restaurant
Etiler Girişi, Aytar Sok. No.6
Etiler
Tel. 264 55 83 - 279 38 37
12.00 a.m.-12.00 p.m.
Turkish cuisine.
All major cards. $$

Evren Fish Restaurant
Çapari Sok. No.4 , Kumkapı
Tel. 517 23 38
Reservations for dinner
12.00 a.m.-12.00 p.m.
Seafood and fish restaurant
(See Kumkapı Page 70)
All credit cards except Amex.
$$

Façyo Restaurant
Kireçburnu Cad. 13 ,Tarabya
Tel. 262 08 98 - 262 00 24
Reservations suggested for
dinner.
12.00 a.m. -12.00 p.m.
The most frequented fish
restaurant on the Bosphorus. It
offers a great variety of tasty,
well-prepared *meze*.
All major cards. $$ - $$$

Filiz
Kefeliköy Cad.80, Tarabya
Tel. 262 01 52
Reservations suggested
12.00 a.m. -12.00 p.m.
Excellent Turkish *mezes* and
food in ordinary setting.
All major cards. $$ - $$$

Fisher Restaurant
İnönü Cad.51, Taksim
Tel. 245 25 76
Reservations for dinner
12.00 a.m.- 3.00 p.m.
6.00 p.m.-11.00 p.m.
A small restaurant featuring
Austrian and Russian special-
ties. Quick service.
Visa, Mastercard, Eurocards.
$$

Four Seasons
İstiklâl Cad. 509, Tünel
Tel. 245 89 41
Reservations recommended
12.00 a.m - 3.00 p.m.
8.00 p.m.-12.00 p.m.
Closed Sundays
Lunch fixed menu if desired
($6). A great variety of food.
Popular with foreigners.
All major cards. $$ - $$$

Galata Kulesi
Kuledibi, Şişhane
Tel. 245 11 60 (3 lines)
Reservations recommended
Restaurant/bar/nightclub
Belly dancer
Amex,Visa,Prestige $$$

Garaj Restaurant
Yeniköy Cad.
Tarabya
Tel. 262 00 32 - 262 04 74
Reservations recommended
12.00 a.m.-12.00 p.m.
A well-known restaurant with
good service and tasty *meze*
and food, especially fish.
All major cards. $$$

Garibaldi
İstiklâl Cad. Perukar Çıkmazı,
Oda Kule, Beyoğlu
Tel. 249 68 95-251 95 91

Reservations necessary
12.00 a.m.-2.00 p.m.
International specialties.
Live music pop and local
All major cards. $$

Gelik
Sahilyolu Mobil Karşısı
Ataköy
Tel. 560 72 83
12.00 a.m.-12.00 p.m.
A very large meat restaurant.
All major cards. $$

Gelik Balık Restoran
Zeytinburnu
Tel. 547 13 20
Reservations necessary (for
groups only)
11.30 a.m.-12.00 p.m.
A very large fish and seafood
restaurant.
All major card. $$

Genoa
Bağ Sok.Gülistan Apt.13/1
Etiler
Tel. 265 92 70 - 265 57 50
Reservations recommended
12.00 a.m.-1.00 a.m.
Restaurant/cafe.
Overlooks the Bosphorus.
Seafood specialties. Good coffee and cakes.
Live music Fridays, Saturdays
Visa, Prestige, Amex. $$

Guang Zhou Ocean Restaurant
İnönü cad. 53
Taksim
Tel. 243 63 79
Reservations for dinner
11.30 a.m.-11.30 p.m.
Popular Chinese restaurant,
quick service.
Visa, Mastercard. $$
(fixed menu for two for $20-30)

Gülizar Cafe
The Conrad Hotel
Beşiktaş
Tel. 227 30 00
7.00 a.m. -12.00 p.m.
Overlooks the Bosphorus.
Hotel's coffee shop, serves
international and Turkish food.
All major cards. $$ - $$

Günay
Büyükdere Cad. Beytem Plaza
Mecidiyeköy
Tel. 230 44 44
Reservations recommended
Open: Thursdays, Fridays,
Saturdays
10.00 p.m.-4.00 a.m.
Live music
(Turkish and pop singers)
No cards. $$$$

Güp Güp Fish Restaurant
Bağdat Cad.510
Bostancı
Tel. (0216) 373 62 39 - 380 94 13
Reservations necessary
12.00 a.m.-2.00 a.m.
Fish specialties.
Visa, Master, Prestige, Eurocard. $$

Hacıbaba Restaurant
İstiklâl Cad. 49 Beyoğlu
Tel.244 18 86 -245 43 77
12.00 a.m.-11.00 p.m.
A Turkish restaurant serving a
great variety of Turkish dishes.
Visa, Diners Club, Amex. $

Hacıbozanoğulları
Ordu Cad. 214, Laleli
Tel. 528 44 92
11.30 a.m.-11.00 p.m.
Delicious kebab varieties.
No cards. $

Hacıdan Ocakbaşı
Aytar Sok, 11
Levent
Tel. 269 04 22 - 23
12.00 a.m.-12.00 p.m.
Closed on religious holidays,
Kebab varieties.
All credit cards except Prestige
$ - $$

Han
Yahya Kemal Cad. 10
Rumelihisar
Tel. 265 29 68
Reservations suggested for
dinner, weekends
12.00 a.m.-12.00 p.m.
A simple fish restaurant with
nice ambiance by the Bosphorus.
All major cards. $$

Hanedan

İskele Meydanı, Barbaros Anıtı karşısı, Beşiktaş
Tel. 260 48 54 - 261 49 82
Reservations suggested for dinner
12.00 a.m. -12.00 p.m.
Meat Kebab and fish served.
All credit cards except Diners Club. $$

Hasır

Beykoz Korusu - Beykoz
Tel. (0216) 322 29 01 - 322 57 57
12.00 a.m. -12.00 p.m.
Turkish meat restaurant in the midst of woods in Beykoz on the Asian side. Crowded over weekends.
All major cards. $$ - $$$

Hasan Balıkçılar Lokantası

Rıhtım Sok. No.8 ,Yeşilköy
Tel. 573 83 00
Reservations for large groups necessary
12.00 a.m.-12.00 p.m.
Very good fish restaurant.
All major cards except Amex. $$

Hıdiv Kasrı Restoran

Çubuklu
Tel. (0216) 331 26 51
Reservations for dinner
12.00 a.m.- 3.00 p.m.
7.00 p.m.-12.00 p.m.
Housed in the Art Nouveau style summer mansion of the last Ottoman Governor (Khedive) of Egypt located in the most thickly wooded areas on the slopes of Çubuklu overlooking the Bosphorus. Small luxury hotel, excellent restaurant, coffee house and beautiful view. (See page 64.)
All cards except Diners Club and Prestige. $$$ - $$$$

Hipodrom Restaurant

Atmeydanı No.74
Sultanahmet
Tel. 516 04 74
10.00 a.m.-12:00 p.m.
Convenient for sightseers. An unpretentious small restaurant with very reasonable prices. Amex,Visa. $

Hünkar Restaurant

Akgün Hotel
Vatan Cad. Aksaray
Tel. 534 48 79
Reservations suggested for dinner especially weekends.
9.00 a.m.- 10.30 a.m.(Breakfast)
12.00 a.m.- 3.00 p.m.(Lunch)
7.00 p.m. - 11.00 p.m. (Dinner)
Turkish and international food.
All major credit cards. $$

Home Store

Park Sok. 4, Çağlayan, Şişli
Tel. 224 56 80
Reservations necessary
8.30 p.m.-4.00 a.m.
Closed Sundays
Very expensive and fashionable restaurant.
Live music on Fridays, Saturdays and Tuesdays.
Disco music after 12.00 p.m.
All credit cards except Diners. $$$$

Huzur (Arabın Yeri)

Salacak İskelesi 20
Üsküdar
Tel. (0216) 333 31 57
12.00 a.m.-12.00 p.m.
Simple fish restaurant with a view of old Istanbul (Blue Mosque, Topkapı Palace and St. Sophia).
You are lucky if you are there at sunset.
No cards. $$

İstiridye Restoran

Nova Baran İş Merkezi, Şişli
Tel. 248 17 58
12.00 a.m.-11.00 p.m.
A small seafood restaurant in the Nova Baran shopping center. Fresh fish cooked in different styles.
No cards. $$

Japan Club

Japanese Restaurant
Barbaros Bulvarı, Mürbasan

Sok., Balmumcu
Tel. 272 86 31 - 266 14 23
Reservations recommended
Lunch:12.00 a.m.-2.00 p.m.
except Saturdays and Sundays.
Dinner: 6.30 p.m.-11.00 p.m.
except Sundays.
Best Japanese restaurant in
town.
Authentic Japanese music
Visa, Amex, Diners, JCB. $$$$

Kaşıbeyaz Meat Restaurant
Çatal Sok., Florya
Tel.663 28 90
Reservations suggested during
the month of Ramazan
12.00 a.m.-11.00 p.m.
A very large kebab restaurant.
All cards except Diners. $$

Kadife Chalet
Bahariye Kadife Sok. 29
Kadıköy
Tel. (0216) 347 85 96
Reservations suggested on
weekends
10.00 a.m.-8.00 p.m. Closed
Mondays
Serves light meals, pastry, tea
and coffee.A small, pleasant
restaurant/cafe in a recently
restored old wooden house
with all the details carefully
planned.
Ottoman and international food.
Live music for special group
arrangements
No cards. $ - $$

Kalamar Restaurant
Çapari Sok. No.19, Kumkapı
Tel. 517 18 49 - 517 75 57
12.00 a.m.-12.00 p.m.
See Kumkapı (Page 70)
Regular Kumkapı music
(gypsy music and belly danc-
ing)
All credit cards, except Diners
Club. $$

Kale Restaurant
Körfez Cad.,Anadolu Hisarı
Tel. (0216) 332 04 09
Reservations suggested
12.00 a.m.-1.00 a.m.

Seafood and fish restaurant by
the Bosphorus
Live music for dinner and a
singer
All major cards. $$

Kallavi 20
Kallavi Sok. 20, İstiklâl Cad.
Beyoğlu
Tel. 251 10 10
12.00 a.m. -12.00 p.m.
An old-style Turkish bar (*mey-
hane*). Good *meze* and kebabs.
Now-a-days fashionable.
Typical Turkish music
No cards. $$

Kapalıçarşı Havuzlu Restaurant
(Covered Bazaar)
Gani Çelebi Sok. 3
Kapalıçarşı
Tel. 527 33 46
12.00 a.m.-6.00 p.m.
Closed Sundays
A simple Turkish restaurant re-
commended for lunch and cof-
fee break in the Covered Bazaar.
All cards except Diners. $

Kapkara Figeyra
Karakol Bostanı Sok. 13/1
Teşvikiye
Tel. 261 45 07
4.30 p.m. -2.00 a.m.
Closed Sundays
Two floor Cafe/Restaurant/Bar
Live music (11.30 p.m.)
Visa.
Fixed menu and beverage $10

Karaca Restaurant
Yahya Kemal Cad. 1/C
Rumelihisar
Tel. 263 34 68 - 265 97 20
Reservations for dinner
12.00 a.m.-1.00 a.m.
A typical fish restaurant.Good
meze and fresh fish, simple but
pleasant ambiance.
All major cards. $$ - $$$

Kazan
Mövenpick Hotel
Büyükdere Cad. 49, Maslak
Tel. 285 09 00
Reservations recommended

6.00 p.m.-11.00 p.m.
Closed Mondays
Very good Turkish food and service.
All Major Cards. $$$ - $$$$

Kazan Restoran
Cumhuriyet Cad. 151/1
Elmadağ
Tel. 232 72 16
Reservations for weekends
12.00 a.m.-4.00 p.m. self-service
Dinner until 11.00 p.m.
Live music (guitar)
Visa, Master Card, Eurocard.
$ - $$ (Lunch - $6)

Kebab's
Manolya Sok.2/1
Bebek
Tel. 257 71 41
Reservations for dinner
12.00 a.m.-12.00 p.m.
Fasıl heyeti (Turkish classical music), Kebabs from different regions of Turkey.
Live music 9.00 p.m.(Tuesdays, Thursdays, Saturdays).
All major cards. $ - $$

Kent Fasıl
Kore Şehitleri Cad..
Zincirlikuyu
Tel. 274 14 07 - 274 14 61
Reservations recommended
8.00 p.m. -4.00 p.m.
Closed Sundays
Interesting for those who wish to listen to the classical Turkish music. Serves *meze*, fish and meat dishes.
Visa, Mastercard. $$

Kervansaray
Cumhuriyet Cad. No:30
Harbiye
Tel. 247 16 30/1 - 246 08 18
Reservations necessary
7:30 p.m. -1:00 p.m.
Turkish restaurant/night club. Turkish and international cuisine.Belly dancing and folk dancing.Tour groups' favorite place. Turkish and internation-al music.
American Express, Diners Club, Visa. $$$$

Kıyı Restaurant
Kefeliköy Cad. 126, Tarabya
Tel. 262 00 02
12.00 a.m.-12.00 p.m.
A nice fish restaurant along the Bosphorus.
All major credit cards. $$$

Kız Kulesi Deniz Restaurant
Salacak Sahil Yolu, Üsküdar
Tel. 341 04 03
Reservations suggested
12.00 a.m.-12.00 p.m.
Spectacular view of the harbor and the Bosphorus. Seafood restaurant.
Live music at the bar
All major cards. $$

Klassis Hotel Restaurants
Silivri
(100 kms from city center)
Tel. 727 40 50
The three hotel restaurants Festus, Cedrus and Actium serves international food in a relaxing resort atmosphere.
All major cards. $$$ - $$$$

Konyalı Restaurants
Topkapı Sarayı (Topkapı Palace)
Sultanahmet
Tel. 513 96 96 (3 lines)
10.00 a.m.-5.00 pm.(lunch only)
Closed Sundays
The only restaurant in the premises of the Topkapı Palace Museum.
Overlooks the Sea of Marmara, Leander's Tower and the Bosphorus.
Amex, Diners, Visa. $$
Group menus: $9-22

Kör Agop Fish Restaurant
Kumkapı
Tel. 517 23 34 (2 lines)
Reservations suggested on weekends
12.00 a.m. -12.00 p.m.
One of the oldest of Kumkapı restaurants. See Kumkapı (Page 70)
All cards except Diners,Amex. $$

Körfez Restaurant
Körfez Cad. 78, Kanlıca
Tel. (0216) 413 43 14
Reservations necessary
12.00 a.m.- 3.00 p.m.
8.00 p.m. -12.00 p.m.
Closed Mondays
By the Bosphorus overlooking
the European castle and Fatih
Sultan Mehmet Bridge. A leading name in fish dishes. The
seabass marinated in salt has a
unique taste which should be
experienced.
All major cards. $$$$

Kosova Restaurant
Turistik Tesisler
Florya
Tel. 573 78 38 - 573 67 82
Reservations necessary only
during Ramazan.
Open 12.00 a.m. -12.00 p.m.
A very large meat restaurant
(Turkish Kebabs)
Visa, Mastercard. $$

Kuruçeşme Divan
Kuruçeşme Cad., 36
Kuruçeşme
Tel. 257 71 50/4
Reservations necessary
12.00 a.m.- 3.00 p.m.
7.00 p.m.-12.00 p.m.
Delicious Turkish and interna-
tional dishes. Along the Bos-
phorus, pleasant atmosphere.
Piano music
Visa, Diners Club, Amex.
$$$

La Corne d'or
Swissôtel
Maçka
Tel. 259 01 01
Closed Sundays
Good French and intenational
cuisine. A pleasant hotel
restaurant with beautiful view
of the Bosphorus.
Live music (7.00 p.m. -11.30 p.m.)
All major cards. $$$ - $$$$

La Coupol
Sheraton Hotel
Taksim

Tel. 231 21 21
7.00 p.m. -12.00 p.m. dinner
The hotel's restaurant featuring
international and Turkish cui-
sine. Breakfast and lunch, open
buffet dinner à la carte.
All major cards. $$

La Delicatesse
Çınar Hotel
Yeşilköy
Tel. 663 29 00
Reservations necessary
7.00 p.m.-11.00 p.m. dinner
Hotel's pleasant restaurant
serving good Turkish food.
Live music
Visa, Amex, Diners. $$$$

La Maison Restaurant
Müvezzi Cad. 63
Beşiktaş
Tel. 227 42.74
Reservations suggested
12.00 a.m.-3.00 p.m.
8.00 p.m. -2.00 a.m.
French restaurant serving good
food and imported French wine.
CD French music
All major cards except Amex.
$$$

La Torretta
Regatta 240
Ataköy Marina
Tel. 560 33 91
Reservations suggested
12.00 a.m.-11.00 p.m.
Italian chef, very good Italian
food - (some imported)
Visa, Mastercard, Amex.
$$-$$$

Le Baron
Mövenpick Hotel
Büyükdere Cad. 49
Üçyol Mevkii
Maslak
Tel. 285 09 00/6132
Reservations necessary
12.00 a.m.- 2.30 p.m.
7.00 p.m.-11.30 p.m.
French specialties.
Classical music
Amex, Visa, Mastercard,
Eurocard. $$$

Le Select
Manolya Sok. 21
Levent
Tel. 268 21 20
Reservations necessary
12.00 a.m. -4.00 p.m.
  7.30 p.m.-1.00 a.m.
Restaurant/bar, international
food in an elegant decor. A
very 'in' place.
Visa. $$$

Leonardo Restaurant
Polonezköy Meydanı No.32
Polonezköy
(0216) 432 30 82
Reservations suggested
Pleasant outing in the woods.
12:00 a.m. -12.00 p.m.
Polish food. Saturdays and
Sundays open buffet and bev-
erage ($10)
Classical, Jazz music
Visa. $$

Liman Lokantası
Yeni Yolcu Salonu üstü
Karaköy
Tel. 244 10 33 - 244 61 13
Reservations suggested
12.00 a.m.-4.00 p.m.
Closed on Saturdays, Sundays
and holidays.
Unpretentious decoration
Located in the harbor with a
view of old Serglio Point.
Good, authentic Turkish food.
All major cards. $$

Marine Club
Meclisi Mebusan Cad. 22,
Salıpazarı
(Deniz Ticaret Odası Binası)
Tel. 251 95 24
Reservations suggested
12.00 a.m.-12.00 p.m.
In the heart of the business com-
munity, a good restaurant.
Live music (lunch and dinner)
All major cards except Diners
Club. $$

Marmara Restaurant
Istanbul Polat Renaissance
Hotel, Yeşilyurt
Tel. 663 17 00

7:00 a.m.- 11.00 p.m.
International food. A la carte
and buffet
All major cards. $$ - $$$

Marmit
İstanbul Cad. 58
Yeşilköy
Tel. 573 85 81
Reservations for weekends
7.00 pm.-12.00 pm.
Mexican and South American
food. No cards. $$ - $$$

Mayna
Ataköy Marina
Tel. 560 80 10 (7 lines)
Reservations suggested
12.00 a.m.-12.00 p.m.
Meat specialties. Pleasant dec-
oration.
All major cards. $$

Mey
Rumeli Hisar Cad. 122
Bebek
Tel. 265 25 99
Reservations for weekends
7.00 p.m.-1.00 a.m.
A fish restaurant with unique
seafood specialties.
All cards. $$

Miyako
Swissôtel
Maçka
Tel. 259 01 01
Reservations suggested
12.00 a.m.-12.00 p.m.
Closed Mondays
Hotel's Japanese restaurant
with excellent food prepared
by specialists.
All major cards.. $$$ - $$$$

Moda Park Restaurant (Koço)
Moda Cad. No.265
Moda, Kadıköy
Tel. 336 07 95 - 337 70 44
Reservations necessary
12.00 a.m.-12.00 p.m.
70 year-old restaurant. It has
Aya Katerina (ayazma=holy
water) and a view of the Sea of
Marmara.
No cards. $$

Monteverdi
Conrad Istanbul Hotel
Beşiktaş
Tel. 227 30 00
Reservations recommended
7.00 p.m.-1.00 a.m.
Closed Sundays
Features northern Itâlian dish-
es. It ranks as the best Italian
restaurant of Istanbul.
All major cards. $$$

Motel Yeşilköy Restaurant
Havan Sok.4,Yeşilköy
Tel. 663 27 70 (3 lines)
Reservations on weekends
11.00 a.m.-12.00 p.m.
Turkish and French cuisine
and seafood.
Amex, Visa, Mastercard. $$

Mövenpick Restaurant
Mövenpick Hotel
Büyükdere Cad. 49, Maslak
Tel. 285 09 00
Reservations suggested
6.30 a.m. -1.00 a.m.
International and Swiss menu.
All major cards. $$

Oba Fish Restaurant
Balta Limanı Cad. 54
Balta Limanı
Tel. 277 99 11
Reservations recommended
12.00 a.m.-12.00 p.m.
Bar/Cafeteria 9.00 a.m.-5.00 p.m.
A spacious Bosphorus restau-
rant serving mainly fish.
Live music in the bar
All major cards except Amex
and Diners. $$ - $$$

Ocakbaşı Restaurant
The President Hotel
Tiyatro Cad. 25
Bayezıt
Tel. 516 69 80
Reservations suggested
Open buffet 12.00 a.m.-3.00 p.m.
Dinner 7.00 p.m.-11.00 p.m.
Turkish kebabs and interna-
tional food.
Live music, oriental dancer,
Turkish music
All major cards. $$

Osteria Da Mario Restaurant
Dilhayat Sok.7, Etiler
Tel. 265 15 96 - 265 51 86
Reservations suggested
12.00 a.m.- 3.00 p.m.
 7.00 p.m.-11.00 p.m.
Italian restaurant serving
excellent Italian specialties
including Italian wine.
Authentic Italian music (live
music on Sundays)
Amex, Visa, Mastercard, Eurocard. $$ - $$$

Pafulli
Kuruçeşme Cad. No.116
Kuruçeşme
Tel. 263 66 38
Reservations recommended
12.00 a.m.-1.00 a.m.
The only restaurant which pre-
pares popular specialties of the
Black Sea region.(*hamsili
pilav, hamsi kuşu, laz böreği*)
Traditional Black Sea music
All major cards, $$

Panaroma Restaurant
The Marmara Istanbul Hotel
Taksim
Tel. 251 46 96
Reservations necessary
7.30 p.m.-1.00 a.m.
Hotel's rooftop restaurant.
Breathtaking view of the
Bosphorus and the Sea of
Marmara. Excellent Turkish
and French cuisine.
Live piano music
All major cards. $$$. .

Pandeli
Mısır Çarşısı, Eminönü
Tel. 527 39 09
Reservations suggested
11.30 a.m.-4.00 p.m.
Closed Sundays and on reli-
gious holidays.
At the entrance of the Spice
Market, an old Turkish restau-
rant decorated with blue
Turkish tiles. It keeps its good
standard. A convenient lunch
place when shopping in the
area. The food is excellent.
All major cards. $$$

Papirüs (Restaurant/Bar)
Ayhan Işık Sok. 5A
İstiklâl Cad.
Tel. 251 14 28
Reservations recommended
12.00 a.m.-2.00 a.m.
One of the oldest bars of
Istanbul. Very friendly atmosphere, usually attended by the
same clientele.
Live guitar music on Thursdays, Fridays, Saturdays
Visa. $$

Park Şamdan
Mim Kemal Öke Cad. 18/1
Nişantaş
Tel. 225 07 10
Reservations recommended
12.00 a.m.- 3.00 p.m.
8.00 p.m.-12.00 p.m.
Stylish and popular restaurant.
Rich menu and good service.
No cards. $$$$

Paysage Restaurant
Hekimler Sitesi, Kanlıca
Tel. (0216) 322 70 60
Reservations for dinner
12.00 a.m.- 3.00 p.m.
7.00 p.m.-12.00 p.m.
Wonderful view of the Bosphorus.
Live music (except Sundays,
Mondays,Tuesdays)
Amex,Visa. $$

Pera Palas Restaurant
Pera Palas Hotel
Meşrutiyet Cad. 98/100
Tepebaşı
Tel. 251 45 60
Reservations necessary
12.00 a.m. - 3.00 p.m.
7.00 p.m. -12.00 p.m.
The restaurant is interesting in
that it is situated in a hotel
with a fin-de-siècle splendor
which has become internationally renowned during the
World War II as a meeting
place of international spies.
Room 411 where Agatha
Christie stayed is an added
attraction. (See page 74).
Live music
All major cards. $$$

Pescatore
Kefeliköy Cad. 29/A, Kireçburnu
Tel. 233 18 19
Reservations suggested
12.00 a.m.-12.00 p.m.
Stylish fish restaurant along
the Bosphorus. Tasty seafood
specialties.
All major cards. $$ - $$$

Piazza
Mövenpick Hotel
Büyükdere Cad. 49, Üçyol
Mevkii Maslak
Tel. 285 09 00
10.00 a.m. -12.00 p.m.
Daily specialties such as
spaghetti, pizza, cakes and pies.
All major cards. $$

Pizza Flora Restaurant
Valikonağı Cad. No.9, Harbiye
Tel. 225 22 26
Reservations necessary in winter
12.00 a.m. -11.00 p.m.
Italian and French cuisine.
Visa, Prestige, Amex, Diners
Club. $ - $$

Pizza Papillon
Selçuklar Sok. 5.Yıl Çarşısı
21/3, Akatlar-Etiler
Tel. 257 39 46
12.00 a.m.-11.00 p.m.
Italian cuisine
All major cards. $$

Pizzamatik
Lamartin Cad. 11/2, Taksim
Tel. 256 28 25 - 414 27 07
11.00 a.m.-11.00 p.m.
Autentic American pizza.
Outside catering service.
No cards. $

Queen Victoria Restaurant
Çalıkuşu Sok.5, Levent
Tel. 281 63 72/3
6.00 p.m.-2.00 a.m.
Shepherd's pie and other traditional British delicacies,popular with expatriots, cosy and
friendly atmosphere, good
range of malt whiskeys.
All major cards except Amex
and Diners. $$

Raquette (Raket) Restoran/Bar
Enka Sadi Gülçelik Tesisleri,
İstinye Yolu
Tel. 276 50 87 - 285 11 46
Reservations suggested
12.00 a.m.-2.00 p.m.
Closed Mondays
Enka Sports Facilities' restaurant by the Olympic size swimming pool. French and Turkish cuisine.
Live music (except Sundays, Mondays, Tuesdays)
No cards. $$

Reşat Paşa Konağı
Sinan Ercan Cad.34/1
Erenköy
Tel. (0216) 361 34 11 - 361 34 87
Reservations necessary
Open 7.00 p.m. -12.00 p.m.
Closed Mondays
A restored old wooden Turkish mansion decorated in Turkish style.
Serves authentic Turkish dishes.Turkish and international cuisine.
Live classical Turkish music on Wednesdays and Thursdays.
All major cards. $$ - $$$

Rejans
Emir Nevruz Sok. 17
Galatasaray
Tel. 244 16 10
Reservations for dinner
12.00 a.m.- 3.00 p.m.
7.00 p.m.-11.00 p.m.
Closed Sundays
At one time it was a very popular restaurant of Istanbul featuring Russian specialties.
No cards. $$

Revan
Shereton Hotel
Taksim
Tel. 231 21 21
Reservation suggested
7.00 p.m.-12.00 p.m.
Hotel's rooftop restaurant with a breathtaking view of the sea.
Excellent Turkish food.
Turkish classical musical
All major cards. $$$

Ristorante Italiano
Cumhuriyet Cad. 6-B,
Elmadağ
Tel. 247 86 40
Reservations on weekends
12:00 a.m.-10.30 p.m.
Closed Sundays
The city's first Italian Restaurant serving good Italian food.
All major cards. $$

Ristorante Rosa
Cumhuriyet Cad. 131
Elmadağ
Tel. 232 42 22 - 241 28 27
11.30 a.m.-11.30 p.m.
Serves Italian food.
All major cards except Prestige.
$$

Ristorante Vito
Osmanzade Sok. No.13
Ortaköy
Tel. 227 65 98
Reservations recommended
12.00 a.m.-12.00 p.m.
Popular Italian restaurant.
No cards. $$

Russian Restaurant
İnönü Cad. Palas Ap. 77/A
Gümüşsuyu
Tel. 243 48 92
12.00 a.m.- 3.00 p.m.
6.00 p.m.-10.00 p.m.
A small restaurant featuring Russian specialties. Popular with students.
Visa. $$

'S' Restaurant
Vezir Köşkü Sok. 2
Bebek
Tel. 287 01 50/1
Reservations necessary
12.00 a.m.- 3.00 p.m.
7.00 p.m.-12.00 p.m.
Closed Sundays
Elegant place with formal atmosphere. It is a very classy restaurant .
Excellent Turkish and French food. Very good service.
Live music
All major cards. $$$

Sanden Restaurant - Catering
İnönü Cad. Miralay Şefik Bey
Sok.9/1, Gümüşsuyu-Taksim
Tel. 251 27 65/66 - 252 49 34
10.00 a.m.-9.00 p.m.
Closed Sundays.
Diet, and vegetarian food plus
regular menus.
Visa, Eurocard. $ - $$

Sarnıç
Soğukçeşme Sok.
Sultanahmet
8.00 p.m.-12.00 p.m.
Closed Mondays
A recently restored former
Roman cistern. A stunning
middle age atmosphere.
Amex, Mastercard, Visa. $$$

Sarnıç Restaurant
Yalı Sok. 3, Beşiktaş
Tel. 261 96 78
Open 24 hours
Turkish and French cuisine.
All major cards. $$

Scala
Çamlık Sok.15, 3. Levent
Tel. 281 57 69
Reservations recommended
10.00 a.m.-12.00 p.m.
(Sundays special arrange-
ments)
Restaurant and bar in a villa.
Warm atmosphere. Inter-
national cuisine. An 'in' place.
Visa. $$

**Schnitzel Unlimited/
Cafe Amadeus**
Köybaşı Cad. 57-59
Yeniköy
Tel. 262 06 35
11.00 a.m.-11.00 p.m.
Reservations on weekends
Closed Mondays
The only schnitzel restaurant
in town. Housed in a restored
old wooden house. Pleasant at-
mosphere. Excellent service. A
great variety of schnitzel. The
one with vegetables, Austrian
pies and cappucino coffee rec-
ommended.
Visa, Eurocard. $$

Seoul
Nisbetiye Cad. 41
Etiler
Tel. 263 60 87
12.00 a.m.- 3.00 p.m.
6.00 p.m.-11.00 p.m.
Closed Sundays
Korean and Chinese food.
All major cards. $$$

Set Balık Lokantası
Kireçburnu Cad.No.18
Tarabya
Tel. 262 04 11 - 262 34 98
Reservations for dinner
12.00 a.m.- 3.00 p.m. (lunch)
7.00 p.m.-12.00 p.m. (dinner)
Seafood specialties.
No cards. $$

Spasso
Hyatt Regency Hotel
Taşkışla Cad. ,Taksim
Tel. 225 70 00
12.00 a.m.- 3.00 p.m. (lunch)
7.00 p.m.-11.00 p.m. (dinner)
Featuring Italian specialties
cooked in the open kitchen.
All major cards except Diners
Club. $$$

Sultanahmet Halk Köftecisi
(Selim Usta)
Divan Yolu Cad. 12/A
Sultanahmet
Tel. 513 14 38
11.00 a.m. -11.00 p.m.
A simple restaurant featuring
Turkish *Köfte* (meatballs) and
white kidney bean salad.
Established in 1920. It is sup-
posed to be the best 'Köfte'
place in Istanbul.
No cards. $

Sunset
Adnan Saygun Cad. Kireçhane
Sok. Ulus Parkı 2, Ulus
Tel. 287 03 57 -58
12.00 a.m.- 3.00 p.m (lunch)
7.00 p.m.-12.00 p.m. (dinner)
Panoramic view of the Bos-
phorus. Arizona decoration.
Californian cuisine.
Restaurant/Gill & Bar.
Visa, Eurocard, Mastercard. $$

Süreyya
İstinye Cad. 26, İstinye
Tel. 277 58 86
Reservations necessary
12.00 a.m.- 3.00 p.m.
  8.00 p.m.-12.00 p.m.
Closed Sundays
Continues Süreyya's, the
founder's, tradition of good
food, quick and best service.
Süreyya is famous for its game
dishes and nice ambiance.
Visa, Diners, Amex. $$$

Susam Restaurant
Susam Sok. 6, Cihangir
Tel. 231 59 35 - 36
Reservations necessary
12.00 a.m.- 3.00 p.m
  8.00 p.m.-12.00 p.m.
Elegant restaurant/bar with a
view of the Topkapı Palace.
International cuisine.
No cards. $$$- $$$$

Sweeties
Vapur İskelesi Cad.No.5
Ortköy
Tel. 227 0287
Reservations necessary on
weekends.
12.00 a.m.- 3.00 p.m.
  6.00 p.m.-12.00 p.m.
A very nice small restaurant
with good food and cosy am-
biance.
Visa, Mastercard, Eurocard. $$

Swiss Farm
Swissôtel, Maçka
Tel. 259 01 01
Reservations necessary
7.00 p.m.-11.30 p.m.
Closed Mondays
Hotel's restaurant. Chalet set-
ting. Swiss dishes.
Swiss folklore music (tape)
All major cards. $$$

Swiss Pub/Bar/Restaurant
Cumhuriyet Cad. 14
Elmadağ
Tel. 247 30 35 - 248 80 49
12.00 a.m.- 2.00 a.m.
Turkish, French, Swiss cuisine.
All major cards. $

Şark Sofrası
Swisshotel
Maçka
Tel. 259 01 01
Reservations suggested.
8.00 p.m.-4.00 a.m.
Turkish restaurant with typical
meze and authentic regional
cooking.
All major cards. $$$ - $$$$

Şans
Hacı Adil Sok. 6. Aralık
(Karakol yanı) 1.Levent
Tel. 280 38 38 - 281 07 07
Reservations recommended.
12.00 a.m. - 3.00 p.m.
  8.00 p.m. -12.00 a.m.
A beautiful villa decorated in a
comfortable style. A popular
place to eat Turkish, Chinese,
Italian and French food.
All major cards except Diners
and Prestige. $$$

Şiribom
Moda Cad. İskeleyolu, 258
Moda
Tel. (0216) 338 35 95
12.00 a.m.-11.00 p.m.
An outstanding kebab house
with delicious *meze* and south-
eastern specialties. Fast service.
No cards. $ - $$

Taksim Sanat Evi
Sıra Selviler Cad. 69/1, Taksim
Tel. 244 25 26
12.00 a.m.-4.00 p.m.
Overlooking the Sea of Mar-
mara. Intellectual atmosphere.
Turkish and French cuisine.
Dinner only on Sundays.
All cards except Diners . $$

Tegik
Recep Paşa Cad. 20
Elmadağ
Tel. 254 71 72 - 254 66 99
Reservations on weekends
12.00 a.m.- 3.00 p.m.
  6.00 p.m.-12.00 p.m.
Korean restaurant featuring
Korean, Chinese and Japanese
dishes. Dinner only on Sun-
days.
All major cards. $$$

Teras
Bayıldım Cad. 10
Maçka
Tel. 260 73 04
Reservations suggested
12.00 a.m.-12.00 p.m.
Nice view and international
cuisine.
All major cards. $$$

The Bistro
Sheraton Hotel, Taksim
Tel. 231 21 21
Reservations suggested
7.00 a.m. -11.30 p.m.
Hotel's snack-bar.
Live-music after 5.30 p.m.
All major cards. $$ - $$$

The Chinese Restaurant
(Çin Lokantası)
Lamartin Cad.17/1
Taksim
Tel. 250 62 63
Reservations suggested
12.00 a.m.- 3.00 p.m.
7.00 p.m.-11.00 p.m.
Closed Sundays
Istanbul's oldest ethnic and
first Chinese Restaurant. For
almost 40 years it has kept its
good standard. Serves popular
Chinese food.
Amex,Visa, Prestige. $$

The Dining Room
Hotel Gezi
Taksim
Tel. 251 74 30
7.00 a.m. -11.00 a.m.(breakfast)
12.00 a.m. -12.00 p.m.
Hotel restaurant overlooking
the Bosphorus. Turkish and
international cuisine.
All major cards. $$$

The Gallery
A.Adnan Saygun Cad., Dostlar
Sitesi A Blok 5/2 Ulus
Etiler
Tel. 263 35 55
12.00 a.m. -12.00 p.m.
Closed Sunday
A popular restaurant/bar fea-
turing international cuisine in
a true art gallery atmosphere.
Amex, Mastercard, Visa. $$

Tiendes Restoran
Nisbetiye Cad.,Seheryıldızı
Sok. 6, Etiler
Tel. 265 02 32
Reservations recommended
9.00 p.m. -5.00 a.m.
Bar/Restaurant Popular place.
Pleasant atmosphere. Favorite
place for after-dinner drinks.
Live music
All major cards except Diners.
$$$

Tuğra
Çırağan Palace Hotel
Kempinski, Beşiktaş
Tel. 258 33 77
Reservations recommended
12.00 a.m.- 3.00 p.m.
7.30 p.m.-11.30 p.m.
Closed Mondays
Hotel's restaurant with impres-
sive setting and excellent ser-
vice featuring Ottoman dishes.
(*Tuğra* is the name of the seal
of the Ottoman sultans).
All major cards. $$$ - $$$$

Üçüncü Mevki
Büyük Parmakkapı Sok. No.9
Gözüm Han, Beyoğlu
Tel. 244 22 23
12.00 a.m.-10.00 p.m.
No cards. $

Uluorta
Gürcü Kızı Sok. No.2
Ortaköy
Tel. 227 31 49
9.00 p.m -5.00 a.m.
Nice view of the Bosphorus
bridge.
Live music (Turkish)
All major cards. $$$

Ulus 29
Akatlar Parkı, Ulus
Tel. 265 61 98 - 265 61 81
Reservations necessary
12.00 a.m.-4.00 p.m.
8.00 p.m.-2.00 a.m.
Very fashionable restau-
rant/bar. Elegantly decorated.
Has a magnificient view of the
Bosphorus. Serves French spe-
cialties prepared by French
chef.

All major cards except Diners Club. $$$$

Urcan
Orta Çeşme Cad. 2/1 Sarıyer
Tel. 242 03 67
12.00 a.m.-12.00 p.m.
An impressive big fish restaurant of good reputation on the waterfront where fish can be selected from the display tank while alive.
Visa, Amex, Diners. $$ - $$$

Veranda Restaurant
Holiday Inn - Crown Plaza Ataköy
Tel. 560 81 00
Reservations suggested
7.00 a.m.-10.00 p.m.
Hotel's pleasant restaurant. Turkish and Mediterranean cuisine. Open shrimp buffet on Wednesdays with live music ($20)
All major cards. $$ - $$$

Verenda
Mahmut Çavuş Sok.10, İstinye
Tel. 277 87 18
Reservations for dinner
12.00 a.m.-3.00 p.m.
7.00 p.m.- 1.00 a.m.
Closed Mondays
Overlooking the Bosphorus, nice ambiance with a veranda in summer.
All majorcards except Diners and Amex. $$ - $$$

Vito Restaurant
Osmanzade Sok. 13
Ortaköy
Tel. 227 65 98
Reservations for dinner
12.00 a.m.-12.00 p.m.
Italian food
Visa, Mastercard, Eurocard. $$

Yakup 2
Asmalı Mescit Sok. 35,
Tünel
Tel. 249 29 25
12.00 a.m. -12.00 p.m.
A popular *meyhane* (Old Turkish style bar).
Visa, Mastercard, Amex. $

Yeşil Ev Restaurant
Kabasakal Cad. 5, Sultanahmet
Tel. 517 67 85 (4 lines)
Reservations necessary
7.00 a.m.-10.30 a.m.(breakfast)
12.00 a.m.- 3.00 p.m.(lunch)
7.00 p.m.-10.30 p.m.(dinner)
Housed in a restored old wooden mansion which is run as a hotel by Touring and Automobile Association of Turkey, serves good Turkish and international food. Meals are served in its pleasant garden during summer months. Adjacent is the hotel's handicraft shopping arcade.
Live music on Thursdays and Saturdays.
All major cards. $$ - $$$

Yedi Gün
İskele Cad. Rumeli Kavağı
Tel. 242 37 98
12.00 a.m.-12.30 p.m.
Popular weekends, delicious fish.
Visa, Mastercard. $$.

Yeditepe Restaurant
Baba Nakkaş Tepe Sok.
Kuzguncuk
Tel. (0216) 333 13 07 - 334 08 03
Reservations suggested
12.00 a.m.-4.00 p.m. (lunch)
7.00 p.m.-1.00 a.m. (dinner)
Fantastic view of the Bosphorus.
Live taverna music
All major cards. $$

Yekta
Vali Konağı Cad.39/1, Nişantaş
Tel.248 11 83 - 225 22 77
11.30 a.m. - 2.30 p.m.
7.00 p.m.-12.00 p.m.
A popular old restaurant with good food.
No cards. $$

Yeni Bebek Restaurant
Cevdet Paşa Cad.123, Bebek
Tel. 263 34 47
12.00 a.m.- 3.00 p.m.(lunch)
7.00 p.m.-12.00 p.m.(dinner)
Along the Bosphorus, an excellent fish restaurant. Pleasant ambiance.
All major cards. $$$

Zeytin & Sardunya
Yıldız Posta Cad. No 25
Gayrettepe
Tel. 274 8713
Reservations recommended
12.00 a.m.-3.00 p.m.(lunch)
7.30 p.m.-3.30 a.m. dinner)
A popular restaurant/bar
Live music after 11.30 p.m.
All major cards except Diners
Club, Amex. $$$

Zihni Restaurant
Muallim Naci Cad. 119
Kuruçeşme
Tel. 258 11 54
Reservations on weekends
7.30 p.m. -2.00 a.m.
Restaurant/Bar along the
Bosphorus. International cuisine.
Live music.
Visa, Diners. $$$

Ziya
Muallim Naci Cad. 109/1
Ortaköy
Tel. 261 60 05
Reservations necessary

7.00 p.m.-12.00 p.m. (restaurant)
2.00 p.m. -3.00 a.m. (bar)
Bar/restaurant with a good
ambiance along the Bosphorus.
Bar serves snacks. The restaurant serves good international
food. Keeps its tradition of
high standard.
All major cards. $$$

Ziya Restaurant
(Nişantaş Ziya)
Mim Kemal Öke Cad. 21/1
Nişantaş
Tel. 225 46 65/62
Reservations necessary
12.00 a.m. -12.00 p.m.
Closed Sundays and between
June 15 - Sept., 15.
Popular restaurant/bar.
International and Turkish cusine.
Features good fish dishes.
The bar has live music and
snacks.
Live music (pop, classic, jazz)
Ziya Restaurant is not related
to Ziya in Ortaköy.
All major cards. $$

CAFES

In the Turkish tradition tea-time has its importance and women especially enjoy tea-time gathering as well as baking. Now Istanbul abounds in cafe houses, mostly in a pleasant settings. Turkish cakes are lighter than the European and American ones and they are very tasty. Ice cream is magnificent. All sorts of coffees, cappucino, expresso, instant and filter coffees and of course Turkish coffee, a wide range of Turkish tea blends are available. Pastry and savory dishes are most delicious. What more do you need to enjoy tea time?

Abdülcabbar
Mis Sok. 11, Beyoğlu
Tel. 243 63 95
8.30 a.m. - 2.00 a.m.
Cafe and Bar. Serves good crepes , coffee and drinks.
Live music (classical and pop)
No cards.

Boulevard Cafe
Mövenpick Hotel, Maslak
Tel. 285 09 00
l0.00 a.m.-11.00 p.m.
Delicious cakes and ice cream.
Tape music
All major cards.

Cafe Caliente
Vapur İskelesi Sok. No.3, Ortaköy
Tel. 260 96 08
12.00 a.m. -2.30 p.m.
6:00 p.m.- 11:30 p.m.
Reservations suggested
Mexican cuisine
Visa, Master Card.

Cafe Çan Çan
Hüsrev Gerede Cad. 87
Narmanlı Apt.,Teşvikiye
Tel. 261 16 16
11.00 a.m. -6.30 p.m.
Çan Çan means chatting. A pleasant place to chat with friends. Light food.
Visa.

Cafe Da Lino
Hamam Sok. 16/1, Bebek
Tel. 265 25 86
8.00 a.m. -9.30 p.m.
Snacks and cakes, smart place.
No cards.

Cafe de Paris
Mim Kemal Öke Cad. 19, Nişantaş
Tel. 225 07 00
12.00 a.m.-3.00p.m.
6.30 p.m.-1.00 a.m.
Closed Sunday lunch
Reservations necessary
Fixed menu (steak, French fries, salad)
French music (tape)
Visa, Amex. $$-$$$

Cafe de Pera
Meşrutiyet Cad. 98-100
Pera Palas Oteli,Tepebaşı
Tel. 251 45 60,
9.00 a.m.-11.00 p.m.
Reservations necessary
Breakfast and light food.
Piano music
All major cards.

Cafe de Pera
İnşirah Yokuşu
Bebek Çıkmazı Sok., 1 Bebek
Tel. 257 10 53
9.30 a.m. -2.00 a.m.
Reservations for weekends
A nice old wooden house, antique decor, elegant tea service. Branch of the Pera Palace Hotel cafe.
Fridays and Saturdays live guitar and piano music.
All major cards.

Cafe Dedikodu
Halâskârgazi Cad. 252/4
Osmanbey
Tel. 225 65 64 - 230 06 45
11.00 a.m.-11.00 p.m.

The name means 'gossip'. Regular clientele exchange gossip on who knows who in town. Tasty light meals, cakes and pleasant atmosphere. No cards.

Cafe Gramafon
Beyoğlu - Tünel
Tel. 293 07 86
9.00 a.m.-1.00 a.m.
At Tünel Square overlooking the nostalgic Istanbul. Coffee, cakes, snacks.
Visa, Mastercard.

Cafe In
Abdi İpekçi Cad.17
Yorulmaz Apt.
Nişantaş 1
Tel. 241 09 36 - 2248990
10.00 a.m. -10.00 p.m.
Closed Sundays
Features delicious sandwiches.
No cards.

Cafe Keyif
Mim Kemal Öke Cad. Nişantaş
Tel. 225 20 19
8:30 a.m.-10.00 p.m.
Closed Sundays
Popular cafe with light meals.
Jazz and pop (CD)
No Cards

Cafe Lebon
İstiklâl Cad.463, Beyoğlu
Tel. 252 98 52
9.00 a.m.-12.00 p.m.
Lebon was Istanbul's one of the most popular coffee houses when Beyoğlu had its charm 30 years ago. Richmond Hotel revived the old Cafe Lebon. Light food and pastry.
Visa.

Cafe Marmara
The Marmara Istanbul Hotel
Taksim
Tel. 251 46 96
8.00 a.m.-2.00 a.m.
Offers French breakfast, light meals, cakes and pastries.
All major cards.

Cafe Opera
Rumeli Cad. 1/4,Nişantaş
Tel. 224 89 90
8.00 a.m.-9.00 p.m.
For coffee breaks, snacks, cakes and ice cream.
All major cards except Diners Club.

Cafe Palazzo
Maçka Cad.35/4,Teşvikiye
Tel. 232 04 51
11.00 a.m. -9.00 p.m.
A popular place with good light meals.
Tape music (jazz,classic,rock)
No cards.

Cafe Park
Vali Konağı Cad.8, Nişantaş
Tel. 224 96 66
12.00 a.m.-22.00 p.m.
Reservations suggested
Antique decor
Tape music
Visa, Eurocard.

Cafe Saray
Çırağan Palace Hotel
Kempinski, Beşiktaş
Tel. 258 33 77
10.30 a.m.-12.00 p.m.
Hotel's coffee house with excellent Bosphorus view and spacious terrace for summer.
All major cards.

Cafe Verde
Rumeli Cad. 17/1
Nişantaş
Second Floor
Tel. 247 53 10 - 246 08 22
10.00 a.m.-8.00 p.m.
Closed Sundays
Popular place with good cakes and sandwiches.Offers a nice break after shopping.
Visa.

Cafe Vienna
Sheraton Hotel, Taksim Square
Tel. 231 21 21
7.00 a.m.-11.30 p.m.
In the hotel lobby.
All major cards.

Cafe Wien
Atiye Sok.5, Teşvikiye
Tel. 233 78 60 - 247 61 72
10.00 a.m.-9.00 p.m.
Excellent setting featuring
Austrian specialties at their best
especially Schnitzel. Pioneered
cafe concept in Istanbul.Visa,
Eurocard, Mastercard.

Çadır Köşk
Yıldız Park, Beşiktaş
Tel. 260 04 54 - 260 07 09
9.00 a.m.-6.00 p.m.
Restored Ottoman buildings in
the Yıldız Park. Serves breakfast, light luncheons, tea, coffee
and cakes in a soothing atmosphere of the park.
Classical tape music
Visa,Amex , Diners.

Çamlıca Cafe
Sefa Tepesi
Tel (0216) 329 81 91
9.00 a.m. -12.00 p.m.
A Touring and Automobile
Association facilities estab-
lished atop Çamlıca, the hill on
the Asian side where one can
have a bird's eye view of the
Bosphorus on clear days.
Ottoman decor. Typical Turk-
ish music and food. Popular
over the weekends for lunch.
Visa, Mastercard, Eurocard.

Gazebo
Çırağan Palace Hotel
Kempinski, Beşiktaş
Tel. 258 33 77
8.00 a.m. -11.30 p.m.
3.00 p.m. -6.00 p.m. teatime
Çırağan's coffee house in the
lobby. Tea, coffee, sandwiches
and drinks.
Live piano music (3.00 p.m. -
6.00 p.m. except Mondays)
All major cards.

Genoa
Bağ Sok. Gülistan Apt. 13/1,
Etiler
Tel. 265 92 70 - 265 57 50
(See restaurants page 125)

Kafe Kaktüs Cafe/Bar
İmam Adnan Sok.4, Beyoğlu
Tel. 249 59 79
9.30 a.m. -2.00 p.m.
Nice atmosphere. Attended most-
ly by intellectuals and artists.
No cards.

Köy Cafe
Holiday Inn Crown Plaza
Ataköy
Tel. 560 81 00
8.00 a.m.-11.00 p.m.
Snacks, delicious cakes and cof-
fee.
All major cards.

Malta Pavilion and Sarı Köşk
Yıldız Park, Beşiktaş
Tel. 260 04 54 - 260 07 09
9.00 a.m.-6.00 p.m.
Restored Ottoman buildings in
the Yıldız Park. Serves breakfast, light luncheons, tea and
coffee, cakes in a soothing
atmosphere of greenery.
Classical tape music
Visa, Mastercard.

Matchka Cafe
Maçka Cad. 35, Teşvikiye
Tel. 240 51 95
12.00 a.m.-4.00 a.m.
Closed Sundays
Reservations for weekends
Snack/bar, restaurant, night club
Live music in the evenings
All major cards.

Myott Cafe
Iskele Sok.14, Ortaköy
Tel. 258 93 17
7.30 a.m.-4.00 p.m.
Closed Mondays
Italian coffee, salad, Muesli,
best cappucino in town.
No cards.

Opera Sanat Galerisi
Hariciye Konağı Sok.
Sağlık Apt.1, Taksim
Tel. 249 92 02
11.00 a.m. -6.30 p.m.
Closed Sundays
An art gallery with a small cafe.

Patiserrie Divan
Divan Hotel, Elmadağ
Tel. 231 41 00
8.30 a.m.-8.00 p.m.
First of its kind in Istanbul, features excellent cakes and pastry and has several branches all over the city. There, you can watch the world go by.
All major cards.

Patisserie Gezi
İnönü Cad., 5/1,Taksim
Tel. 251 74 30
7.30 a.m. -9.30 p.m.
Delicious cakes and coffee.
All major cards..

Romantica
Fenerbahçe Park, Kalamış
Tel. (0216) 336 38 28
9.00 a.m. -6.30 p.m. (on weekends 9.00 a.m. -11.00 p.m.)
In the middle of a beutiful park by the seaside.
It serves only coffee, tea, pastries and drinks.
3.00 p.m. -6.00 p.m. on Fridays, Saturdays, Sundays
Visa, Mastercard, Euro card.

Taş Cafe/Bar
Köybaşı Cad. 88
Yeniköy
Tel. 262 21 06
2.00 p.m. -2.00 a.m.
Closed Tuesdays
Coffee and homemade cakes and their specialties "*Taş Kebab*".
Live music except Sundays and Mondays.
No cards.

Vakko
İstiklâl Cad. 123
Beyoğlu
Tel. 251 40 92
10.00 a.m.-7.00 p.m.
Inside the fashion store of Vakko serving light meals and coffee with nice decoration and pleasant atmoshpere.
All major cards.

Vakkorama
Osmanlı Sok. 13
Taksim
Tel. 251 15 71
9.30 a.m.-7.00 p.m.
Serves healthy salads.
All major cards.

Fast Food

TURKISH FAST FOOD

Most of the internationally known fast food companies operate in Istanbul as indicated below. They are the same as elsewhere. However, the Turkish fast food chain which started a few years ago, can be of more interest to foreigners. It has been established by Borsa Restau-rant which has a century-old experience of excellent Turkish cuisine tradition behind the operation.

Borsa Fast Food
It has two places near Tak-sim square:
Borsa Fast Food in Beyoğlu, Istiklal Cad. Tel. 245 14 70
Borsa Fast Food inTaksim Square, Gezi Dükkanları,
Tel.245 43 43

INTERNATIONAL FAST FOOD

Dairy Queen
Büyükdere Cad., 15/A, Şişli

Kentucky Fried Chicken Galleria, Ataköy and Levent

McDonald's
Nişantaş, Taksim, Şişli, Fenerbahçe, Şaşkınbakkal, Kadıköy, Karaköy,Bayezıt

Pizza Hut, Etiler,Taksim, Şişli (NovaBaran), Caddebostan, Bahariye Cad., Moda, Ataköy

Wimpy
Istiklal Cad. 249, Beyoğlu

Pizzamatik, Lamartin Cad. 11/2, Taksim

BARS

Turks do have a bar tradition. According to some sources *Meyhane* (pub, bistro, tavern) existed since the days of Fatih Sultan Mehmet the Conqueror. Most probably, an institution inherited from the Byzantines. There were several types of *meyhanes* according to the standards of the clientele. And one type was called "*Koltuk meyhanesi*" where people were standing and leaning on the bar while drinking and chatting with friends before going home. Each meyhane was generally named after its owner. They served only *rakı* and wine always accompanied by *meze* served in mini plates. Although Meyhanes were declared outlaw on and off, they kept on reopening and establishing the new ones. Acccrding to the records, after the reign of Murat IV, Istanbul had about 1000 meyhanes and about 300 illegal ones. Now some of the bars try to recreate the meyhane atmosphere.

Always
Yeni Sülün Sok., Levent
Tel. 280 73 97
6.00 p.m.-2.00 a.m.
Closed Sundays
A popular bar, good music.
Visa.

Anahtar
Divan's Bar/Patiserrie
Kuruçeşme Cad. 36, Kuruçeşme
Tel. 257 71 50
Patisserie:2.00 p.m.-6.00 p.m.
Bar:6.00 p.m.-2.00 a.m.
Pleasant atmosphere.
All major cards.

Andro Bar
Elmadağ Cad., 4Taksim
Tel. 232 54 66
10.00 p.m.-04.00 a.m. (open Mondays, Wednesdays, Fridays, Saturdays)
Disco music.
No cards.

Arena
Nisbetiye Cad. 6, Etiler
Tel. 270 01 08 - 268 64 26
11.30 p.m.-04.00 a.m.
Reservations necessary
Closed Sundays
Live Turkis pop music and disco.
All major cards

Pub Avni
Cumhuriyet Cad. 239
Harbiye
Tel. 246 16 11
12.00 a.m.-02.00 a.m.
Closed Sundays
Has regular customers. Snacks for lunch and supper.
Visa card.

8 1/2 Otto e Mezzo
Halâskâgazi Cad. 53/1,Harbiye
Tel. 241 61 54
11.00 a.m.-2.00 a.m.
Bar and restaurant featuring pasta dishes.
Pop music.
No cards.

Babıâli Wine Bar
Hotel Merit Antique Istanbul, Laleli
Tel. 513 93 00
12.00 a.m.-2.00 a.m.
5.00 p.m.-7.00 p.m.Happy hours.
Soft live music
All cards except Diners Club.

Bade Bar
Çınar Hotel
Yeşilköy
Tel. 663 29 00
4.00 p.m.-12.30 a.m.
With the view of the Sea of Marmara.
Live music
All major cards.

Bebek Bar
Cevdet Paşa Cad.15, Bebek
Tel. 263 30 00
12.00 a.m.-1.00 p.m.
Reservations recommended
Along the Bosphorus. Terrace
bar in summer. It's famous for
its refined and steady clientele.
Live music between 11.00 p.m.-
1.00 a.m.
All credit cards.

Beyoğlu Pub
İstiklâl Cad. 140/17, Beyoğlu
Tel. 252 38 42
12.00 a.m.-2.00 a.m.
Restaurant/Bar
(See Restaurants page 120)
Live music
All major cards.

Bilsak
Sıraselviler Cad.,Soğancı Sok.7
Cihangir
Tel. 243 28 99
12.00 a.m.-2.00 a.m.
Restaurant/Bar page. 121)

Cine Bar
Yeşilpınar Sok. 2, Arnavutköy
Tel. 257 74 38
5.30 p.m.-3.00 a.m.
Reservations recommended
Restaurant/Bar
Live music (Turkish)
Visa, Mastercard.

Cool Bar
I.Cadde 104
Arnavutköy
Tel. 257 37 07
9.00 p.m. -4.00 a.m.
A dancing bar.
Live music on Wednesdays,
Fridays, Saturdays.
No cards.

Çiçek Bar (Arif'in yeri)
Billurcu Sok. 25
Beyoğlu
Tel. 244 26 19
6.00 p.m.-2.00 a.m.
Closed Sundays.
A popular meeting place of
artists and journalists.
Visa & Prestige Card.

Dadaist
İstiklâl cad.,
Beyoğlu
Tel. 252 60 88
6.00 p.m. - 4.00 a.m.
Owner Bedri Baykam, famous
Turkish painter. Usually
attended by artists.
Rock music.
Master card & Visa.

Doruk
Holiday Inn Crown Plaza
Ataköy
Tel. 560 81 00
12.00 a.m.-2.00 p.m.
Restaurant/Bar
(See Restaurants 123)
All major cards..

Ece Bar
Tramvay Cad. 104, Kuruçeşme
Tel. 265 79 49
6.00 p.m.-2.00 a.m.
Restaurant/Bar
(See Restaurants 123)
Visa Card.

English Pub
President Hotel- Tiyatro Cad.
25, Bayezıt
Tel. 516 69 80
Happy hour: Monday-Thurs-
day 5.00.m.p -7.00 p.m.
A bar with a nice atmosphere.
All major cards.

Fly Inn
Nisbetiye Cad. 10
Etiler
Tel. 257 62 86
6.00 p.m.-3.00 a.m.
Interesting decor. Very popu-
lar for weekends.
Rock music.
All major cards.

Fondip
Cevdet Paşa Cad. 386, Bebek
Tel. 263 2280
7.00 p.m.-3.00 a.m.
No cards.

Gurme
Birinci Cad. No.138/A
Arnavutköy-İstanbul

Tel. 263 25 25
5.00 p.m.- 4.00 a.m.
Reservations necessary
All international cocktails and
snack bar.
Pop, live music
All major cards.

Hayal Kahvesi
Parmakkapı Sok 19, Beyoğlu
Tel. 244 25 58
11.00 a.m.-4.00 a.m.
Reservations suggested
Cozy place for drinks, light
meals and nice music.
Live music between 11.00 p.m-
2.00 a.m.
No cards.

Kadeh Bar
Nisbetiye Cad. No.24, Levent
Tel.268 66 60
9.00 p.m.-4.30 a.m.
Reservations necessary
Restaurant/bar. Performance
of most popular pop singers.
Live music
All credit cards.

Kalem Bar
Otobüs Durağı arkası, Bebek
Tel. 265 04 48
12.00 a.m.-2.00 a.m.
A popular small bar.
Live piano music
All major cards except Amex,
Diners.

Koala Cafe/Bar
1. Cadde, Arnavutköy
Tel. 263 66 27
2.00 p.m.-2.00 a.m.
Reservations necessary
Lunch available and Sunday
Breakfast.
Live music (except Sundays,
Mondays,Tuesdays)
Visa, Mastercard.

Living Room
Emirgan Cad.18, Emirgan
Tel. 229 28 37
7.00 p.m.-4.00 a.m.
Overlooking the Bosphorus.
Live music
No cards.

Lounge Bar
Conrad Hotel, Beşiktaş
Tel. 227 30 00
10.30 a.m.-2.00 a.m.
Live jazz music
All major cards.

Merhaba Bar
The Marmara Istanbul Hotel
Taksim Square
Tel. 251 46 96
Lobby Bar of the hotel.
Live music (3.30 p.m.-8.00
p.m.) except Mondays.
All major cards.

North Shields
Marina-Ataköy
Tel. 559 20 18
2.00 p.m.-1.00 a.m.
Typical English Pub.
All major cards..

Orient Bar
Pera Palas Hotel,Tepebaşı
Tel. 251 45 60
10.30 a.m.-2.00 a.m.
Early 19 century atmosphere.
Nostalgic.
All major cards.

Papirus
İstiklâl Cad. Ayhan Işık Sok.
5/A, Beyoğlu
(See Restaurants page 132)

Sherlock Holmes British Pub
Çalıkuşu Sok. 5, Levent
Tel. 281 63 72
6.00 p.m.-2.30 a.m.
Closed Sundays
A very authentic British Pub.
Turkish and English bar staff.
Popular with foreigners.
Happy hour 6.00 p.m.-8.00 p.m.
All cards except Amex,Diners.

Sis Bar
Vapur İskelesi Sok. 4/6
Ortaköy
Tel. 259 48 58
12.00 a.m. -2.00 a.m.
Features crepes, coffee etc.
11.00 p.m. - 2.00 a.m.
Live rock music
No cards.

Süleyman Nazif Bar
Vali Konağı Cad. 3
Nişantaş
Tel. 225 22 43/44
6.00 p.m.-1.30 a.m.
Closed Sundays.
Ottoman architecture. Cozy
and comfortable.
Jazz-Pop music
Visa, Master Card, Eurocard.

Susam
Susam Sok. 6
Cihangir
Tel. 251 59 35
Restaurant /Bar
(See Restaurants page 135)

Şaziye Bar
Abdi İpekçi Cad. 24/26
Maçka
Tel. 232 41 55 - 231 14 01
7.00 p.m.-12.00p.m. bar (then a
disco)
Reservations necessary
Very popular bar.
Billiards, backgammon and
video games.
Disco music Sundays and
Mondays 11.00 p.m.-1.00 a.m.
Live music/singer
All major cards except Amex.

Taksim Sanat Evi
Sıraselviler Cad. 65/1
Taksim
Tel. 244 25 26
6.00 p.m.-4.00 a.m.
Reservations recommended
Restaurant /Bar
Live music except Sundays,
Mondays and Wednesdays
All major cards.

Zihni Bar
Bronz Sok., Nişantaş
Tel. 233 90 43
6.00 p.m. - 10.00 p.m.
A very popular bar in town,
keeps its high standard.
Visa, Diners

Ziya Nişantaş
Mim Kemal Öke Cad. 21/1
Nişantaş
Tel. 225 46 62 - 225 46 65
Restaurant/Bar.Has no branch.
(See restaurants page 13)

Ziya (Ortaköy)
Muallim Naci Cad. 119
Kuruçeşme
Tel. 261 60 05
Restaurant/Bar.
(See restaurants page 138)

NIGHT CLUBS

Galata Tower Night Club
Şişhane
Tel. 245 11 60
Belly dancer
Open every night

Kervansaray
Elmadağ
(at the arcade entrance of the
Istanbul Hilton)
Tel. 247 16 30 - 31 246 08 18
Belly dancer, floor show and
folk dancing. Favorite night
club with groups.
Open every night

DISCOS

Andromeda Disco (Summer)
Gümüşyolu Cad., Nakkaştepe
Tel. (0216) 310 53 95
On Wednesdays, Fridays, Saturdays only

Andromoda Disco (Winter)
Elmadağ
Tel. 246 01 68
On Wednesdays, Fridays, Saturdays

Club 29 (Summer)
Paşabahçe Yolu 24/3, Çubuklu
Tel. (0216) 322 28 29
Open every night

Dolphin
Hotel Demirköy, II.Kısım, Ataköy
Tel. 560 98 13
On Fridays, Saturdays, Friday
matinée

Exit
Nisbetiye Cad., 24, Levent
Tel. 268 66 60
Open every night

Garaj (Winter)
Taksim
Tel. 262 00 32 - 262 04 74
Wednesdays, Fridays and
Saturdays only

Memo's Disco
Salhane Sok.10/2, Ortaköy
Tel. 261 83 04
Open every night

Pasha (Summer)
Muallim Naci Cad., Ortaköy
Tel. 227 17 11
Open every night
On Sundays no disco only
movie show and bar

Selamlık Disco (Winter)
Reşat Paşa Konağı, Erenköy
Tel. (0216) 361 34 11
Only Fridays and Saturdays

Şaziye (Winter)
Eytam Cad., 21, Maçka
Tel. 232 41 55 - 231 14 01
Open every night

MOVIE THEATERS

Istanbul abounds in movie theaters, and the latest international movies come to Istanbul very quickly. Tickets can be purchased ahead of time especially for the popular films. They usually cost around $3 - $6. Our listing provides selected movie theaters on the European side of Istanbul. Some of them are within walking distance from the Hilton hotels.

Akmerkez 1 & 2 & 3
Akmerkez, Etiler,
Tel. 282 05 05

As 1 & 2
Cumhuriyet Cad.,
Cebeltopu Sok. 7, Harbiye
Tel. 247 63 15

Atlas
İstiklâl Cad., 209
Kuyumcular Pasajı
Beyoğlu
Tel. 243 75 76

Beyoğlu
İstiklâl Cad.,
Halep Pasajı 140, Beyoğlu
Tel. 251 32 40

Dünya
İstiklal Cad.,
Fitaş Pasajı 24-26, Beyoğlu
Tel. 252 01 62

Emek
İstiklâl Cad.,
Yeşilçam Sok. 5, Beyoğlu
Tel. 293 84 39

Fitaş
İstiklâl Cad.,
Fitaş Pasajı 24-26
Beyoğlu
Tel. 249 01 66

Fitaş Cep
İstiklâl Cad.,
Fitaş Pasajı 24-26
Beyoğlu
Tel. 249 01 66

Gazi
Halâskârgazi Cad., 214
Osmanbey
Tel. 247 96 65

Kent 1 & 2
Halâskârgazi Cad., 281
Şişli
Tel. 241 62 03

Lale 1 & 2
İstiklâl Cad., 85
Beyoğlu
Tel. 249 25 24

Mövenpick 1 & 2
Mövenpick Hotel
Maslak
Tel. 285 06 95

Nova Baran
Nova Baran Plaza
Şişli
Tel. 240 35 58

Parliament Cinema Club
Hillside Club, Alkent
Etiler
Tel. 263 18 38

Ortaköy Kültür Merkezi
Dereboyu Sok.,
Barbaros Pasajı 110
Ortaköy
Tel. 258 69 87

Site
Halâskârgazi Cad., 291
Şişli
Tel. 247 69 47

Sinepop
İstiklâl Cad.,
Yeşilçam Sok., 22
Beyoğlu
Tel. 251 11 76

CULTURAL

EVENTS

OPERA, BALLET, SYMPHONY

The State Opera, Ballet, Orchestra and Theater perform at the Atatürk Cultural Center (AKM) in Taksim. The AKM box office (Tel. 251 5600) issues monthly programs.

Interestingly enough, most Turkish artists have reached international standards and some even international renown. Foreign visitors enjoy philharmonic concerts, chamber music, opera, ballet and musicals. Turkish, like Italian, goes very well with the opera. The Western musicals also have been staged with great success. As theater is in Turkish, it may not be easy for you to follow unless it is a play you have seen before.

CONCERT HALLS

Atatürk Kültür Merkezi (AKM)
Taksim
Tel. 251 56 00

Cemal Reşit Rey Konser Salonu
Harbiye
(next door to the Istanbul Hilton)
Tel. 248 53 92

ART FESTIVALS

International Film Days sponsored by the Istanbul Foundation of Culture and Arts takes place annually in April.
The annual Istanbul International Art Festival (June 15 - July 31). The Festival is part

of the prestigious Confederation of International Music Festivals of Geneva. For more information:

İstanbul Kültür ve Sanat Vakfı (Istanbul Foundation for Culture and Arts) at Yıldız Sanat ve Kültür Merkezi, Yıldız, Beşiktaş.
Phone: 260 90 72 - 258 74 9 7 - 8.

FOREIGN CULTURAL OFFICES

Their activities generally cover lending libraries, language classes and sponsorship of exhibits, lectures, concerts and films.

Austrian Cultural Office
Silahhane Cad., 101/12
Teşvikiye
Tel. 236 15 81

British Council
Cumhuriyet Cad., 22-24
Ege Han, Elmadağ
Tel. 252 74 74

Casa d'Italia
Meşrutiyet Cad., 161
Tepebaşı
Tel. 293 98 48 - 251 04 87

French Cultural Center
Istiklal Cad., 2,Taksim
Tel. 249 07 76

German Cultural Center
Odakule
Galatasaray
Tel. 249 20 09

Spanish Cultural Center
Tomtom Kaptan Sok., 37
Beyoğlu
Tel. 225 21 53

U.S.I.S (United States Information Service)
Meşrutiyet Cad., 108
Tepebaşı
Tel. 251 36 02

TRAVEL

TOURIST INFORMATION

The Ministry of Tourism Offices provide information on sights and hotels, and free hand out brochures, maps and booklets.

Atatürk International Airport
Tel. 663 63 63

Istanbul Hilton Arcade
Elmadağ
Tel. 233 05 92

Karaköy Sea Port
Yolcu Salonu, Karaköy
Tel. 249 57 76

The Turkish Touring and Automobile Club
Büyükdere Caddesi
Şişli Meydanı
Şişli
Tel. 231 46 31
Issues international traffic licences, provides car rescue service and has several books about Istanbul on sale. They have their own food and beverage outlets as indicated in this guide.

TRAINS

Traveling by train in Turkey is not the best way. The most comfortable train trip is to Ankara by night sleeper. Tickets should be purchased on reserved seat basis in advance.

Haydarpaşa Train Station (for Anatolian bound trains) Information phone: (0216) 336 20 63 - 336 04 75

Sirkeci Train Station (for European bound trains) Information phones: 527 00 50 - 527 00 51.

BOATS

Boats going up the Bosphorus, to Kadıköy and Üsküdar, and to places in the Sea of Marmara dock near the entrance to the Golden Horn. Those sailing to ports in the Black Sea as well as those going to Europe leave from Karaköy. The boats to the islands of Marmara and Avşa leave from the Sirkeci quay, while those to İzmir dock below Gülhane Park. There are also hydrofoils to Avşa and Marmara that leave from Yenikapı. See also page 17: " İstanbul Deniz Otobüsleri ".

Car ferries to Izmir and return are very pleasant. One does not need to have a car on the boat. The ferries leave on Fridays at 3:00 p.m. and return Mondays leaving Izmir at 2:00 p.m. giving enough time for passengers to discover Izmir and its environs including Ephesus and Virgin Mary's last home.

Turkish Maritime Lines
Information telephones:
244 4233 (for domestic lines),
249 9222 (for cruises to Europe)

Karaköy Yolcu Salonu
(embarkation point of cruises)
Tel. 244 1001

USEFUL TURKISH AIRLINES
TELEPHONE NUMBERS
Airport Tel. 663 64 00
Reservations: Tel. 663 63 63
Airport (Domestic and international lines): Tel.663 64 00
Cargo reservation:
Tel. 663 46 00
THY General Directorate:
Tel.663 63 00
Taksim office (open from 7.00 a.m. to 8.30 p.m.)
Tel. 252 11 06

INTER-CITY BUSES

The bus network is great in Turkey. You can go anywhere you like by bus and and be comfortable. Fellow passengers and the crew are hospitable and helpful to foreigners. The leading bus companies use the most modern buses generally imported from Ger-many including the double deckers where one has a chance to have a non-smoking level.

The buses have toilet facilities, air conditioning as well as beverage services and snacks.

Travelling by the following bus companies is as comfortable as airplanes. They all have hostesses or stewards.

The following three companies have services to various European destinations as well.

Pamukkale Turizm
Taksim
Tel. 249 27 91
Destinations: Western and Southern Turkey

Ulusoy Seyahat
Merter
Tel. 582 36 36
Destinations: Western and Southern Turkey, Black Sea coast and Ankara.

Non-stop executive service between Ankara and Istanbul are very popular.
Duration: 5 hours.

Varan Turizm
Taksim
Tel. 251 74 81
Destinations: Southern and Western Turkey and Ankara. Non-stop business line between Ankara and Istanbul.
Duration: 5 hours.

Car Rental

Avis
Airport Tel. 663 06 46
Istanbul Hilton Office: 248 7752

Airtour
Taksim Office: 232 84 86

Budget
Airport Tel. 663 08 58
Taksim Office: 253 96 53

Europcar
Airport Tel. 663 0746
Taksim Office: 254 7788

Hertz
Airport Tel. 663 08 07
Taksim Office: 248 71 01

Lets
Airport Tel. 573 45 02
Taksim Office: 255 24 31

TRAVEL

AIRLINES

Adria (Slavonian Airways)
Ordu Cad., 206/1
Laleli
Tel. 512 42 31

Aeroflot
Mete Cad., 30, Taksim
Tel. 243 47 25

Air China
Cumhuriyet Cad., 235/2
Taksim
Tel. 232 71 12

Air France
Taksim Square
Tel. 256 43 56

Alia (Jordanian Airlines)
Cumhuriyet Cad., 163/2
Tel. 230 40 74

Alitalia
Cumhuriyet Cad., 15/7
Elmadağ
Tel. 231 33 91

American Airlines
Cumhuriyet Cad., 47/2
Taksim
Tel. 237 20 03

Austrian Airlines
Sheraton Oteli, Taksim
Tel. 232 22 00

Azerbaijan Airlines
Cumhuriyet Cad., 39/1,Taksim
Tel. 237 42 01 - 02

British Airways
Cumhuriyet Cad., 10
Elmadağ
Tel. 234 13 00

Delta Airlines
Hilton Arcade
Elmadağ
Tel. 231 23 39

Egypt Air
Cumhuriyet Cad., 337
Harbiye
Tel. 231 11 26

EL AL (Israil Airlines)
Rumeli Cad., 1
Nişantaş İş Merkezi
Kat 4
Nişantaşı
Tel. 241 02 43

Emirates Airlines
Halâkârgazi Cad., 69
Harbiye
Tel. 232 32 16

Finnair
Hilton Arcade
Istanbul Hilton
Elmadağ
Tel. 234 51 30

Gulf Air
Cumhuriyet Cad., 213
Harbiye
Tel. 231 34 50

Iberia
Topçu Cad.,
Uygun Apt., 2/2
Taksim
Tel. 255 19 68

Iran Air
Vali Konağı Cad.,17
Harbiye
Tel. 225 02 55

JAL (Japanese Airlines)
Cumhuriyet Cad., 141/6
Elmadağ
Tel. 241 73 66

Kazakhstan Airlines
Recep Paşa Cad., 3/3
Taksim
Tel. 250 67 72

KLM
Abdi İpekçi Cad., 8
Nişantaşı
Tel. 230 03 11

KTHY (Northern Cyprus Turkish Airlines)
Büyükdere Cad., 56/B
Mecidiyeköy
Tel. 246 51 37

Kuwait Airlines
Cumhuriyet Cad., 30, Elmadağ
Tel. 240 40 81

Libyan Arab Airlines
Halâskârgazi Cad., 103
Harbiye
Tel. 232 49 76

LOT (Polish Airlines)
Cumhuriyet Cad., 91/2
Elmadağ
Tel. 241 57 49

Lufthansa
Büyükdere Cad.,
Maya/Akar İş Merkezi K. 3
Esentepe
Tel. 288 10 50

Malev (Hungarian Airlines)
Cumhuriyet Cad., 141/14, K.1
Elmadağ
Tel. 241 09 09

MAS (Malaysian Airlines)
Cumhuriyet Cad., 171/2
Elmadağ
Tel. 230 71 30

Middle East Airlines
Cumhuriyet Cad., 30, Harbiye
Tel. 248 22 41

Olympic Airways
Cumhuriyet Cad., 171/A
Elmadağ
Tel. 246 50 81

PIA (Pakistan Airlines)
Cumhuriyet Cad., Elmadağ
Tel. 233 05 71

Qantas (Australian Airlines)
Cumhuriyet Cad., 155/1
Elmadağ
Tel. 240 50 32

Sabena
Topçu Cad.,Uygun Apt., 2/1
Taksim
Tel. 254 72 54

SAS (Scandinavian Airlines)
Cumhuriyet Cad., 26/A
Elmadağ
Tel. 246 60 75

Saudi Arabian Airlines
Cumhuriyet Cad., 31/33
Taksim
Tel. 256 48 00

Singapore Airlines
Halâskârgazi Cad., 113
Harbiye
Tel. 232 37 06

Swissair
Cumhuriyet Cad., 44
Elmadağ
Tel. 231 28 50

Syrian Air
Sheraton Hotel, Taksim
Tel. 246 17 81

Tarom (Romanian Airlines)
Cumhuriyet Cad., 125
Elmadağ
Tel.230 73 09

Tunisair
Vali Konağı Cad.,
Bizim Apt. 8/1, Nişantaş
Tel. 241 70 96

TWA (Trans World Airlines)
Cumhuriyet Cad., 193
Elmadağ
Tel. 234 53 27

THY (Turkish Airlines)
Atatürk Havalimanı,
Yeşilköy
Tel. 663 63 00 (35 lines)
Taksim Tel. 252 11 06 (3 lines)

Uzbekistan Airlines
Cumhuriyet Cad.,39/4, Taksim
Tel. 237 19 93/94

TRAVEL AGENTS

Airtours
Gül Sok., 5, Levent
Tel. 232 35 00

Anadol Tourism
Cumhuriyet Cad., 261
Harbiye
Tel. 233 78 41

Arar Tours
Şehit Ahmet Sok., 4/3
Mecidiyeköy İşmerkezi
Mecidiyeköy
Tel. 274 29 22

Art Tours
Valikonağı Cad., Polat Apt. 77
Nişantaşı
Tel. 231 04 87

Bumerang Tourism
Rıhtım Cad.,
Veli Alemdar Han, K.8
Karaköy
Tel. 251 73 80

Bosfor Tourism
Mete Cad., 14/3, Taksim
Tel. 251 70 00

**Catoni Maritime Travel
Service**
Rıhtım Cad., ICI Han 231
Tophane
Tel. 251 50 60

Değer Tourism
Cumhuriyet Cad., 349/7
Harbiye
Tel. 232 41 00

Dorak Tours
Cumhuriyet Cad., 247/5
Harbiye
Tel. 248 33 34

Duru Turizm
Cumhuriyet Cad., 243
Harbiye
Tel. 231 90 00

Efes Tur
Yıldız Posta Cad., 38/2
Gayrettepe
Tel. 274 55 10

Elitur Tourism
Cumhuriyet Cad., 151/2
Elmadağ
Tel. 240 10 33

Entaş Tourism
Büyükdere Cad., 33
Şişli
Tel. 241 15 65

Esin Tour
Cumhuriyet Cad., 47/2
Taksim
Tel. 254 77 88

H.W.Feustel
Meclisi Mebusan Cad.
139/A
Fındıklı
Tel. 251 83 00 (11 lines)

Irem Tour Tourism
İnönü Cad., 44/6, Taksim
Tel. 293 28 45 (2 lines)

Kenantour
Hilton Hotel,
Harbiye
Tel. 230 87 14

Kongresist
Cumhuriyet Cad., 193
Harbiye
Tel. 246 22 49

Kültur Tourism
Cumhuriyet Cad., 243/4
Harbiye
Tel.247 18 93

Magister Tourism
Halâskârgazi Cad., 321/2, Şişli
Tel. 246 30 26

Marveltur Tourism
Sıracevizler Cad., 60/A
Şişli
Tel. 247 14 18

Miltur Milliyet Tourism
Cumhuriyet Cad., 193
Elmadağ
Tel. 246 04 20

Navas Tourism
Lamartin Cad., Cecile Apt., 51
Taksim
Tel. 250 84 70

Pamfilya Tourism
Yzb. Kaya Aldoğan Sok,. 7/1
Zincirlikuyu
Tel. 274 38 40

Pasha Tours
Taksim Cad., 97, Taksim
Tel. 235 01 45

Plan Tour
Cumhuriyet Cad., 131/1
Elmadağ
Tel. 230 22 72

Setur
Cumhuriyet Cad., 107
Harbiye
Tel. 230 03 36

Sultan Tourism
Cumhuriyet Cad., 87/1
Elmadağ
Tel. 233 60 98 (2 lines)

Tantur
Gazeteciler Sitesi
Yazarlar Sok., 17, Esentepe
Tel. 272 49 74

Tek-Ser Tourism
Cumhuriyet Cad., 211/1
Harbiye
Tel. 230 02 61

TGI Travel Agency
Cumhuriyet Cad., 155/1
Elmadağ
Tel. 240 50 32

Tura Tourism
Cumhuriyet Cad., 129
Elmadağ
Tel. 241 60 82

Türk Ekspres Tourism
Istanbul Hilton, Elmadağ
Tel. 231 46 46

VIP Tourism
Cumhuriyet Cad., 269/2
Harbiye
Tel. 241 65 14 (4 lines)

Vista Travel Agency
Cumhuriyet Cad., 233
Harbiye
Tel. 230 00 56

Visitur Travel Agency
Cumhuriyet Cad., 129/8
Elmadağ
Tel. 241 40 40

For further information:
**Association of Turkish Travel
Agencies (TURSAB)**
Tel. 275 06 98 (2 lines)

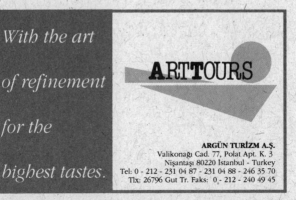

CONSULATES

Australia
Tepecik Yolu 58
Etiler
Tel.257 70 50

Austria
Köybaşı Cad., 46, Yeniköy
Tel. 262 49 84

Bangladesh
Ayşe Sultan Korusu
Bebek
Tel. 265 06 72

Belgium
Sıraselviler Cad., 73
Taksim
Tel. 243 33 00

Bulgaria
Adnan Saygun Cad., 44
Ulus Mah., Etiler
Tel. 269 22 16

Canada
Büyükdere Cad., 107/3
Gayrettepe
Tel. 272 51 74

Chile
Setüstü Derya Han
Kabataş
Tel.245 01 83

China
Ortaklar Cad., 14
Mecidiyeköy
Tel. 272 52 00

**Czech and Slovakian
Republics**
Abdi İpekçi Cad.,
Dramalaı Apt. 71
Maçka
Tel. 247 50 30

Denmark
Bilezik Sok., 2
Fındıklı
Tel. 245 03 85

Italy
Tomtom Kaptan Sok., 15
Beyoğlu
Tel. 243 10 24

Japan
İnönü Cad., 24
Gümüşsuyu
Tel. 251 76 06

Libya
Miralay Şefik Bey Sok., 3
Gümüşsuyu
Tel. 251 81 00

Malaysia
P.K. 108
Levent
Tel. 247 17 28

Malta
Vişnezade Cami Meydanı
Efe Apt., Kat 5 Daire 14
Beşiktaş
Tel. 227 60 81

Mexico (Honorary)
145 Emirhan Cad.,
Atakule, Ortaköy
Tel. 259 32 11

Monaco
Cevdetpaşa Cad., 164/17
Bebek
Tel. 263 39 89

Netherlands
İstiklâl Cad., 393
Beyoğlu
Tel.251 50 30

Norway
Rıhtım Cad.,
Frank Han 89/3
Tophane
Tel. 249 97 53

Pakistan
Abidei Hürriyet Cad.,
Hacıonbaşılar İşhanı
Şişli
Tel. 233 58 01

Poland
Büyük Çiftlik Sok., 5/7
Nişantaş
Tel. 232 03 61

Portugal
Okçu Musa Cad., 52/2
Bankalar Cad.,
Karaköy
Tel. 250 11 30

Romania
Sıraselviler Cad., 55,
Taksim
Tel. 244 35 55

Russian Federation
İstiklal Cad., 443,
Tünel
Tel. 244 26 10

Saudi Arabia
Akıncı Bayırı Sok., 8
Mecidiyeköy
Tel. 275 43 96

Spain
Vali Konağı Cad., 33
Başaran Apt.,
Harbiye
Tel. 225 21 53

Sweden
İstiklal Cad., 497
Beyoğlu
243 57 70

Switzerland
Hüsrev Gerede Cad., 75/3
Teşvikiye
Tel. 259 11 15

Thailand (Honorary)
Ferah Sok.,
Ege Binası
Teşvikiye
Tel. 231 15 85

Syria
Maçka Cad., 59/5,
Teşvikiye
Tel. 275 43 96

U.K.
Meşrutiyet Cad., 34
Tepebaşı
Tel. 293 75 40 - 252 64 36

U.S.A.
Meşrutiyet Cad., 104
Tepebaşı
Tel. 251 36 02

Yugoslavia
Vali Konağı Cad., 96/A
Nişantaş
Tel. 248 11 33

FOREIGN WOMEN'S ASSOCIATIONS
Please note that contact names
and telephone numbers will
most likely change because
new officers are elected each
May for the following year.

**International Women of
Istanbul**
Contact. Ms. Lynn Saka
Tel. (0216) 336 22 25
Ms.Elizabeth Mercer
Tel. 265 43 39

**American Women of
Istanbul**
Contact. Ms. Dorian Seagrave
Tel. 262 41 38

**Turkish American Women's
Coffee Group**
Contact. Ms. Gülsevin Biren
Tel. 246 05 41

MOSQUES
All the mosques are open to worship.

CHURCHES

Catholic Churches
St. Antoine
Istiklâl Cad., 325
Beyoğlu
Tel. 244 09 35

St. Esprit Cathedral
Cumhuriyet Cad., 205/B
Harbiye
Tel. 248 09 10

St. Louis de Francis
Postacılar Sok., 11
Beyoğlu
Tel. 244 10 75

Church of the Assumption
Cem Sok., 5
Moda
Tel. (0216) 336 03 22

Orthodox Churches
Aya Triada
Meşelik Sok., 11/1
Taksim
Tel. 244 13 58

**Greek Orthodox
Patriarchate**
Sadrazam Ali Paşa Cad.,
35/5
Fener
Tel. 527 03 23

Protestant Church
German Protestant Church
Emin Cami Sok., 40
Aynalıçeşme
Beyoğlu
Tel. 250 30 40

Anglican Church
St. Helena's Chapel
British Consulate grounds
Galatasaray
Tel. 244 42 28

Union Church of Istanbul
Postacılar Sok.,
Beyoğlu
Tel. 244 52 12

Armenian Churches
Armenian Patriarchate
Şarapnel Sok., 20
Kumkapı
Tel. 527 03 23

Üç Horan
Balık Pazarı
Beyoğlu
Tel. 244 13 82

SYNAGOGUES

Synagogues
Chief Rabbinate of Turkey
Yemenici Sok., 23
Tünel
Beyoğlu
Tel. 243 51 66 - 293 8794

Neve Shalom
Büyük Hendek Cad., 67
Beyoğlu
Tel. 244 15 76 - 293 62 23

Ashkenazy
Yüksek Kaldırım, 37
Karaköy
Tel. 244 29 75

USEFUL INFORMATIONS

Time
Time is GMT + 3 hours in winter

GMT + 2 hours in summer

Shopping hours
Monday - Saturday
9:00 a.m. - 7:00 p.m.

Voltage
220 V AC, 50 cycles

Weights and Measures
Metric system of weights and measures.
One meter (100 cm) is equal to about 39.7 inches.
One kilogram equals 2.2 pounds.

Currency
Turkish Lira (TL) decimal.
Coins: 500, 1000, 2500, 5000 TL
Notes: 10,000, 20,000, 50,000 , 100,000, 250,000, 500,000 TL.

Currency Regulations
Foreign currency import and export is unrestricted if declared.

KDV (Vat)
Value Added Tax is included in the prices and is registered on the bills.
Make sure you get your receipt.

Tipping
It is customary to tip around 10 percent of the bill in the restaurants, bars and cafes. Taxi drivers do not expect to be tipped.
Hairdressers do.

COMMUNICATIONS

Major PTT Offices
Galatasaray PTT
Beyoğlu PTT
Taksim PTT
Şişli PTT
Sirkeci PTT is open 24 hours for all postal services provided by Turkish PTT.
Yeşilköy PTT is open seven days a week for all services offered by Turkish PTT.
Contact your PTT office in the hotel for more information.

Special PTT Services
APS (Express Mail Service)
Every post office accepts express mail until 5:00 p.m. during week days for domestic and international destinations.

ALO Post
Call telephone number 169. If you telephone up to noon for courier service, delivery to destinations within Istanbul is in the afternoon. Don't call in the afternoon.

Express Mail and Parcel Services
DHL
(for international deliveries)
Tel. 275 08 00 (10 lines)
Yurtiçi Kargo
(for domestic deliveries)
Tel. 231 65 06 - 231 00 29

Telephones

Telephone Tips
To dial a direct Long Distance call from Istanbul within Turkey dial (0) then the area code plus the number you are calling. For international calls dial first (00) then the country code, the area code and the number you are calling.

Istanbul codes

Istanbul has two area codes: European side (0) 212 and Asian side (0) 216. Even while dialling from Istanbul you use the area code. You need to dial (0) 216 if you are dialing a number on the Asian side from the European side. As we assume most of our readers are living on the European side, we only included (0) 216 in the phone numbers when necessary.

Codes for some major cities

Adana	322
Ankara	312
Antalya	242
Bursa	224
Diyarbakır	412
Gaziantep	342
İçel	324
İzmir	232
Muğla	252
Samsun	362
Trabzon	462
Bodrum	252 (313) or (316)
Kemer	242 (814)
Marmaris	252 (412) or (413)

PRESS, RADIO AND TV
FOR FOREIGNERS

Press. The only English language daily is "Turkish Daily News".

All the leading foreign newspapers and magazines are available in the international bookstores and the hotel's bookstores.

Radio. Turkey has state radio stations as well as an innumerable private radio stations, mostly on FM airing Western music. Among them are Radio Blue (98.0), Classic FM (94.5), Power FM (100.0), Best FM (98.4) and Number One (102.5), TRT 3, FM(88.2) might interest foreigners with classical, popular hit, jazz, rock and Latin American music.

News Broadcast in Foreign Languages on television

TRT 3 FM - English, French and German news broadcasts are aired after the Turkish news at 9:05 a.m., 12:05 a.m., 2:05 p.m., 5:05 p.m., 7:05 p.m.,10:05 p.m.

TV 2 broadcasts news in English and German around 10:30 p.m. after the Turkish news broadcast.

In Antalya Lara Tourism Radio broadcasts news in English, French and German at 8:30 a.m., 10:30 a.m., 12:30 p.m., 6:30 p.m., 9:30 p.m.

Television. Turkey has 10 TV channels, private and state run, plus all the major international TV channels that can be obtained through satellites.

SPORTS

The Istanbul Hilton offers the most extensive sports facilities compared to other hotels in town: tennis, swimming, squash, sauna, and fitness center.

Istanbul has some sports clubs running on a membership basis in the fields of water sports, tennis, riding, carting, hunting, shooting, flying, gliding and golfing.

Istanbul Golf Club

(Büyükdere Caddesi, Harp Akademileri, Ayazağa, Tel. 264 07 42accepts non-members on a daily basis except Saturdays and Sundays. All the necessary equipment can be rented including shoes for less than $50. For reservations please telephone Mr. Necdet Karacaoğlan.

Kemer Golf & Country Club
Kemerburgaz
Tel. 239 19 13
It is only half an hour away from Istanbul. The nine-hole course maintains highest international standards. Experienced non-member golfers can play every day except Mondays.

Alkent Hillside Club
Alkent, Etiler
Tel. 257 71 15
Offers fitness and sports facilities including racquetball. Non-members can utilize facilities against a daily fee.

Vakkorama Gym
Osmanlı Sokak
Taksim
Tel. 251 15 71
Offers step and gym classes.

Hunting and Shooting Club
Avcılık ve Atçılık Kulübü
Poligon Cad., 1, İstinye
Tel. 277 89 05
Members can bring guests to the club.

Ice Skating
Galleria Shopping Mall
Ataköy
Tel. 560 85 50

Istanbul Atçılık Kulübü
(Istanbul Riding Club)
Binicilik Sitesi,
Üçyol
Maslak
Tel. 276 14 04
Non-members are accepted to the club for riding.

FLORISTS
Florists in Istanbul have good taste and make beautiful floral arrangements. They deliver to any address without any extra charge. When ordering a flower, rest assured that it will be delivered to the given address at the requested time. Some florists, such as Sabuncakis have been in the business for generations.

Inci Mis Tel. 240 47 91
Defne Tel. 234 08 39
Lotus Tel. 247 60 27
Sabuncakis Tel. 248 10 31

BEAUTY SALON
Janine
Şakayık Sok., Nil Apt. 45/8
Daire 2,
Nişantaş
Tel. 247 32 05
Facial and body care, massage. Appointment essential.

HOSPITALS

Private Hospitals

The American Hospital
Güzelbahçe Sok., Nişantaş
Tel. 231 40 50

The Armenian Hospital
Yedikuyular Cad., 6/1
Elmadağ
Tel. 248 47 62

Florence Nightingale Hospital
Abidei Hürriyet Cad., 290
Çağlayan
Tel. 224 49 58

The German Hospital
Sıraselviler Cad., 119, Taksim
Tel. 251 71 00

The Greek Hospital
Hastaneler Yolu Cad.,
Zeytinburnu
Tel. 547 16 00

Intermed Check-up Center
Teşvikiye Cad., Bayer Apt.,
143, Nişantaş
Tel. 225 06 60

The International Hospital
Yeşilyurt
Tel. 574 78 02

The Italian Hospital
Defterdar Yokuşu 37
Tophane
Tel. 249 97 51

The Jewish Hospital
Hisarönü Cad., 46-48
Ayvansaray, Balat
Tel. 524 11 56

La Paix French Hospital
Büyükdere Cad., 22-24
Şişli
Tel. 246 10 20

The European Hospital
(Avrupa Hastahanesi)
Mehmetçik Cad.,
Cahit Yalçın Sok.,
Mecidiyeköy
Tel. 288 30 08

State Hospitals

Bakırköy Hospital (for
Psychological and
Neurological Diseases)
Bakırköy
Tel. 543 65 65

Çapa Hospital
Millet Cad.,
Çapa
Tel. 534 00 00

Cerrahpaşa Hospital
Kocamustafapaşa Cad.,
Cerrahpaşa
Tel. 588 48 00

Etfal Hospital
Etfal Sok.,
Şişli
Tel. 231 22 09

Haseki Hospital
Millet Cad.,
Haseki
Tel. 589 59 50

Haydarpaşa Heart Hospital
Haydarpaşa
Tel. (0216) 349 91 21

Haydarpaşa Numune Hospital
Selimiye
Tel. (0216) 345 46 80

Marmara University Hospital
Tophanelioğlu Cad., 13/15
Altunizade
Tel. (0216) 340 01 00

Taksim Ilk Yardım (First Aid)
Sıraselviler Cad.,
Taksim
Tel. 252 43 00

BUSINESS

INDEX

<small>BUSINESS HOURS</small>
Private Sector
Monday - Friday
9.00 a.m. - 6.00 p.m

Banks
Monday - Friday
9.00 a.m. - 12.00 a.m.
2.00 p.m. - 4.00 p.m.

Weekends
Saturday and Sunday

<small>OFFICIAL HOLIDAYS</small>
January 1   New Year Day
April 23   Atatürk Memorial
and Youth and
Sports Day
August 30 Victory Day
October 29 Republic Day

Religious Holidays
March 13 - 15
The Ramazan Feast
May   21 - 24
The Sacrifice Feast
The dates of religious holidays
vary annually acccording to
the Islamic calender and move
ten days ahead each year.

BANKS
Al Baraka Turkish Finance
House
Büyükdere Cad. Akabe
Ticaret Merkezi, 78
Mecidiyeköy
Tel. 274 99 00 -267 07 37

Akbank
Sabancı Centre, Levent
Tel. 270 00 44

Arap Türk Bankası
Vali Konağı Cad. 1
Nişantaş
Tel. 225 05 10

Avrupa-Türk Yatırım
Bankası
(Euroturk Bank)
Yapı Kredi Plaza
C Blok Kat 14, Levent
Tel. 279 70 70 (10 lines)

Banco di Roma
Tünel Cad., 18
Karaköy
Tel. 251 09 17

Bank Mellat
Büyükdere Cad.,
Binbirçiçek Sok.1
1 Levent
Tel. 269 58 20 - 29

Bank of New York
Büyükdere Cad., 108
Enka Han Kat 4
Esentepe
Tel. 275 81 92 - 93

Banker's Trust Co.
Büyükdere Cad.,
Yapı Kredi Plaza
B Blok Kat 11,Levent
Tel. 280 16 20

Banque Indosuez (Eurotürk)
Yapı Kredi Plaza
Büyükdere Cad., C Blok
20/21, K. 7
Levent
Tel.288 20 00 (20 lines)

Birleşik Yatırım Bankası
Cumhuriyet Cad. l6/3
Elmadağ
Tel. 231 66 66 (8 lines)

Chemical Bank
Abdi İpekçi Cad.,
Polat Palas 63
Maçka
Tel. 241 75 99 - 231 40 11

Citibank N.A.
Abdi İpekçi Cad. 65
Nişantaş
Tel. 288 77 00

Credit Lyonnaise
Setüstü Haktan İşhanı 45/4
Kabataş
Tel. 251 63 00 (10 lines)

Egebank A.Ş.
Büyükdere Cad., 106
Esentepe
Tel. 288 74 00

Faisal Finance Institution
Kemeraltı Cad., 46,
Tophane
Tel. 251 65 20
   (10 lines)

Finansbank A.Ş.
Büyükdere Cad., 123
Gayrettepe
Tel. 275 24 50 (15 lines)

Garanti Bankası
Buyükdere Cad., 63
Maslak
Tel. 285 40 40

Habib Bank Limited
Geçit Sok.,
Hacıonbaşılar İş Hanı,
Şişli
Tel. 246 02 20 (3 lines)

Hollantse Bank
İnönü Cad., 13/17, Taksim
Tel. 293 88 02

İktisat Bankası T.A.Ş
Büyükdere Cad., 165
Zincirlikuyu
Tel. 274 11 11

İş Bankası
(Altınbakkal Branch)
Cumhuriyet Cad., 209
Harbiye
Tel. 230 54 80

Koç Bank
Barbaros Bulvarı
Morbasan Sok., C Blok
Balmumcu
Tel. 274 77 77

Midland Bank
Cumhuriyet Cad., 8/2
Elmadağ Han, Elmadağ
Tel. 231 55 60

Osmanlı Bankası
(Ottoman Bank)
Bankalar Cad., 35/37
Karaköy
Tel. 252 30 00

Pamukbank T.A.Ş.
Büyükdere Cad., 82
Gayrettepe
Tel. 275 24 24

Sakura Bank
Büyükdere Cad., 108/A
Esentepe
Tel. 275 29 30

Saudi American Bank
(SAMBA)
Cumhuriyet Cad., 233
Harbiye
Tel. 230 02 84

Societe Generale Bank
Büyükdere Cad.,
Yapı Kredi Plaza
B Blok K.11,
Levent
Tel. 279 50 51 (11 lines)

Tasarruf ve Kredi Bankası
(Bank of Bahrain)
Bahçeler Sok., 14
Soyak İş Hanı Kat 1
Mecidiyeköy
Tel. 275 07 36 (3 lines)

Türk Boston Bank A.Ş.
(Bank of Boston)
Yıldız Posta Cad., 17
Esentepe
Tel. 274 52 22

Türkiye Emlak Bankası A.Ş.
Büyükdere Cad., 45, Levent
Tel. 285 22 50

Türk Ekonomi Bankası
(TEB)
Meclisi Mebusan Cad., 35
Fındıklı
Tel. 251 21 21

Türk Merchant Bank
Cevdet Paşa Cad., 288
Bebek
Tel. 257 76 84

Tütünbank
Yıldız Posta Cad., 21, Esentepe
Tel. 274 52 80

Uluslararası Endüstri ve Ticaret Bankası (INTER-BANK)
Büyükdere Cad., 108/C
Esentepe
Tel. 274 20 00

Vakıf Bank (Elmadağ Branch)
Cumhuriyet Cad., 16
Elmadağ
Tel. 246 30 92

West LB
Nisbetiye Cad.,
Erdölen İş Merkezi 38/1
Levent
Tel. 279 25 37

Yapı Kredi Bankası
Büyükdere Cad.,
Yapı Kredi Palaza A Blok
Levent
Tel. 280 11 11

Yatırım Bank A.Ş.
19 Mayıs Mah.,
Dr. Şevket Bey Sok., 5, Şişli
Tel. 225 70 90 (5 lines)

Ziraat Bankası (Şişli Branch)
Halâskârgazi Cad., 401
Şişli
Tel. 248 50 80

BUSINESS ASSOCIATIONS

DEİK (Dış Ekonomik İlişkiler Kurulu)
Foreign Economic Relations Board
İstiklâl Cad., 286/9, Beyoğlu
Tel. 243 41 80 (4 lines)
Fax. 243 41 84

İGEME (İhracatı Geliştirme Merkezi)
Export Promotion Center (Istanbul Branch)
Halâskârgazi Cad., 220/3
Osmanbey
Tel. 233 06 77
Fax. 230 02 77

İSO (İstanbul Sanayi Odası)
Istanbul Chamber of Industry
Meşrutiyet Cad., 11, Beyoğlu
Tel. 252 29 00 (10 lines)
Fax. 249 39 63

İTO (Istanbul Ticaret Odası)
Istanbul Chamber of Commerce
Gümüşpala Cad., 84
Eminönü
Tel. 511 41 50
Fax. 526 21 97

Istanbul Ticaret Borsası
Istanbul Commodities Stock Exchange
Zahire Sok., 5
Bahçekapı
Eminönü
Tel. 522 95 91
Fax. 511 76 54

TUSİAD (Türk Sanayici ve İşadamları Derneği)
Turkish Industrialists' and Businessmen's Association
Meşrutiyet Cad., 74
Tepebaşı
Tel. 249 54 48 - 249 19 29 - 249 08 95 - 249 07 23
Fax. 249 09 13

YASED (Yabancı Sermaye Derneği)
Association for Foreign Capital Coordination
Koza İş Merkezi B Blok Kat 1
Barbaros Blv., Mürbasan Sok., Balmumcu
Tel. 272 50 94 (2 lines)
Fax. 274 66 64

İMKB (İstanbul Menkul Kıymetler Borsası)
Istanbul Stock Exchange
Rıhtım Cad., 245, Karaköy
Tel. 251 59 06 (4 lines)
Fax. 252 50 00

TUGİAD (Türkiye Genç İş-adamları ve Sanayicileri Derneği)
Young Businessmen's and Industrialists'Association of Turkey
Korukent Sitesi R Blok, 3
Levent
Tel. 274 9 974-75
Fax. 280 09 97

TABA (Türk-Amerikan İşadamları Derneği)
Turkish-American Businessmen's Association
Fahri Gizdem Sok., 22/5
Gayrettepe
Tel. 274 28 24 - 288 62 12
Fax. 275 93 16

FOREIGN CHAMBERS OF COMMERCE

British Chamber of Commerce
Meşrutiyet Cad., 34
Tepebaşı
Tel. 249 04 20
Fax. 252 55 51

Danish Chamber of Commerce
Dilhayat Sok., 9, Etiler
Tel. 265 8829
Fax. 265 8828

Italian Chamber of Commerce
Meşrutiyet Cad.,161
Tepebaşı
Tel. 244 22 68
Fax. 252 5885

Israel Commercial Attache
Vali Konağı Cad., 73
Nişantaş
Tel. 225 10 40
Fax. 225 10 48

JETRO
Japanese Foreign Trade Association
Şakir Kesebir Sok., 36
Balmumcu Plaza 4
Daire 12
Balmumcu
Tel. 274 03 89
Fax. 288 07 39

Official German Economic Bureau
Resmi Alman Ekonomi Bürosu
Muallim Naci Cad., 118/4
Ortaköy
Tel. 259 11 95 - 96
Fax. 259 19 39

Spanish Chamber of Commerce
Vali Konağı Cad., 17
Harbiye
Tel. 225 21 91
Fax. 225 2193

Swiss Chamber of Commerce
Hüsrev Gerede Cad., 75/3
Teşvikiye
Tel. 259 11 15
Fax. 259 11 18

Turkish-French Commerce Association
Istiklâl Cad., 8
Taksim
Tel. 251 0017
Fax. 252 5175

TRADE FAIR ORGANIZERS

Afeks A.Ş.
Akyol Sok., 61
Fındıklı
Tel. 243 4220
    243 1546 (3 lines)
Fax. 251 6159

**CNR Uluslararası Fuarcılık
ve Ticaret A.Ş.**
Çoban Çeşme Kavşağı
Hava Limanı Karşısı
Yeşilköy
Tel. 663 0881
    663 0945
Fax. 663 0975

**INTERTEKS Uluslararası
Fuarcılık A.Ş.**
Hilton Convention and
Exhibition Center
Elmadağ
Tel. 225 0920 (12 lines)
Fax. 225 0933

Tüyap A.Ş.
İstanbul Sergi Sarayı
Meşrutiyet Cad.,
Tepebaşı
Tel. 245 5202
Fax. 267 1851

HELICOPTER RENTAL
MAŞ Havacılık
İç Hatlar Binası Kat 3
Atatürk Havalanı
Yeşilköy
Tel. 573 6355
    663 0403
Fax. 574 055553
VIP class helicopter for 10
passengers

Genel Havacılık
Özel Hangarlar Bölgesi
Yeşilköy
Tel. 541 2917(3 lines Fax. 541
2923
Helicopter for four passengers

AIRPLANE HIRE

MAŞ Havacılık
İç Hatlar Binası Kat 3
Atatürk Hava Alanı, Yeşilköy
Tel. 573 3275 - 663 00403
Fax. 574 0553

TGI Havacılık
Cumhuriyet Cad., Hava
Palas 155/1, Elmadağ
Tel. 232 5205
Fax 241 5552
Hansa jets for eight people.
Comfortable and spacious
sitting. Full standing and
walking room.

LIMOUSINE HIRE
Inter Limoousine Service
Harbiye Office: 246 0393
(Chauffeur-driven luxury cars)

COURIER SERVICES (with
motorcycle)
Es Kurya. Tel. 280 8066
Kurye Tel. Tel. 275 0760
Star Kurye. Tel. 272 5781

SELECTED FOREIGN NEWS
AGENCIES
Associated Press Tel. 522 3052
Reuter Tel. 2775 08870 -72

BUSINESS SERVICES
**IBS International Business
Services**
Abdi İpekçi Cad., 59/4, Maçka
Tel. 231 0480
Consulting, business research

TRANSLATIONS OFFICE
ALFA Translation Bureau
Halâskârgazi Cad., 38
Sinan Apt., Daire 16, Harbiye
Tel. 246 4530 - 247 0870
Fax. 240 1636

REAL ESTATE
Ma Maison Tel. 277 0177
Turyap   Tel. 272 5909